DEFIANT

DREAMS

THE JOURNEY OF
AN AFGHAN GIRL
WHO RISKED
EVERYTHING FOR
EDUCATION

DEFIANT
DREAMS

SOLA MAHFOUZ &
MALAINA KAPOOR

BALLANTINE
BOOKS
NEW YORK

Published in the United States by Ballantine Books,
an imprint of Random House, a division of
Penguin Random House LLC, New York.

BALLANTINE is a registered trademark and the colophon
is a trademark of Penguin Random House LLC.

LIBRARY OF CONGRESS CATALOGING-IN-PUBLICATION DATA
NAMES: Mahfouz, Sola, author. | Kapoor, Malaina, author.
TITLE: Defiant dreams: the journey of an Afghan girl who risked everything
for education / Sola Mahfouz and Malaina Kapoor.
DESCRIPTION: First edition. | New York: Ballantine Books, 2023.
IDENTIFIERS: LCCN 2022048205 (print) | LCCN 2022048206 (ebook) |
ISBN9780593359761 (hardcover) | ISBN 9780593359778 (ebook)
SUBJECTS: LCSH: Mahfouz, Sola, 1996- | Sex discrimination in
education—Afghanistan. | Girls—Education—Afghanistan. | Women—
Social conditions—Afghanistan. | Afghanistan—Social conditions—21st century.
CLASSIFICATION: LCC LC2410.A3 M35 2023 (print) | LCC LC2410.A3 (ebook) |
DDC 371.82209581092 [B]—dc23/eng/20221207
LC record available at https://lccn.loc.gov/2022048205
LC ebook record available at https://lccn.loc.gov/2022048206

Printed in Canada on acid-free paper

randomhousebooks.com

9 8 7 6 5 4 3 2 1

FIRST EDITION

Title-page image from Adobe Stock

Book design by Barbara M. Bachman

To my mother, whose positive outlook toward life,
like light in a dark lane, gave me the courage to go
through the darkest time of my life with defiance

—SOLA MAHFOUZ

For my family, who has given everything
to give me everything

—MALAINA KAPOOR

DEFIANT DREAMS IS A WORK OF NONFICTION. However, some names, identifying details, and locations have been changed for security reasons. The name Sola Mahfouz is also a pseudonym.

DEFIANT
DREAMS

I BEGAN TO GROW UP THE DAY MY MOTHER WARNED ME TO stop laughing. She was terrified that even my momentary giggle could bring a strange man to our door, ready to yell, kidnap, or even kill to silence the sounds of a young woman. Don't dance outside your room, she'd warn me. Don't sing in the hallways, where the sound can carry. I was eleven years old.

I was more interested in playtime than in my mother's fears. I escaped the thick heat of Kandahar, my Afghan hometown, by jumping through the water pump inside our family compound, shielded by walls so tall they kissed the cloudless sky. I dragged a speaker into the kitchen to blast the Bollywood music I'd heard on TV, flinging my arms into the air and moving with my sisters and cousins to the strong beat. Outside my home, bombs were exploding. Soldiers patrolled the streets, and the Taliban shot to kill. But in those days, I still woke up mostly oblivious to how brutal a place my country was to live in. I was excited just to race my brothers or buy fried snacks at the crowded bazaar, my skirt hiked up above my knees and the dusty wind sweeping through my tangled hair.

Just before my twelfth birthday, my female cousins and I were biking in our courtyard. We were the only girls in our entire neighborhood who were allowed to ride bicycles. However, we still had to stay behind the walls that closed in our sprawling family compound, where I lived with my parents, siblings, and cousins. I perched precariously on a metal-frame bicycle far too big for me and raced freely in the waning sun, giggling. One of my cousins burst into a popular Bollywood song, and we all sang along, laughing harder and harder as we pedaled across the small squares of pavement that framed the garden.

Suddenly, something came sailing over the walls. Before we could figure out what it was, we heard a group of boys just outside the compound erupt in laughter, whooping at their victory. Their voices were sharp and caustic, and we froze at their tone. They roared even louder once they realized they'd silenced us.

Eventually, after the sound of their voices receded into the alleyways behind our house, I turned to see what the boys had thrown over. Two unidentifiable packages lay just a few feet away from me. Immediately, I grew afraid. I wondered for a moment if the packages might be bombs or containers of acid meant to blind or disfigure us. I stepped forward for a closer look and then recoiled in disgust. The boys had thrown two large plastic sacks stuffed with excrement. One of them burst and leaked across the grass and toward our rose bushes. The awful scent assaulted our senses, but we stood still, stunned and horrified and unable to move.

After that day, I listened to my mother's warnings. I began to understand her fear. I started to live the same life as so many women and girls in Afghanistan, trapped within the four walls of our kitchen. I was deeply jealous of my brothers who would go on road trips together, talk politics, and speak of visiting bazaars and enjoying street food. By age thirteen, I rarely left the house. When I did go outside, I viewed the world through the crisscross slats cut into my first burqa.

PART
ONE

IN SECRET, BABA LOVES TO DANCE. MY FATHER'S BARE FEET move slowly across the embroidery on our Afghan carpet, as the sleeves of his dove-gray *kameez* billow to a beat emanating from a portable stereo. My mother peeks out of the kitchen, laughing softly as he throws his arms into the air. Like most Afghan men, Baba is guarded, steeled by the memories of war and the demands of a patriarchal culture. His tufted beard and piercing black eyes often intimidate. In photographs, he rarely smiles. But music betrays him, forcing a sheepish, mischievous grin across his face.

As a young girl, I was ashamed by these glimpses into my father's more joyful dispositions. Our family and our province are ethnically Pashtun. In Pashtun culture, the strength of a man and the honor of his family are determined by his stoicism and authority. He is expected never to display emotion.

A man is also obligated to keep a tight rein on the women in his household. In the most traditional communities, it is the deepest shame for a man to ever allow his wife or daughters to be seen, even through the whispered shadows of a doorway.

Men in Afghanistan spend lazy afternoons under the dusty shade of local pomegranate groves, gather at restaurants to enjoy Indian biryani and cans of ice-cold Coca-Cola, and maneuver motorcycles every morning into the city for work. Women spend their days indoors, with only a brief respite to drink tea with friends before lunch. They squat low to the ground and sweep cracked tiles with brooms made of dried grass, the embroidered hems of their *salwaar kameez* dresses just brushing the floor. They wring sopping-wet, hand-washed laundry and hang it on clotheslines to dry. In the evenings, as a hazy dusk falls on the city, the women emerge from the kitchen. They serve elaborate meals to their husbands and sons, meals that they have taken the entire day to prepare: lamb soup with vegetables and coriander, rice crispy with crystallized sugar, lentil stews, fresh tomato salads, half-moon flatbreads studded with caraway seeds. It is only after the men eat that many women do, spooning cold leftovers onto their plates from behind the kitchen doors.

Baba could never devote himself completely to this culture of conservatism. He grew up with a gravely ill father, so his mother filled the traditional male role at home. He was one of only a handful of university-educated men in our province. He had spent years in the bustling capital city of Kabul and even visited Russia, a land devoid of restrictions in the name of religion. So he never forced the women in our house to inform him when they left for the bazaar or to visit a friend. He let his daughters go to school. When no other fathers would, he danced, listened to his children sing, and allowed us all to take photographs and watch movies.

The neighbors gossiped about us: *Did you know he allows his little girl to go swimming in that river near the pomegranate groves? Look, look! His wife's sleeves aren't long enough to cover her wrists.* I was ashamed that my father was seen as weak. Why, I wondered, did he care so much about preserving our little delights and liberties, even in the face of ridicule?

Perhaps it was because he understood what I didn't yet: in Afghanistan, freedom is transient and every small happiness is fleeting, forever threatened by the weight of tradition and the crossfire of war.

IN 1952, BABA WAS born in Kandahar, a city ringed by mountains and accented by teal-blue mosques and brightly painted food stalls. The streets are without lane markings and swell with people. A cacophony of blaring horns and sputtering motorcycles pierces the air, and smells of stale oil and roasted meat emanate from open-air butcheries and street vendors. A thick, dusty heat snakes through the city, enveloping gray buildings, slinking between the folds of ubiquitous blue burqas and pastel turbans.

Baba grew up in the decades after the British retreated from their occupation of our country, as an exhilarating spirit of patriotism surged across the nation. Under colonial influence, Afghanistan had been a poor country, one without electricity or a basic educational system. But independence offered the promise of cultural and institutional reform, led by King Zahir Shah and his cousin, Prime Minister General Mohammed Daoud Khan. Beginning in 1953, Khan enacted widely popular social measures centered on women's rights. Most notably, he lifted restrictions on women entering the workforce and allowed them to decide on their own whether to wear a veil in public.

As a part of his broader push toward modernization, the prime minister also solicited investment and military assistance from foreign nations. Brimming Cold War tensions served Afghanistan well, as both Moscow and Washington poured money into the country in an attempt to secure political influence. In northern Afghanistan, the Soviets were dominant. They spearheaded massive infrastructure projects, improved the education system, and funded scholarships for young Afghans. In the south, where Kandahar is located, the United States had more influence. American engineers flew in to help build new highways, dams, and electric power plants. They started construction on the Kandahar International Airport, whose terminals were meant to have the same grandeur as those in neighboring India and Pakistan, with state-of-the-art underground refueling stations and massive airport hotels for travelers who would spend layovers in Kandahar while traveling between Europe and East Asia. Local schools suddenly offered English lessons taught by volunteers from the Peace Corps. It wasn't uncommon to witness groups of sixteen- and seventeen-year-old boys belting out American nursery rhymes like "The Itsy Bitsy Spider."

Americans affiliated with government-aid organizations or private contractors settled in southern Afghanistan. In Kandahar, many lived in homes or barracks erected at Manzel Bagh, a palace gifted to a private contracting company by the king. The nearby city of Lashkar Gah was nicknamed "Little America" for the number of American vacationers

and workers who stayed there. As a child, I heard many stories of what my family thought of these visitors from the
West. "They were wealthy and so different—we loved to
just peek at them as they walked down the street," my aunt
would tell me. "But . . . well, they were a little uncultured,"
someone would chime in, before describing the brazen
assurance with which American women walked through
Kandahar. "They let doors slam behind them! When they
would eat dinner—Sola!—they spoke so loudly, their voices
carried to the next house over."

As a child, Baba was mostly oblivious to this whirlwind
of change occurring outside his door. Instead, he was consumed by domestic troubles. His father, whom I called
Agha Jan, had been struck with an undiagnosed illness,
likely diabetes. That left Baba's mother, whom I called Ana
Bibi, to care for their ten children and help provide for the
family.

In the beginning, Agha Jan's illness was not too serious,
and he tried to maintain his dominance as the patriarch of
the household. As Baba remembers him, his father was a
simple man. He was set in his ways, stuck in the past, and
cantankerous about the cultural liberalization occurring
around him. In contrast, Ana Bibi, came from an educated
family, though she herself never attended school. She possessed a fierce intellect and often wielded it against her husband.

For instance, Agha Jan did not believe that girls should
be allowed to attend school. Ana Bibi disagreed but bro-
kered a compromise. "Our daughters will attend school
until fifth grade," she said. "After that, we will pull them
out."

Agha Jan agreed. But somehow their daughters never seemed to reach the fifth grade. One girl supposedly failed the fourth-grade final exam several years in a row. Another seemed suspiciously old for her class, but Ana Bibi promised she was still finishing second grade. Agha Jan was confused and exasperated. "How can these girls *still* not be in the fifth grade?!" he would ask. But somehow he trusted Ana Bibi, who cleverly managed to educate five of her six daughters right underneath her husband's nose.

In the late 1960s, when Baba was a young teenager, his father was struck with constant, debilitating pain that forced him to quit his job as a driver. He soon became bedridden, leaving Ana Bibi with the responsibility of supporting the children and paying for his medical care. She expanded her small sewing business and sold clothes to neighbors and friends. But it wasn't enough. So Baba got a job after school laying bricks for the Kandahar International Airport, helping to construct the characteristic arches that line the building today. When that project was completed, he moved through a series of odd jobs before landing at the local ice factory as a teenager. At the time in Kandahar, there was no refrigeration, so Baba's job was to pack and deliver ice at four in the morning to all the restaurants and shops in the city. His bosses refused to provide him with food or any breaks, so he sneaked slices of bread from home and ate them when no one was looking. He was paid just ten afghanis, or around ten U.S. cents, per day.

Meanwhile Agha Jan grew sicker, lying listless in bed for days at a time. Baba often considered leaving school to work full-time and provide better for the family, but Ana Bibi refused to allow him to quit. "You must study hard and make it to university," she insisted. "You have to leave Kandahar and make something better for yourself." So, urged on by his mother, Baba continued at school. He split long days between the ice warehouse and his science classrooms. He spent nights studying, squinting at calculus problems in the unsteady candlelight.

AS BABA GREW OLDER, the political modernization in Afghanistan continued. King Zahir Shah attempted to transition the country into a constitutional monarchy, where political parties would have influence and power alongside the king. A traditional assembly of tribal elders and community leaders approved Shah's new constitution, which created representative bodies made up mostly of elected officials. In 1965, spurred by these increasing political freedoms, a group of men met secretly at the home of Nur Mohammad Taraki to form the Marxist People's Democratic Party of Afghanistan (PDPA). The group became especially attractive to young people with its promises of equality and progressive social reform. But it faced stiff political competition from another rising group, the Islamic Society. Members of the society, known as Islamists, were firmly against the recent trends toward liberalization. Deeply religious and conservative, they valued a return to an Afghanistan of the past by whatever means necessary, including violence.

As the two political parties gained momentum, King Zahir Shah—likely afraid of what he'd unleashed—stalled the reforms he had promised to enact, effectively nullifying major elements of the new constitution. This only increased tensions between the Communists and the Islamists as they tried to assert their authority against the increasingly unpopular monarchy.

In 1970 Baba was accepted to the brand-new Kabul Polytechnic University in Afghanistan's capital city. He left his home in Kandahar and settled into a campus whose vibrancy rivaled that of many Western universities. At college, Baba was exposed for the first time to Afghanistan's political forces. Universities had become centers of national political expression, and groups with affiliations ranging from Chinese Maoism to the Egyptian Muslim Brotherhood sprang up across campuses. Baba regularly stumbled upon peaceful protests by the university gates and fended off eager recruiters from a range of ideological groups. Most disagreements on campus stemmed from the fundamental question of Communist versus Islamist, which seemed to infiltrate every classroom and conversation.

Baba faced enormous pressure to join one of the student political groups. Maintaining any sense of neutrality between the Communists and the Islamists was nearly impossible, and he believed it would serve only to anger both political behemoths. So he sided casually with the Communists but refused to commit to attend their innumerable peaceful protests or serve as a recruiter of other students. He was going to college with one goal: to land a job that could support his large family. Baba couldn't afford the dangers and distractions that would come with political engagement.

His unyielding neutrality ultimately served as a boon.

Baba was able to make many friends across political, ethnic, and religious lines. Though he often forwent college parties in order to study, he still managed to find a circle of friends who spent evenings together enveloped in puffs of cigarette smoke, laughing about everything and nothing at all. Years later, when some of my brothers and cousins were able to leave Afghanistan to attend college, my father would wink at them and say, "Don't forget to have fun!" It wasn't until I heard stories from a family friend about Baba's time at university that I understood the mirthful, remembering look I'd seen in his eyes.

But Baba's collegiate escape from his troubles at home didn't last long. Just months into his first year, he received word that Agha Jan had taken a turn for the worse. Alone, Baba boarded a rickety, overcrowded bus bound for Kandahar. He gazed blankly out the mud-splattered window, steadying himself by grasping the tattered seat in front of him. Once he arrived home and saw how ill his father was, Baba decided to take Agha Jan back with him to Kabul to seek medical treatment. By then, diabetes had caused his father to lose control of his legs. Baba carried him across his shoulders through the streets of Kabul, searching for a doctor who might be able to help him. When Baba finally found an open office and lowered Agha Jan onto the dilapidated examination table, the doctor confirmed what the family had feared: Agha Jan's disease was incurable. He lived for only a few more painful weeks before dying at home in Kandahar, tucked into the bed he'd been confined to for Baba's entire adult life.

After the burial, Baba wondered what was going to happen to Ana Bibi. He couldn't imagine leaving his mother alone in Kandahar to fend for herself as he returned to his carefree university life in Kabul. So he sat down to talk with her, steeling himself for her reaction to what he was about to say.

"I am the head of the family now," he began. "I won't go back to school. Instead, I'll get whatever job I can to support you. Who will look after you if I am so far away, wasting precious time studying?" Ana Bibi stood up and met his eyes with an unmoving gaze. Her response would become a legend in our family, a story told to me often as I grew up.

"*I* am the head of this family," she said, emphatically. "And you absolutely must go back to university."

Her outburst made him hesitate, but he refused to yield.

Ana Bibi grabbed Baba's wrist and pulled him roughly toward the front door. "Look out there," she said, pointing to the dirt path just outside their home. "I will disown you and you will never again enter through this door unless you swear to me you will continue your studies."

Faced with that ultimatum, my father boarded a bus back to Kabul Polytechnic a few weeks later. Though Agha Jan had been sick for many years, the finality of his death made Baba solemn, introspective. He devoted himself to circuit diagrams and physics courses and little else.

IN 1973 THE AFGHAN monarchy was unstable and clinging to power, threatened by the surging popularity of the Communist and Islamist political parties. Sensing an opportunity, former prime minister Daoud Khan partnered with a faction of the Communist PDPA and staged a coup. Khan eradicated the country's monarchy and declared a new Republic of Afghanistan. He also enacted several modernization policies that built on what he had accomplished as prime minister a decade earlier. For his newfound alliance with the Afghan Communists, Khan earned the nickname "the Red Prince."

Yet soon after he seized power, Daoud Khan pivoted away from Afghan Communism. He demoted and transferred government officials aligned with the PDPA and decreased Afghanistan's dependence on the Soviet Union, instead making deals with wealthy Islamic nations like Iran and Saudi Arabia. Khan also courted American government officials and investors, urging them to continue financing development efforts in the south of the country. When asked to explain his foreign policy strategy, Khan was apparently known to say, "I'm lighting my American cigarette with a Soviet match."

When Daoud Khan came into power, my father had just graduated from Kabul Polytechnic. At the time, all men were required to complete a mandatory service in the Afghan military. Given his college degree, Baba was considered an intellectual and so was required to complete only a six-month military mission with limited exposure to dangerous conditions. He served alongside Mohammad Najibullah, a future president of Afghanistan. When Baba returned to Kabul, he took a well-paying job in the mining industry, surveying potential resource-rich sites. He rented a small house in western Kabul and sent for his mother, brother, and younger sister to move in with him.

Living with his family again, Baba found it impossible to dodge the topic of marriage. At thirty, he was considered the perfect age to settle down with a wife. In Afghanistan, most marriages are arranged, and it is extremely rare for a couple to have a "love match" and get engaged without the help of their families. Instead, a young man's mother and sister bring him potential wives to choose from. They take note of his preferences: Tall or short? Educated or not? Fair-skinned or darker? Then they tell anyone they know to keep an eye out for a suitable girl.

Baba had few requirements. He wanted to marry some-one educated, and his family would never consider a woman from outside their ethnic group, the Pashtuns. Millions of Pashtuns live throughout South Asia, most of them Mus-lim, united by the soft-toned Pashto language and the Pash-tunwali code of conduct that emphasizes principles of family honor, hospitality, and the protection of women.

So Ana Bibi, acting on recommendations from family members and friends, visited dozens of families to assess in person if a suggested girl was right for her son. As is cus-tomary, she was shown into the house of every potential daughter-in-law and given the chance to speak with her mother. Then the girl would have to enter demurely, her hair draped loosely in a scarf to project modesty. She would wear delicate clothes and intricate jewelry to try to im-press Ana Bibi. The girl would never stay longer than two minutes—that was all the time Ana Bibi needed to assess her beauty.

If Ana Bibi was dissatisfied, she would not return for an-other visit. However, if she liked the girl, she would make preparations for Baba to meet her in person.

But my father wasn't eager to marry anyone whom his mother presented. And so he stayed an unmarried man in Kabul, working during the day and gathering with his friends in the cool evenings, waiting unhurriedly for the right girl.

MY MATERNAL GRANDMOTHER, ANA JANA, WAS CON-sidered an unlucky woman. In 1942, at age seven-teen, she was married off to a dried-fruit merchant. Within the next three years, she gave birth to two daughters. They both died, and a few years later her husband did too. After the funeral, as is the custom in Afghanistan, Ana Jana re-mained with her husband's parents in their family home. In the beginning, her parents-in-law were struck by an all-consuming grief at the loss of their son. But their sadness quickly turned to virulent anger that they directed toward Ana Jana. In tearful outbursts, they declared her the cause of all their suffering. They insisted it was her presence that had killed their son, her shortcomings that had given them sickly granddaughters instead of healthy grandsons.

As Ana Jana shrank from these blistering accusations, she also had to fend off advances from her husband's brother. In Pashtun culture, it is tradition for a man to marry his brother's widow in order to take care of her and keep her within the family, even if he has to take her on as a second wife. But Ana Jana couldn't bear the thought of marrying her brother-in-law, a married man who leered at every woman he saw and beat his wife.

My mother's father, Agha, lived next door to Ana Jana. At just seventeen, he became deeply affected by the predicament of his young neighbor. One morning he approached his own father and declared his intent to marry Ana Jana and rescue her from her miserable living conditions. Agha's parents were horrified. "She is nine years older than you are!" they shouted. "She's bad luck, she's a widow!" They told Agha that he had his whole life ahead of him, that there was no reason to settle down so abruptly. They threatened to withhold any financial support and refused to pay for his wedding. Not surprisingly, Ana Jana seized the opportunity to marry Agha. Despite his family's objections, my grandparents wed in 1952 in a modest ceremony in Kandahar.

Agha and Ana Jana moved into a small house on the outskirts of the city. In 1955 Ana Jana gave birth to my aunt, Yasmin. Five years later my mother, whom I call Moor, was born.

In this second marriage, Ana Jana had only the two children, which was unusual in a time when most families numbered upward of ten. People gossiped about how she'd failed to give birth to any sons and insinuated that she was bad for her young husband, that maybe she was cursed.

Moor remembers Ana Jana as a quiet, almost silent woman. She was a devout Muslim who woke up early every morning to read her Quran. She prayed five times every day, first at the crack of dawn and finally after sunset, as the muddy streets and thatched roofs outside their home faded into blackness. By the time Moor woke up in the mornings, her mother was sequestered behind the doors of their small kitchen. She stayed there for most of the day, chopping onions, grinding spices, and washing dishes as her husband went to work and her daughters played.

Agha was the indubitable head of their household. He had the exuberance and forceful personality of a former revolutionary. As a young teenager, he'd been a member of the political group Weekh Zalmian (Awakened Youth). Their goal was to promote Afghan liberalization in the decades after the country became fully independent. Agha spent hours debating causes like socialism and women's rights, heady from thick clouds of hookah smoke and the aura of intellectualism that surrounded him.

Though Weekh Zalmian disbanded before Yasmin and Moor were born, Agha remained deeply committed to its principles. He supported reformist policies that advanced gender equality and political representation. He wanted his daughters to grow up in a modern Afghanistan, one that eschewed religion and outdated cultural norms in favor of scientific thought and personal freedoms. Ana Jana disagreed. Her own conservative Islamic values contrasted sharply with Agha's progressive idealism. But even though she was married to a liberal who spoke eloquently on the issue of women's rights, she was powerless to object. In Afghanistan, the man of the house always has the final say, regardless of his political leanings.

One autumn afternoon just before Moor was born, her family attended a reunion of former Weekh Zalmian families. They didn't know it, but the gathering would soon explode into a cultural firestorm, drastically altering Kandahar's political landscape. The group planned to defy traditional Afghan customs that required men to have long facial hair and women to wear burqas. Agha followed the men into one room, where they stood together and shaved their beards. Tufts of hair fell to the ground and blanketed the concrete floors.

My grandmother and Yasmin entered another room with all the Weekh Zalmian wives. Around them, women struggled out of their burqas and into Western-style coats that brushed against their ankles. Ana Jana stood uncomfortably in the corner, clutching Yasmin's hand. She did not change her clothes. To her, removing a burqa in public was akin to stripping naked.

As the women around her undressed, they spoke excitedly of a banquet that the governor of Kandahar was hosting that evening for former Weekh Zalmian families. Ana Jana listened silently. She gathered that the dinner was another attempt to promote Afghan modernization. In direct opposition to how meals were usually conducted in Afghanistan, the governor planned to seat men and women next to each other that night. Ana Jana was horrified. Like most Afghans, she believed it was the gravest offense for a man to sit beside another's wife. It was an insult to the husband's pride and an affront to the woman's dignity.

In a rare display of conviction, Ana Jana yanked Yasmin through the front door and marched home. Later that evening, Agha met her at home and asked her to join him at the dinner banquet. Ana Jana refused. Shocked by her uncharacteristic boldness, Agha yelled and threatened to divorce her if she didn't oblige. Ana Jana insisted she would not sacrifice her modesty to dine with him among other men, and Agha stormed away.

Agha returned home early the next morning, their fight forgotten. He assured Ana Jana that the dinner had been harmless. But within a few days, he was proven wrong. Word of the governor's party spread among religious conservatives living in Kandahar. Islamists and religious leaders known as mullahs harnessed the public disaffection with the governor's actions through impassioned speeches delivered at local mosques.

The religious ideologues grew even angrier at news of the events following the banquet. Apparently, on the night of the party, a former Weekh Zalmian member had brought his servant to the dinner. His wife, like Ana Jana, had refused to attend, and the man presumed that in such a large crowd, no one would notice the difference. But the next day a guest reported him to the governor. "Who is this man to come and ogle our wives without showing us his own?" he asked angrily. In an attempt to make peace, the governor asked the former member to display his wife at the homes of several prominent figures who had attended the previous evening's party.

The governor's actions sparked instant controversy. Local mullahs and their followers were enraged. "Have our women become showpieces?" they demanded. "Will we allow them to be paraded around Kandahar upon orders from the Afghan government?" The so-called modernizers, they claimed, were stripping Afghan women of their bodily integrity and stripping the Afghan nation of its moral compass.

In the early 1960s, tensions boiled over. Religious conservatives set fire to the new girls' school in Kandahar. They declared that it was against Islam for women to be educated, and that the modernizers would pay the price for driving Afghans away from their religion.

Agha and Ana Jana learned of the attack when Yasmin came home from school early, sobbing. Her bare feet were scraped and blistered, her skin was blackened with soot. She had crouched under her desk and watched flames consume the classroom door. Somehow she managed to escape and run home, losing her shoes in the chaos.

The arson was an affront to the Afghan government's policies of modernization. Police forces mobilized throughout Kandahar, but the religious conservatives were undeterred. They orchestrated the burning of Kandahar's cinema, another symbol of modernization.

In response, the police arrested anyone even faintly suspected of involvement in the violence. They stopped people in the street and asked, "Do you think it is acceptable for a woman to show herself in public?" The Afghans who responded no were promptly arrested.

It was a time of heightened extremes in Kandahar. Many women faced an impossible choice between betraying their religious beliefs and relinquishing their personal freedoms. And in either case, men were still the ones dictating the way women should look and behave.

GROWING UP, MOOR WAS mostly oblivious to the cultural and political strife occurring around her. She was the younger child, and her father chose to shelter her even more than he had Yasmin.

When Moor was five years old, Agha enrolled her in the same, newly repaired all-girls school in downtown Kandahar that her sister attended. He was so devoted to his daughters' education that he soon moved the entire family into a new rental home at the center of the city so that the girls could be closer to school. They excelled there, continuing on to secondary school even as many other female students dropped out. Agha insisted that education would be his daughters' ticket to illustrious careers or futures living abroad. He believed it should always be their first priority. So unlike their other classmates, Moor and Yasmin didn't spend hours every day with their mother, learning all the domestic skills necessary to be a desirable wife. They never sat by the stove learning to fry spices, watching as they browned in the shimmering oil. They were never instructed on how to prepare tea for their future mothers-in-law, how to steep the loose tea leaves in a pot and stir in the sugar and milk rapidly, how to pour the tea into a glass while it was still at a rolling boil. They didn't learn how to prepare a lunch for their future husbands, or how to wrap a diaper on a baby.

The girls in Moor's school got married one by one—her sister was one of the lucky ones allowed to graduate. Moor heard stories of their bejeweled green wedding gowns; of their husbands, some of them angry, some indifferent; and of her friends' first times giving birth. Meanwhile Agha asked her questions about her geography diagrams and her physics exams. He cajoled Ana Jana into letting Moor study instead of doing laundry or preparing dinner. My mother adored him.

Moor's friends couldn't comprehend the life she lived. Their lives were filled with the constant drudgery of household responsibilities. They came from large families and took care of their younger siblings—from the age of eight or nine, they usually had a baby on their hip and a toddler by their side. Their own fathers never took an interest in their studies unless it was to wonder aloud why their daughter was wasting her time. But Moor's life was strikingly different. Her father was thrilled when, a few months before her graduation from secondary school, she declared her desire to attend university and major in chemistry.

MY MOTHER WAS ACCEPTED into Kabul University in 1978. College life surprised her. Though Kabul University lacked the glamour and prestige of an international college, the campus was imbued with a vibrancy she had never experienced. Like any modern college student, Moor was ready to reinvent herself and throw herself into new experiences. She exchanged her conservative *salwaar kameez* for skirts and short-sleeve blouses and sported a fashionable bob haircut that she rarely covered with a veil. She lived alongside Communists and Islamists in a dormitory that buzzed with political activity.

Moor drank milk tea with her roommates every morning, sharing her extra sugar packets with girls who liked their cups sweeter. She ate dinner every night at an affordable college cafeteria that served meat only once a week, and so she subsisted mostly on rice, potatoes, and lentils. On the weekends, she explored Kabul with packs of friends, both male and female. They visited luscious gardens, lounging on stone benches set among scarlet buds. She and her friends loved attending concerts—one summer night she even managed to catch the wildly popular singer Ahmad Zahir at the historic Gardens of Babur. During a break from classes, she traveled without her father as a chaperone for the first time and hauled her luggage onto a mud-splashed bus headed to Kandahar. She chatted and laughed with her friends the whole ride home, sandwiched between them in a row smelling of sweat and motor oil and someone's groceries.

But just a few months after she enrolled in college, the mood on Kabul University's campus turned tense. President Daoud Khan was in deep political trouble. On top of a recent nepotism scandal, he faced intense criticism for abandoning the Communist principles that had allowed him to take power. Multiple factions of the Communist PDPA, including the party's student chapters, organized massive demonstrations against his government. Khan's retaliation followed swiftly. He ordered the arrest of leftist opposition leaders and called for politically motivated assassinations.

The Communists were undeterred by the government's response. Instead, as Daoud Khan's popularity continued to plummet, they saw an opportunity. PDPA member Hafizullah Amin made contact with allies in Afghanistan's army in an attempt to garner support for a coup. His bid was successful, and on April 27, 1978, the PDPA overthrew the government. They killed Daoud Khan and eighteen members of his family, and installed Nur Mohammad Taraki as the leader of the new Democratic Republic of Afghanistan.

Taraki declared himself a leader for the people and promised not to be unduly influenced by the Soviet Union, though he did sign an Afghan-Soviet friendship treaty. Throughout his tenure, he instituted Marxist land reforms and social policies that pushed equality for Afghan women. However, these reforms were extremely unpopular, especially among religious conservatives living in rural areas. Violent antigovernment riots broke out across the country.

Though many Afghans didn't support the new regime, they stayed silent because Taraki and his supporters quickly cracked down on dissent. One of Moor's school friends was kidnapped and taken in for questioning by the government. His only offense was his long beard, which government officials took to be a sign that he was a radicalized, anti-Communist Muslim.

Moor began to worry for her own safety. She was a practicing Muslim, used to praying five times a day. She was afraid Taraki's supporters might single her out on campus for her beliefs. Soon her fears came true. She faced regular interrogations about her religious beliefs from fellow students who were ardent supporters of the new regime. In an attempt to calm the situation, she told them that her father was a Marxist who held a government job. That seemed to satisfy them, but by that point her carefree university days were over. She felt uneasy, as though someone were watching her, waiting for a fatal misstep.

Later that year Moor applied for a scholarship to finish her studies in Russia. For decades, the Soviet Union had offered opportunities for promising students to attend university in Moscow, in an attempt to secure influence in the Afghan government and to expose young Afghans to the perks of life under Soviet-style leadership. Every applicant to this program was eager to visit a completely different country, one rumored to have towering feats of modern architecture, dazzling school campuses, and uncrowded, peaceful streets. But the girls were the hungriest for opportunity. Even if their fathers were liberals, even if their mothers let them leave the house with their hair uncovered and go on dates, they were still imprisoned by a culture and community that believed they deserved less.

A few years earlier my aunt Yasmin had been awarded one of the highly coveted Soviet scholarships. She had traveled to Kabul and boarded a plane with thirteen other lucky young Afghan women. She was just seventeen years old, as she left the language, country, and family that had defined her existence. It was impossibly expensive to phone home, so for the six years that she was there, earning a degree in psychology, she didn't even hear the voices of her parents or sister. Agha was proud of Yasmin beyond measure. But Ana Jana was inconsolable, mourning for her faraway daughter as though she had died.

Soon after Moor applied, she received news that she had been accepted into the same scholarship program as Yasmin. She was ecstatic. But Ana Jana wept uncontrollably and begged her not to go. "I cannot lose both of my daughters," she cried. She tried to convince Moor that Russia was an infidel nation, that she would scarcely find another Muslim there. My mother waited for Agha to take her side and admonish Ana Jana for stamping out their daughter's dreams.

But by then Agha was tired and unwilling to live an additional six years alongside his wife's unrestrained grief. He told my mother she would have to convince Ana Jana herself.

Moor approached her mother gently, but her arguments were futile. Ana Jana was sick with desperation and threatened to starve herself unless her daughter promised to stay in Afghanistan. My mother lay awake at night, racked by guilt and indecision.

Eventually, Moor quietly shelved her dreams of a new life in Moscow. As a dozen young Afghan women boarded the international flight without her, she packed her suitcases for the bus ride back to Kabul.

ON FEBRUARY 14, 1979, U.S. ambassador to Afghanistan Adolph Dubs was killed under suspicious circumstances. In response, the U.S. government withdrew all aid from the country. This forced President Taraki to turn to the Soviet Union, as antigovernment riots grew increasingly out of hand. Along with military assistance, Soviet officials allegedly offered Taraki some political advice. They claimed that his close colleague Hafizullah Amin was growing greedy and would soon be a danger to Afghanistan's stability. They suggested Amin be removed from power.

Amin, the man who had engineered the PDPA coup, did indeed have significant influence over the new Communist government. He initially served as a deputy prime minister but became prime minister in March 1979. That same year, on September 14, Amin was called to Kabul for a meeting that turned out to be a trap. He was ambushed with gunfire but managed to escape. In a shocking turn of events, Amin used his supporters in the military, arrested Taraki, and orchestrated a coup, installing himself as Afghanistan's new president.

Amin's reign was ruthless. He targeted politicians, intellectuals, and religious figures who posed even the slightest threat to his grasp on power. The scholars and professors teaching Moor at Kabul University were suddenly in danger. One of Moor's beloved teachers was abducted and died when Amin's supporters threw him out of a flying helicopter. Evidence of these vicious murders lay in warehouses, where thousands of watches were stacked high, all stolen from Amin's victims. They were sold later at local bazaars for significant sums.

Moor and Yasmin were afraid for their father. Agha was considered an intellectual and was known to harbor ideals antithetical to Amin's beliefs. One evening a friend stopped by his home with a warning: government officials were likely surveilling him and assessing his loyalty. From then on, Agha panicked anytime he heard the sound of screeching tires outside his front door, convinced that Amin's people were finally coming for him. He passed evenings in his living room, peering through the windows, jumping at errant footsteps or roving car beams.

HAFIZULLAH AMIN'S TERRIFYING REGIME lasted only one hundred days. The Soviet Union had grown dissatisfied with his hold over Afghanistan, aware that his ruthless leadership style was threatening the country's stability and fueling opposition groups. After taking power, Amin had reached out to the United States to ask for their renewed support, further jeopardizing the USSR's political and military influence.

As a result, the Soviet Union invaded Afghanistan in December 1979. KGB special forces killed Amin as he lay in bed at the Tajbeg Presidential Palace in Kabul. In a series of attacks, Soviet troops seized critical Afghan military and government facilities. Then they installed a new leader named Babrak Karmal, who hailed from Amin's rival faction within the PDPA.

The Soviet invasion spurred seismic changes at Kabul University. Moor's Afghan professors were swiftly replaced by Soviets. The heads of every academic department were also replaced. Soon many of the textbooks provided to students were written in Russian. Moor enrolled in language classes to keep up.

One evening in February 1980, as Moor and her classmates were on their way to Russian class, they noticed a peaceful anti-Soviet protest unfolding just outside the school's campus. Some friends tried to persuade them to skip class and go home, in case things escalated, but Moor wasn't afraid. Until that point, most of the violent anti-Soviet clashes had occurred outside Kabul. The city felt insulated and safe.

By the time Moor finished class, the sun had set. The air was bitterly cold, and everyone rushed to get home. But they didn't get far. The small protest they'd witnessed on their way to class had erupted, and thousands of people now filled the street, chanting angrily and yelling "Allahu Akbar" (God is great) to protest the Soviets' antireligious stance. In response, the Soviets fired into the crowd. People screamed, and the demonstrators split in different directions. Moor was stuck in the center of Kabul, hemmed in by the clamoring crowd.

Luckily, she was just a few streets away from the house of a family friend. She and another girl fled there, and the family cracked open the door to let them in. Moor called Agha to tell him she was safe. He was dizzy with relief—he had thought she'd died in the violence.

Over three hundred people were killed in the riots. Now residents of Kabul had to grapple with the fact that their country was at war with the Soviets.

Amid this turmoil, Moor graduated from Kabul University with a degree in chemistry in 1982. She returned to campus just a few weeks later, this time as an instructor within the chemistry department.

Now that their younger daughter was settled professionally and financially, Agha and Ana Jana began to consider the question of her marriage. Agha's only condition on this subject had been that she wait until after her college graduation. He thought she might even secure a "love match" at Kabul University and avoid the complexities of an arranged marriage altogether.

But despite the freedom she found at college, Moor had always been a bookish, quiet girl. She never dated. Eventually, her parents began fielding requests and setting up meetings with potential matches. Early in their search, they received a marriage proposal from my father's family. A year earlier he had offered to marry Moor's older sister. But

Yasmin had become a free spirit, emboldened by her years in Russia. She refused the marriage request on the grounds that she was in love with someone else, a man she'd eventually marry and live with in Pakistan.

So in 1981 Baba's family tried again. This time they requested that Moor be the one to join their family.

THE FIRST THING MOOR NOTICED WHEN SHE MOVED INTO Baba's house was that the kitchen cabinets were bolted closed. A few onions and heads of garlic sat idly on a shelf in the pantry, but almost everything else—pomegranates, cardamom, sweets, flour—was locked firmly within the cupboards. Ana Bibi, Moor's new mother-in-law, held the key and refused to give it to my mother. For the past decade, she'd been a widow, running her large family with an iron fist. She claimed Moor was too ignorant and irresponsible to be trusted with unfettered access to the family's food.

My mother didn't know how to respond to Ana Bibi's spiteful words. She had married into the family only a few days earlier, in a small ceremony held at their relative's house. She had secretly wanted her wedding to be a traditional multiday affair. She'd imagined wearing a bright green Afghan bridal gown and imported gold-tipped shoes, spooning copious amounts of catered food onto her plate, dancing in a large hall until the early morning. But Agha persuaded her to have a smaller wedding so she and Baba could save money for their new family.

After the wedding, Moor traveled with Baba's family to their house in Kote Sangi, one of Kabul's busiest neighborhoods. The house bordered a main street teeming with foot traffic and packed with dozens of vendors who all day long called out, "Snacks, fresh and hot, snacks!" Drivers maneuvered around the crowds, honking insistently and gesturing at people to get out of the way. The house had just two bedrooms. My parents at least had their own, but my father's younger brother Ali Kaka, his younger sister Ama Shirina, and his mother, Ana Bibi, all shared the other one. They all used one outdoor bathroom equipped with a squat toilet.

Moor tried to settle into her new home. As Baba's wife, she was expected to contribute the most to household chores. She cooked massive five- or six-course spreads for her new household at lunch and again for dinner. Afterward she stood alone in the small kitchen, scrubbing all the dishes. In the few spare hours when she wasn't cooking, she would hand-wash laundry or sweep all the floors.

In spite of Moor's efforts, Ana Bibi harbored an instant, inexplicable distaste toward her. Ana Bibi's animosity only increased after it became clear that my mother was simply not very good at household tasks. Since Agha had insisted she forgo all domestic lessons with her mother in favor of academic studies, Moor was left unable to cook, clean, or host to Ana Bibi's satisfaction. She burned vegetables, oversalted stews, and missed spots when she scrubbed the kitchen countertops. "My own daughters are educated and they can prepare a basic meal," Ana Bibi would mutter. "So why can't you?" Sometimes she yelled a Pashto obscenity at her that roughly translates to "You are such a good-for-nothing that you couldn't even feed a donkey!"

Moor's relationship with Ama Shirina, Baba's younger sister, wasn't any better. In Afghanistan, direct relatives of the man of the house have a higher standing than those who marry into the family. Since Ama Shirina was related to Baba by blood, she held inherent power over Moor. She was younger than my mother and still in college, but she never helped with a single household chore. She often yelled at Moor to cook her favorite food or clean up a mess she had made. It would have been unthinkably disrespectful for my mother to refuse.

Moor's only escape from this pernicious environment was her job at Kabul University. She split her time there between teaching courses on nutritional science and conducting research on the nutritional benefits of different kinds of milk. When she wasn't in the lab or the classroom, she sat in the chemistry department offices grading problem sets and writing academic papers. Her best friend from her college years worked in a nearby building, and they often ate lunch together, snacking on fruit and tea as they traded stories about their favorite students or their upcoming research deadlines.

Moor flourished at Kabul University. Her career was the dream that Agha had instilled in her so many years earlier. But soon Ana Bibi managed to influence her professional life, too. Every time Moor brought home a paycheck, her mother-in-law pocketed most of it, leaving her only a tiny allowance of her own money. My mother never said anything to stop her, and neither did Baba. He believed the strife between Ana Bibi and his new wife was a

women's issue, something they had to solve between themselves.

A few years later, Ali Kaka got married, and his wife
moved into the already-full household. Moor's new sister-
in-law had grown up in a larger, more conservative house
than Moor had and was well used to being on the lower end
of the pecking order. She was agile, able to appease Ana
Bibi and get what she wanted. In the afternoons when Ana
Bibi was out visiting friends, my aunt picked the lock on the
cabinets and stole dried fruits and nuts. Once she even
sneaked into a storeroom through an open window and
hauled out armfuls of hidden pomegranates.

Moor could never bring herself to join in on these escapades. She didn't know how to fight for what she wanted,
because she'd never had to do it before. She was too afraid
of breaking rules or showing disrespect to Ana Bibi's age
and authority. And so Ana Bibi continued to play the part
that so many Afghan mothers-in-law play, the harsh discipli-
narian, unrelenting critic, and unquestioned authority. Ana
Bibi herself had withered under the gaze of her husband's
mother, but that experience inspired no empathy. Instead of
liberating her new daughter from a life she knew so well,
she took an incomprehensible, twisted pleasure in enforc-
ing it.

As Moor grappled with her new environment, she also
had to contend with the shifting political situation in Afghanistan. Fighting against the Soviets intensified. Extrem-
ist resistance groups were spurred on by growing public
support and became known collectively as the mujahideen,
which translates to "those engaged in jihad." They received
billions of dollars' worth of financial contributions from

countries, including the United States and Pakistan, that had their own geopolitical reasons for wanting to undermine the Soviet-backed Afghan government.

Like many educated Afghans, my family wanted the Soviets to retain control over the country. They believed a Soviet Afghanistan would be more stable and modern than a radical Islamic guerrilla government. Many of my relatives had received high-paying jobs and exceptional education as a result of Soviet investment. The USSR seemed an infinitely better choice than the fledgling mujahideen.

Years later, when I asked my parents to tell me stories from this period, they never uttered a bad word about the Soviets. But others murmured their distaste for the Russian invaders. They told me that Soviets had been the "lowest of all humans" without any religion or sense of morality to guide them. It became common in Afghanistan to curse at someone by calling them the daughter or son of a Russian.

The Soviets controlled major urban centers, but the mujahideen had more influence in the Afghan countryside. In an attempt to curtail popular support for the resistance fighters, the Soviets dropped bombs on rural areas, leading to the mass migration of millions of Afghans to neighboring Pakistan and Iran.

My parents rarely saw an actual guerrilla fighter, since the mujahideen couldn't penetrate Kabul. But the situation was very different in Kandahar, my parents' childhood home. Baba and Moor heard horrifying accounts from their friends and families about the brutal mujahideen regime there.

One story was especially painful for my mother. Moor's childhood neighbor lived in Kandahar and was married to an official in the Soviet-backed government. One afternoon a rowdy group of mujahid fighters showed up at her door-step and demanded she tell her husband to quit his job. She refused, and they cursed at her in Pashto. She swore back at them, and they recoiled, leaving almost as fast as they came. But in the middle of the night, the fighters returned to avenge their honor. They murdered Moor's friend in cold blood.

My parents heard stories about atrocities committed by the highest-ranking Kandahari mujahid warlords. One mujahid was known for casually leafing through photos of students at local girls' schools. When he found a young girl who looked attractive to him, he would appear at her father's doorstep with a rifle in one hand and a handsome dowry in another. The implication was that he'd shoot the man if he didn't hand over his daughter.

There were stories too of bribery, looting, and assault. Many of my parents' friends were forced to hand over their college-educated daughters to satisfy lecherous, violent mujahid fighters. Those who crossed the mujahideen faced torturous and even deadly consequences. One Kandahari mujahid was known for submerging his victims in honey, then setting them in front of a swarm of bees. Others simply shot and killed anyone who dared to stand up to them.

My parents were lucky to live away from this chaos. Their friends and family wanted desperately to join them but couldn't: all the roads from Kandahar to Kabul were controlled by the mujahideen.

IN 1983 THE SOVIET-AFGHAN war escalated. Fighting between the mujahideen and Soviet forces reached the heart of Kabul and killed scores of civilians. My parents were soon used to being woken up in the middle of the night by the thundering, dull echo of a rocket strike. Over and over again they ran to their landlord's basement across the street to take cover.

One night a rocket hit the house next door to theirs. Ashen debris rained down over the street, and the ground shook from the blast's impact. My parents waited in their basement shelter, unsure whether their house had survived. In the morning, groups of neighbors crowded around the rubble to survey the damage. They found a little girl's body lying in what was left of the hallway outside her bedroom. She had been running toward her parents, frightened by loud noises from the rockets that killed her. The girl's death horrified my mother. Just a few months earlier she had found out she was pregnant with her first child. She couldn't bear to wonder what it would be like if that little girl had been hers, if she had lost a child in an instant. She spent nights filled with restless dreams, then nights with no sleep at all. She lay awake all night, drifting off finally when she heard the clinking of tea saucers as Ana Bibi started break-fast the next morning.

My eldest sister, Aisha, was born that summer. She was adorable, I'm told, with a head of black hair and big ques-tioning eyes. Everyone loved her except for Ana Bibi, who was upset that Moor hadn't given her a grandson. "You are unlucky, just like your mother," she hissed at Moor. "Can you only give birth to girls?" But just a few years later my brother Nadir was born, which appeased Ana Bibi for a while.

As Aisha learned to walk and Nadir said his first words,

the power balance between the Soviets and the mujahideen was shifting. At the end of 1986, the United States and
other countries increased the number of weapons they supplied to the mujahideen. Most impactfully, they sent over
antiaircraft Stinger missiles that could be fired at Soviet
planes from a mujahid's shoulder. Both Soviet and Afghan-
government troops saw their air fleets neutralized. The Soviets, no longer able to attack the mujahideen from the air
unencumbered, lost their military advantage.

The Soviets blamed Afghan president Babrak Karmal for
Afghanistan's new troubles. He stepped down in 1986, supposedly due to bad health. Karmal was succeeded by Mohammad Najibullah, the former head of Afghanistan's secret
police who had once served alongside Baba in the Afghan
military. Najibullah had embraced the nonreligious, strictly
Communist Soviet ideology. He even called himself Najib,
forgoing the *ullah,* meaning "God," part of his name. As
head of the secret police, he had been known for his profound ruthlessness and for the pleasure he took in torturing
mujahid prisoners with skewers and electrocutions. There
are even stories that he enjoyed removing the eyes of prisoners with a metal spoon. The Soviets hoped his reputation
and ferocity would reverse their string of bad luck in the
war to control Afghanistan.

But Najibullah did not behave as the Soviets expected
him to. He was aware that the Soviets were losing ground
in Afghanistan and were even considering withdrawing
their forces. So instead of aligning with Communist ideology, he began to paint himself as a nationalist. He established the National Compromise Commission in an attempt
to reconcile Communist and mujahideen forces, and he al-

lowed more parties to enter Afghanistan's political sphere. But average citizens still knew Najibullah mostly for his life-long callous brutality. His attempts at national unity appeared insincere, inspiring deep distrust and rendering him an unpopular leader.

By February 1989, the war in Afghanistan had become too complicated and costly for the Soviets. Under the new president, Mikhail Gorbachev, the USSR withdrew its final troops. Najibullah remained president of Afghanistan and was left to fend off the growing mujahideen threat on his own.

LEFT WITHOUT A COMMON Soviet enemy to fight, the muja-hideen turned their focus on one another. Tensions among different resistance groups flared, and fighting broke out in Kabul between Pashtun mujahideen and those from other ethnic groups. At the time, my family members were the only Pashtuns in their neighborhood, so they were suddenly in tremendous danger.

One day in the spring of 1991, Baba heard about the violence and called Moor from work. "We have to leave Kabul tonight," he said. "They will kill us all once they realize we are Pashtuns." My mother was at home since it had become too dangerous for her to continue her job at the university. Baba made her promise not to leave the house until he procured a car to take them to Kandahar.

Moor and Ana Bibi moved quickly through the house, packing bags and preparing food for the road. Soon it became impossible to ignore the fighting going on around them. They heard screams that sounded as if they were

coming from right outside the door. As she packed, Moor
would be interrupted by a wail so loud and anguished, she
couldn't stand to imagine what had caused it.

At dusk, my father arrived home. In order to get out of
Kabul, he had managed to enlist the help of a Tajik friend
who served in a faction of the mujahideen. My family, including Baba's brother and his wife, climbed into the back
of a waiting armored vehicle packed with Kalashnikovs. As
little Aisha and Nadir stumbled past a seat stacked high with
the rifles, two men turned around from the front seat to
give orders. "I am taking you to Kandahar," the driver said
to my parents. "Whatever you do, do not speak in Pashto. If
you do, we will not make it out alive."

Inside the car, an eerie silence settled.

In the late evening, as my brother and sister fell into
an uneasy sleep, their vehicle rolled to a stop at a makeshift checkpoint. The mujahideen fighters standing guard
pounded on the windows. Then they yanked open the car
doors. My family was huddled together in the back seat. For
a moment, Ana Bibi, paralyzed by fear, forgot the warning
the driver had given them. "Please don't hurt us!" she murmured in Pashto. "We have children here!"

The men stopped abruptly. "What did she just say?" they
barked.

The driver spun around, glaring briefly at my grandmother. "She's just an old woman, she's not making any
sense," he said quickly.

The mujahid guards gazed suspiciously. My parents silently willed them to move on. "Go, go," the guards finally
said, ushering my family through the checkpoint.

They arrived in Kandahar early the next morning. When

they woke, Aisha and Nadir's ears still rang with the sounds of artillery fire.

My family did not return to Kabul for a year. In Kandahar, Baba was restless. It had been seventeen years since he had lived in his hometown, and he found the city cramped, sticky with painful memories of poverty and loss. But Moor settled into provincial life more easily, willing to sacrifice the independence and modernity she'd found in the city for the safety of her childhood home.

In the winter of 1992, my father's business partner called to say that the fighting had died down in Kabul and it was safe to return home. So my parents packed their bags and drove out of Kandahar while the rest of the family, including Ana Bibi, stayed behind.

My parents and siblings moved into a sixth-floor apartment in Macroyan Kohna, a district in the center of Kabul made up of dull gray high-rise complexes built by the Soviets. Aisha and Nadir enrolled in school and settled into a routine. They woke up every morning before sunrise with my mother, to pray and get ready for the day. Then they left for classes that ran from six in the morning until the late afternoon. In the evenings, they studied by electric light, a luxury they hadn't had access to in Kandahar.

Later that year mujahideen fighters from several factions ousted Najibullah from power. They formed a fragile government and developed a power-sharing agreement, granting two-year terms to the leaders of various mujahideen factions. But the unsteady peace was short-lived. After serving for two years, President Burhanuddin Rabbani refused to relinquish power to his agreed-upon successor.

Fighting among mujahideen groups resumed, and the country again descended into conflict.

Rockets began to fall on Kabul. They were launched primarily by Gulbuddin Hekmatyar, leader of the Hezb-e-Islami, or the Islamic Party, a radical faction of the mujahideen. Hekmatyar became known colloquially as the "Butcher of Kabul" and "Rocketyar" for the hundreds of strikes he orchestrated on Afghanistan's capital that likely killed thousands of civilians. My mother had two new children by now, my older brother Yousef and my older sister Roya, who was a newborn baby. Moor and Baba heard muffled explosions coming from just a few miles beyond their Macroyan Kohna apartment. They waited uneasily to see what would happen next.

One night a rocket hit so close to their apartment that the window next to baby Roya's crib shattered. Fortunately the curtains were heavy enough to prevent the glass from flying into the room, but Moor and Baba were shaken. They moved the entire six-person family out of the apartment and into a makeshift shelter in the basement of their building.

They lived in the shelter for one week. The basement was usually home to Kabul's stray cats and dogs, but now it was crowded with dozens of their neighbors. My mother stopped preparing complete meals, and the family survived on pots of rice she cooked on rapid trips back upstairs to the apartment. They all waited together, alternating between collective, somber silence and petty bickering fueled by stress and uncertainty, hearing only fragments of news. One day a rocket strike killed two people outside their complex, and the next, a rocket killed my parents' next-door neighbor.

Then the temperature in the basement began to drop. Outside it started to snow. My parents decided it was too dangerous for their family to remain in Kabul. One day in January 1993, they fled to Shahr-e Naw, a neighborhood in northwestern Kabul that they had heard was relatively safe. They planned to leave for Kandahar the next day, but the roadways out of Shahr-e Naw were crammed with people. People shoved their way into overfilled buses and cars headed out of the city. There was no room on any vehicle for a family as big as mine. My parents shivered in the bitter cold and scanned the roads desperately, looking for a way out.

Suddenly, they heard the sounds of rocket fire approaching. Another attack on Kabul had begun, and they were exposed, standing amid throngs of people. They ran through the streets, looking for shelter, and finally found a store-keeper willing to take them in. They huddled in his small snack shop for hours as the temperature continued to drop and the sun sank in the sky. Two-year-old Yousef began to sob violently.

Finally, the shopkeeper turned to Baba and said, "Brother, you have young children. If they do not die from these rockets, they will die from the cold. You have to find another place to stay."

Baba remembered he had an old friend who lived just a few streets away in Shahr-e Naw. If they could make it to his house, they might be able to shelter there for a few days while they found a way out of Kabul.

My family stayed with Baba's friend for a week. His family gave my siblings warm clothes and fed my parents as they searched for a way to escape the capital. A week later a ceasefire was called among the mujahideen groups, and my family finally found a car willing to take them out of the city. For the second time in as many years, my parents traveled back to their childhood home to live with Baba's brother and his family.

But Kandahar would not prove to be the oasis my parents had hoped for. The various mujahideen factions in the city were at war with one another, this time along tribal rather than ethnic lines. The result was a state of absolute anarchy. Lootings and murders became even more common. Children were abducted, then sold as sex slaves or abused at mujahideen bases. One of my female cousins who lived in Kandahar spent her days entirely indoors. She was afraid that if she stepped outside, someone would storm their property and kidnap her. And the mujahideen continued to govern the chaos with unpredictable brutality.

It was against this volatile, terrifying backdrop that a one-eyed mullah named Mohammad Omar stepped onto the national stage. His burgeoning group of fighters promised a return to order, morality, and traditional Afghan culture. They called themselves the Taliban.

CHAPTER
FOUR

There's a hauntingly beautiful shrine at the center of Kandahar called Kirka Sharif. Its immense teal dome and azure spires rise against the mountainous landscape. Bright yellow and green painted motifs line the structure's exterior, together resembling the most intricate Afghan carpet. Secured between the building's sacred walls is a series of nested silver boxes containing a cloak that once belonged to the Prophet Muhammad. On many days, a sea of turbans and *kameez* fills the shrine's gated courtyard as Afghans offer prayers from the holy site.

Kandaharis say that after Taliban leader Mullah Omar took over their city, he went to Kirka Sharif to procure the cloak. According to local legend, if a man touches or even looks at the garment, he has a mandate from God to rule over the nation.

Perhaps out of fear of the Taliban's leader, the keeper of Kirka Sharif allowed Mullah Omar to take the cloak out of its secure hold. Omar then climbed to the roof of a local mosque, overlooking a large crowd. A bulky turban was balanced atop his head, the loose end falling casually across his shoulder. Where his right eye should have been was a concave hole, covered by his drooping eyelid. But in spite of this uninspiring appearance, the cloak conferred a solemn sense of authority. For a full thirty minutes, Mullah Omar stood in silence, his arms outstretched and contained by sleeves that had once draped over the Prophet Muhammad. Rumor has it that the crowd exploded with cheers and adoration. People stretched their hands toward Omar, as though trying to touch the sacred garment. Some were so overcome with religious devotion that they fainted.

In securing possession of Muhammad's cloak, Mullah Omar gained the legitimacy he needed to fuel his conquest of all Afghanistan. That same year he would lead the Taliban in a fateful invasion of Kabul.

IT WAS THE SPRING of 1994 when most Kandaharis first heard about the Taliban. They learned that the burgeoning group was a small band of religious-minded Pashtun fighters, dedicated to ridding the city of the moral corruption that flourished under mujahideen rule. Many Talibs were Afghan refugees who had fled to Pakistan during the Soviet invasion. There they were educated in conservative madrassas, or religious schools, that received funding and support from the Pakistani government.

The Taliban's beginnings in Afghanistan are shrouded in myth. It's difficult to separate the truth about the militant group's origins from the legends that were spread later on to bolster their religious and political legitimacy. But all the stories share a common component: they highlight the contrast between the mujahideen's debauchery and the supposed virtue of the Taliban.

One such origin story supposedly took place at a mujahideen compound located in Kandahar. Apparently a warlord had just kidnapped two teenage girls, shaved their heads, and brutally raped them at his base. Outrage grew in the local community against this incident, but no one had the capacity to stand up to the all-powerful mujahideen. But one afternoon the Taliban stormed the mujahid's compound with just thirty scraggly fighters and sixteen rifles shared among them. They liberated the girls and hung the mujahideen commander from the barrel of a tank, displaying his body for all to see. The incident was a preview of the kind of justice the Taliban would exact in the coming years.

As stories like this one spread, membership in the Taliban swelled. Some Kandaharis claim the Taliban's ranks grew to thousands of men in just a few days, all dressed alike in jet-black turbans and long beards. In accordance with *sunnah*, or the traditions of the Prophet Muhammad, they lined their eyes with a smear of black powder. From their wardrobe to their ideology, the group evoked a sense of order and strong discipline that Afghans craved.

On November 3, 1994, the Taliban took over Kandahar. They sacrificed only twelve of their fighters in exchange for control of Afghanistan's second-largest city. It is still unclear how the Taliban managed to defeat the mujahideen so quickly. Some people believe that Pakistan, intent on gaining control of the region, bribed mujahideen commanders to surrender to the Taliban. The interior minister of Pakistan, General Babar, even referred to the Taliban victors as "our boys," which adds some credence to this theory.

But at the time, none of this mattered. The Taliban were celebrated in Kandahar for their military victory. My parents, like so many of their neighbors, were flooded with relief. They had been so afraid for my siblings during the mujahideen time, worried they would be kidnapped and abused. Now they thought things would change. It seemed as though, at least in Kandahar, Afghans might have a shot at security and peace.

I WAS BORN TWO YEARS after the Taliban seized Kandahar. During her pregnancy with me, my mother looked beautiful, I was told, and even more youthful than her thirty-six years. My family used to tell me she exhibited a radiant glow, as though there were something special about the child she was carrying. According to Afghan superstition, if an expectant woman is extremely healthy, she will give birth to a boy. Everyone around Moor assumed this would be the good fortune to come from her perfect pregnancy: a son to follow my sister Roya, who had been born three years earlier. Neighbors, relatives, and even Ana Bibi told my siblings to expect a new baby brother.

When my mother's time drew near, Ana Bibi made arrangements for a midwife to come to the house to help with the delivery. All Kandahar's maternity wards were closed because most doctors had fled the city when the mujahideen came to power. The only obstetrics doctor remaining was a woman who closed her doors at night. She was still scarred by the brutalities that had taken place under the cover of darkness in the years before the Taliban. If a woman went into labor after dark, as my mother did, she had to give birth without a doctor's help.

I arrived early on a summer morning in 1996 with a mop

of curly brown hair and a nose too large for my tiny face. My mother was thrilled to see me, relieved the delivery had gone smoothly at home. But the rest of the bedroom fell silent with surprise, then disappointment. After a few minutes, my aunt ventured outside to break the news to my siblings. Aisha, twelve years old at the time, was preparing breakfast, carrying a tray full of water glasses to the rest of the family. "Aisha," my aunt began tentatively, as though trying to shield her niece from devastating news, "you have a new sister." Shocked, Aisha dropped the tray she was carrying. A dozen glasses shattered across the kitchen floor, covering the tile in hundreds of shards.

I cried so hard the day I was born, my parents thought something was wrong with me. Hours passed, and still I wailed uncontrollably. There was no way the obstetrics doctor could come since she had so many other emergencies to deal with. Going to Kandahar's run-down hospital was not an option, as my family knew the wards were rife with infection. Moor watched me helplessly, praying for my recovery. My maternal grandmother, Ana Jana, who was in Kandahar for my birth, wished for something different. "Don't be sad that she is a girl," she said to my family, trying to comfort them. "She will not live through the night."

But in spite of Ana Jana's prediction, I was alive the next morning. My parents named me Sola.

Slowly, as weeks passed, the rest of the family recovered from their shock. Aisha played with me in the afternoons and learned how to swaddle me in a blanket. On some nights, my aunt rocked me to sleep. My brothers tiptoed around me curiously, poking at my toes and fiddling with my blanket.

But my birth remained a profoundly unhappy occasion for my paternal grandmother, Ana Bibi. She grieved my birth the way one would a death and roamed the house cloaked in sadness, barely offering up conversation or a smile. For four months, longer than the Islamic mourning period, she refused to feed me or hold me in her arms.

MOOR WAS THE ONLY one who adored me from the moment she saw me. She rarely left my side, at first as she recovered from her delivery and then as she began to cook dinners again and wash piles of dishes and discipline her four elder children.

Perhaps I was a welcome distraction from the dystopia unfolding around her. Just weeks after the Taliban took over our city, my parents realized they had been wrong to assume the new leaders would provide respite from the fear they'd felt living under the mujahideen. The group had taken over most of Afghanistan by that point, moving swiftly from province to province and encountering little resistance from mujahideen-weary villagers and city dwellers. Just a few months after I was born, they took over Kabul and declared Afghanistan an Islamic emirate with Mullah Omar at its helm. Though few Afghans knew it at the time, the Taliban were also harboring terrorist mastermind Osama bin Laden, who in turn was providing them with generous financial support.

In the name of Islam, the Taliban banned television, music, games, photographs, and most schools. My siblings hid their photographs and posters of Bollywood stars under our woodstove. The roads in Kandahar were strewn with broken cassettes and videotapes that had been confiscated and destroyed by the Taliban. My sister Aisha was forced to stop attending school, and my sister Roya didn't have a chance to start. My brother Nadir, who was eleven, eventually quit because he did not want to adhere to the stringent new guidelines for schoolchildren.

The Taliban had a strict dress code for their citizens. Men were required to wear black turbans and long, untrimmed beards. Almost overnight, Baba shed his image as a youthful father and turned older somehow, more imposing. Any hint of a smile was hidden behind his sprouting new facial hair. "Western-style" collars like the kind on men's dress shirts were also banned. Only the single-layer collars on traditional Afghan *kameez* were allowed. One day my brother ventured out of the house for a quick errand wearing an old shirt with a Western collar. The Talib who caught him cut the offending collar off, his knife wavering just inches from my brother's newly bearded face.

One of my male cousins was just a teenager when the Taliban took over. One evening, on the way to have dinner at our house, he decided to try a new hairstyle. He squinted into the car's blurry mirror, adjusting each strand carefully. Technically the hairstyle he wanted didn't conform to Taliban dress code, but he didn't think anyone could see him. But a Talib spotted him through the dusty window of his family's sedan. The Talib waved the car off the busy road, forced my cousin out of the car, and shaved his head, right there on the street. Though that experience gave my cousin a jolt of reality, it wasn't enough to dissuade him from doing it again. Just a few weeks later, again on the way to our house, he started to style his beard in a manner contrary to Taliban regulations. This time the Talib who caught him arrested him and threw him in a jail cell for three days. "I was sitting with criminals!" he told us when he got out, visibly shaken. "There were murderers next to me. What did I do to deserve the same punishment as them?"

My mother seemed to have it the worst, though. During the days of the mujahideen, in order to stay safe from lawless fighters, she'd stopped teaching at Kabul University and traded her long skirts and breezy scarves for a full burqa. But she'd clung to the hope that her withdrawal was temporary, that once the turmoil from the fighting settled, she'd return to her former life.

When the Taliban came to power, however, they brought a sense of permanence. A quieter militancy tightened around the city, wrapping women in a constant chokehold, mandating they wear burqas and banning them from the workplace. These new edicts handed down by Mullah Omar went uncontested. Moor realized with a gradual, sinking dread that she would never return to teaching, that her own daughters would never experience the respect and dignity that comes from having an education. She tried relentlessly to convince my father to move the family to Pakistan so we could all attend school. But he refused. "No one else is leaving," he told her. "Why should we? I cannot make money in Pakistan—my business is here. Our whole lives are here."

In her role as the eldest child, Aisha tried to persuade my mother to accept their new life. She was almost a teenager at this time, a young girl who had lived through the incomparable brutality of civil war. She'd seen people shot, stared at dead people lying in the streets. Her education and even her freedom seemed a small price to pay the Taliban for the end of war. But Moor had lived something better than her daughter had. She struggled to let go of what the past had promised.

Moor's burqa, made of deceptively cheery sky-blue material, was weighty and restrictive. The Afghan burqa is the most confining covering for women in the world. The tent-like fabric obscures women's shoulders, arms, and legs. Without any sleeves or openings for the face, it strips them of their sense of humanity, reducing them to sky-blue monoliths.

My brother Nadir, just eleven at the time, wasn't used to seeing Moor in a burqa. He had to learn to walk with her through Kandahar's streets and guide her as though she were blind. He yanked her out of the way of jutting curbs and errant passersby, worried that she couldn't see anything at all. She could see a little, of course, through the openings in the mesh screen just before her eyes. But his innocent assessment was generally right. Moor had lost her independence, her personality, her full view of the outside world. As she walked down the streets of Taliban-controlled Kandahar, supervised by her young son, she must have felt as though she really had gone blind.

THE TALIBAN ALWAYS LOOMED NEAR. After they took over Kandahar, they went from house to house confiscating weapons to prevent even the possibility of armed resistance to their rule. Later they conducted random raids in an attempt to catch people watching movies or playing games.

Many of our friends were detained after they were caught playing cards or trimming their beards.

One afternoon in 1999, soon after she gave birth to my younger brother, Javid, my mother invited some friends over for tea and snacks. Their husbands dropped them off and drove away. As the women walked up the path to our front door, one of them told a joke that sent everyone into peals of laughter. Then they knocked for my mother to let them in and lingered for hours, pouring cup after cup of green tea.

Several hours later, as my mother was cleaning up stray saucers and dessert crumbs, she heard a firm rapping on the door. My uncle, who was at home with her at the time, cracked it open. As he peered out, he locked eyes with a Talib.

"Three women were here this morning," the Talib spat. "They were laughing. Who were they?"

My uncle knew if he revealed their names, my mother's friends could be beaten or even killed. "I don't know," he responded, trying to appear nonchalant. "No one was laughing here."

"Don't lie to me!" the Talib yelled. "Where are those women?"

"I don't know."

"You tell me right now who they were and where they live, or I will throw you in jail!"

"I don't know. Sorry, brother."

Angered by my uncle's perceived insolence, the Talib grabbed his wrists and pulled him into a waiting van. My mother watched through the window, horrified. In the hours that followed, no one called to tell us where my uncle had been taken or what they were doing to him. He returned over twelve hours later, his face hollow from a night spent in a grimy Taliban prison cell.

There wasn't always a man to take the fall for an offending woman. And when the Taliban caught women disobeying the rules, they could concoct punishments even more elaborate and painful than imprisonment. Many Kandahari women took a risk every day by leaving home without a man to go shopping or visit relatives. Their husbands and sons were usually at work or out with friends, unwilling to accompany them. So the women just moved quickly through the streets and kept their heads down as they sped away on rickshaws, praying a Talib would not come along and find them.

Two of Moor's friends were alone at the bazaar one day when the Taliban spotted them. The Talibs shoved the women into the back of a pickup truck and drove them all around Kandahar. "Look at these shameful women!" they shouted into a megaphone as they cruised by crowds of people. My mother's friends lowered their heads, mortified. After an hour, the Talibs grew tired and drove the women home.

Another friend of my mother's was not so lucky. I have a foggy memory of walking to her house with Moor, opening the front door, and freezing at the sight of the woman's bloodied, swollen legs. The Taliban had caught her out alone and whipped her repeatedly. Even today I can picture what she looked like at that moment, a grown woman humiliated and bruised and sobbing on her living room floor.

———

THE TALIBAN COMMITTED OTHER atrocities that we didn't witness personally, some so heinous they're too painful to speak of. They burned villages and presided over mass killings. In Kabul, the Taliban transformed a soccer stadium into a public execution arena. They staged stonings, amputations, and killings in front of scores of spectators. Some people came voluntarily to watch the murders, while others were coerced by the Taliban. *This could happen to you,* the Talibs seemed to be warning the hushed crowds.

I was just a toddler in those days, thankfully too young to understand the horrific violence occurring around me. Instead, I spent my time playing with my cousins and siblings, whom I alternately adored and bickered with incessantly. When I turned three in 1999, my grandmother Ana Bibi sent me with all the other children in the family to study the Quran at a neighbor's house. I was too young to learn very much, so I spent most of my time chatting with my cousins. In the afternoons, we came home to the smell of Moor frying papads, paper-thin lentil crisps that melted in our mouths. Once Moor wouldn't let us eat any more, my cousin Mojdeh and I would go outside to play. Our favorite pastime on blistering hot days was to gather buckets of water from a nearby mosque and pour them over each other, screaming with exhilaration as the cold liquid gushed down our backs. Sometimes we poured so many buckets on each other that we flooded the entryway to our house. Water trickled toward the front door, and we'd look at each other worriedly, certain we'd invited a serious scolding. But then the hot sun would beam down on us again, and we'd race back to the mosque for more water, shrieking with laughter the whole way there.

In 2000, when I was four, our entire joint family moved. Baba and my uncle had gathered their savings and designed a compound, still in Kandahar, for all nine of us to live in. The property was sweeping. There were two double-story structures, one for our family and one for my cousins. Our house had five bedrooms and a massive modern kitchen with a stove and a refrigerator, though we rarely had electricity to power it. The building's doors were outlined in decorative wooden frames, the exterior walls accented with sea-green tiles, the foundation lined with a border of rough-cut stones. The large garden would grow to be filled with pale yellow roses and sprawling grapevines. Tall, cylindrical columns marked the corners of the compound's verandas, and high walls surrounded both buildings, protecting us from the prying eyes of any power-hungry Talibs. Though occasional hints betrayed our urban location—the din of street vendors, persistent films of dust that coated everything, the roar of a passing Taliban convoy—our new compound still felt like an oasis.

BY 2001, THE TALIBAN controlled 90 percent of the country. To refer to the Afghan government was to refer to the Taliban. Police officers, teachers, and even neighbors were Talibs. In contrast to the flawed and unpopular leaders who had preceded them, the group seemed invincible.

On September 11, 2001, as per her evening ritual, my

mother turned on the radio. With television banned, the BBC radio broadcast was one of the few ways to understand what was going on in the rest of the world. That night my family learned that there were buildings in America called the Twin Towers and that they had fallen. They learned about the hijackers on four airplanes and about the thousands of people who were dead. The house fell into an uneasy silence as everyone strained to listen.

A few weeks later my family was still discussing the attack. We had learned that a terrorist named Osama bin Laden was likely responsible. He was a part of a terrorist group known as al-Qaeda. My grandmother Ana Bibi was nervous. "Do you think what has happened in America will affect us?" she asked at dinner one evening. My father and my uncle actually laughed at her. They couldn't imagine that a tragedy from so far away could ever have an impact on Afghanistan.

They were unbelievably wrong. On October 7, an American coalition launched a full-scale invasion of Afghanistan in retaliation against the Taliban, who were protecting Osama bin Laden and other al-Qaeda leaders. Unfazed by the Americans' actions, Mullah Omar came onto the air, urging Afghans not to flee the country, but to stay and fight for Taliban rule. "Don't be a coward!" he boomed, his voice crackling across the airwaves. But my parents had seen enough war. They decided we would relocate to Pakistan until the fighting subsided. Our joint family left Afghanistan that same month, in a van filled with everyone except for my uncle and my brother Nadir, then sixteen years old. The two of them had decided to remain in Kandahar, even amid the deadly fighting, to protect our compound from attacks and lootings.

We could drive only as far as the border, then had to cross into Pakistan by foot because no Afghan vehicles were allowed on Pakistani soil. The border was chaotic, a scene that haunted me for months in my nightmares. Luggage handlers thronged around us, snatching our suitcases and demanding payment for their services. Pakistani border agents yelled out instructions and berated offenders. Some agents, fueled by an inexplicable rage, grabbed Afghans trying to cross over and beat them with electric cables, ignoring their screams for mercy. I watched these scenes unfold with horror as Moor pulled me urgently through the crossing. I couldn't understand what the men lying on the ground, writhing in pain, had done wrong, and I was terrified the agents would come after my father next. Eventually, though, we made it across unscathed and piled into one of the taxi vans lining the border in Pakistan.

That afternoon we arrived at Baba's sister's house in Quetta, a major city about ninety miles from the border. When I was younger, we had often visited my aunt on long vacations, and at first this trip felt no different to me. My cousins and I ran shrieking through the house playing tag and our own made-up games. We gaped at the manicured parks and play structures in Quetta that didn't exist in Kandahar. We ate my aunt's cooking and watched hours of Bollywood movies that the Taliban forbade.

But soon I realized this journey to Pakistan was different. My Quetta aunt and uncle were too nice. They engaged us in long conversations, took us on outings, fed us an irresponsible amount of sweets. Meanwhile my parents were distracted and tense. They sat in front of the TV watching the news religiously and spoke in low tones I strained to hear.

I came to understand how worried my parents were one afternoon just a few days after our arrival. My sister Aisha was watching a Bollywood movie in an adjoining room while I sat among the adults, entertaining myself. Suddenly, she burst in on us. "He died!" she exclaimed, before dissolving into tears. Baba stood up, his face suddenly grave. "Who died, Aisha?!" he asked firmly. "Who?"

"Akshay Kumar!" my sister responded between sniffles. Kumar was a famous Indian actor who was performing the lead role in whatever movie she'd been watching. She was crying, we soon realized, because his character had died.

Baba was furious. "How can you say something like that when there is real fighting going on in our own country!" he yelled. "I thought someone we knew had really died! Don't you ever scare us like that again."

A few days later our family left for Karachi, a port city on the Arabian Sea, to live with some relatives from my mother's side: my four cousins, my aunt, my uncle, and Ana Jana, who had moved to Pakistan. We were now twelve people in total, sharing a tiny three-bedroom flat in Karachi's poor area. Our apartment complex was rickety and coated with dust. Each unit had a small balcony that looked out onto the congested, noisy street clogged with air pollution. Residents used the balcony ledge to hang up their wet laundry. Pink blouses, blue towels, and cream-colored pants formed a kind of modern mosaic across the facade of the building.

Baba didn't stay with us in Karachi. Having secured our passage across the country, he left to go home and be with my uncle and brother.

Back in Kandahar, he tried to protect our house and his office from rampant looting. He kept close watch on my mother's expensive gold jewelry, carrying it with him across town as he moved between both his properties. But his biggest problem was right next door. We had some Arab neighbors who my parents had recently come to suspect might be members of al-Qaeda. Baba grew afraid that the Americans would mistakenly bomb our house in their attempt to take out the terrorists living next door. He took to spending cold nights trying to fall asleep outside in a faraway gutter, believing he was safer in the streets than in his own home.

Things were calmer on our side of the border. Moor sent Roya and me to the same religious school, or madrassa, to keep us occupied during the day. Since we had crossed into Pakistan illegally, we didn't have the necessary paperwork to enroll in a formal academic school.

At madrassa I learned to read the Quran, studied the Arabic alphabet, and practiced reading religious passages. I have happy memories of how, during our breaks, we would run to the madrassa snack shop and buy fistfuls of lollipops and candies that had never been available to us in Kandahar.

Perhaps to distract us from our uncertain existence, Moor often took us shopping in Karachi's glittering bazaars. In Kandahar, the street vendors had never sold ready-made clothes, only bolts of fabric. But in Karachi, rows of stalls were lined with dazzling outfits I'd never seen before: teal gowns sewn with hundreds of tiny mirrors, bright pink scarves trimmed with golden thread, maroon blouses heavy with ornate embroidery. Moor laughed as my eyes widened with each turn through the bazaar. She bought me bangles, nail polish, a pair of sandals. Years later, in my dreams, I'd be back in those Karachi markets, twirling between stalls and clutching my presents, surrounded by a display more staggering than I'd even been able to imagine.

Months passed. Eid al-Fitr, the biggest holiday in Islam, came and went. Despite all the new experiences I had in Karachi, our family's separation still weighed on me. We watched the news incessantly, peering at BBC reports for a glimpse of Kandahar. We missed my father and Nadir so much that we took to watching the same Bollywood movie over and over again in the evenings because it featured an actor who looked like my brother. Even though I was very young, I shared the sense that we were suspended in time, waiting for something to occur that was too far beyond our control.

I N 2001, BEFORE WE LEFT KANDAHAR FOR KARACHI, MY
sixteen-year-old sister Aisha received a marriage proposal.
For months, overbearing aunts and neighbors and even perfect strangers had been pressuring my mother to get her
eldest daughter married. Moor hadn't married Baba until
she graduated from university, but in Taliban-controlled Afghanistan Aisha had no hope of ever finishing her education.

The man who wanted to marry Aisha was thirty-five
years old. My sister was ready to accept the marriage, to
bow to the desires of her elders. "I thought this was how a
woman's life is," she told me years later.

But my eldest brother, Nadir, then sixteen, was furious.
"I will never speak to you again if you arrange this marriage," he told Moor. "But this boy is nice," my mother
would say. "The boy will take care of Aisha." This only
made Nadir angrier. "How can you call him a boy?" he
shouted. "You are marrying Aisha off to an old man!"

The women clamoring around my mother vehemently
disagreed with Nadir's assessment. They told Moor not to
worry about it, that marriage was the best thing that she

could do for her daughter. My grandmother Ana Bibi even declared the age difference would be a benefit for Aisha. "You know, an old man has the most love to give to a pretty girl," she said, laughing suggestively. In all the years since she first married Baba, Moor had never summoned the courage to disagree with these women. She made arrangements for the man's family to visit our home in Kandahar and finalize the engagement. But within days of her sending the invitation, the Americans invaded Afghanistan. In the commotion of war, Aisha's engagement was forgotten.

My mother laughed with relief as she told me this story many years later. I was amazed at how she'd almost made such a terrible mistake with her daughter, but a war had saved her.

TWO MONTHS AFTER THE American invasion of Afghanistan, on December 7, 2001, the Taliban surrendered control of Kandahar, losing their final piece of Afghan territory. American forces had been triumphant, reducing Taliban control from 90 percent of the country to almost none in just a matter of months. In January 2002, six months after my fifth birthday, Baba took an eighteen-hour bus ride from Kandahar to Karachi to pick us up. We wanted to stay in Karachi with him to celebrate Eid and the end of the war, but he insisted we return home right away.

The first sign that things had changed in Afghanistan was when my father pulled into a shop and bought two brand-new television sets to replace the ones we'd been forced to get rid of after the Taliban invasion. When we arrived at the compound, I jumped out of the car with my cousins and my siblings Roya and Javid. The weather was warm—it felt like spring even though it was the dead of winter. Since our gardener hadn't left Kandahar during the fighting, the garden was beginning to bloom. Though the flowers hadn't blossomed yet, the vegetables were ripe and ready to be picked. That afternoon my uncle fried okra on an outdoor stove as we sat on the veranda, marveling that we were finally home. I ran around the garden with my siblings and cousins, relishing the space of our sprawling compound.

Returning to Kandahar, I felt as if I were seeing my city in color for the first time. Though burqas still proliferated, men walking in the streets now wore more fashionable clothes and had close-shaven beards. The bazaar stalls were stuffed with imported clothing from Pakistan that women could wear under their burqas: gold earrings inlaid with jewels, high-heeled sandals, and brightly colored dresses adorned with intricate embroidery and small, circular mirrors.

Though the Americans had been in Kandahar for only a few months, they cultivated a secure, hopeful environment that spurred unprecedented modernization. The streets I remembered as alternately muddy and dusty, depending on the weather, were now paved with smooth concrete. Grassy parks like the ones we'd seen in Karachi opened up, as did an amusement park with rickety Ferris wheels and a carousel. A local shrine near the Arghandab River called the Shrine of Baba Wali had been redesigned, and its newly painted teal-and-white dome gleamed in the sunlight. We started going there for picnics and hikes along the adjacent trails.

It even smelled different in the city. During the Taliban

time, any perfumes containing ethanol were banned, since alcohol is forbidden by the Quran. Instead, women had worn what my cousins and I referred to as "Islamic perfume"—an unpleasantly strong, headache-inducing scent that lingered everywhere. Now the light imported aromas were back, carried gently by the warming breeze.

There was a spirit of collective giddiness in Kandahar those first few months, a sense of happy disbelief at how prosperous and safe Afghanistan had suddenly become. Aid money poured in. Friends of ours who had once been unable to afford even a bicycle were now building stately compounds with glass windows and paved walkways. It wasn't uncommon to witness large, impromptu festivals held during class breaks at the newly reopened local schools. Throngs of people would gather around street vendors, and boys would buy snacks and sweets for girls they wanted to impress. Eventually, some official would order an end to the party and mandate his students return to class.

I cherished the changes that accompanied our return to Afghanistan. The simplest of things felt like the most incredible adventure. Baba bought a secondhand car and drove my siblings and me around the city in the evenings, letting us peer out of open windows at construction sites and passing open-air rickshaws. Sometimes on especially warm nights, he would buy us a treat from the new ice cream vendor who sold an American-style "international" novelty instead of the thick, cardamom-laced Afghan ice cream we were used to. The man would bend down and hand us an overflowing cone, then leave to find his next customer, punctuating his steps with warbling cries of "Ice cream! Ice cream!"

We didn't just stay in Kandahar. For the first time in my life, we felt safe moving throughout the country. We drove west to Lashkar Gah, the city that had once been known as "Little America," and dined on fried fish from the nearby river. On another trip, we visited a private park with dozens of freshwater swimming pools. As I splashed my cousins with the lukewarm water, my sister unpacked homemade kebabs and poured generous cups of Pepsi from two-liter bottles. At the time in Afghanistan, sodas were incredibly expensive, and people who could afford to drink them were the epitome of cool. I returned home from that trip and bragged to my friends that on my vacation, we "drank Pepsi as though it was water."

On the way home from these trips, we had to drive through security checkpoints. My sister Roya and I thought the Western soldiers were so heroic and stately. Since they spoke English, we believed they were all from America, though later we realized some were from other countries, including Canada. We hoped to get lucky and have one of them assigned to check our car rather than an Afghan army officer. Anytime we encountered a foreign soldier, my father would approach him confidently and make conversation with the few English words he knew as we whispered excitedly in the background. We felt no animosity toward the Americans for invading our country. In defeating the Taliban, they had saved us from an undisputed evil and propelled Afghanistan to heights it hadn't seen in decades. If anything, we were a little starstruck by their presence.

In my excitement at our new TVs and sudden vacations and encounters with foreigners, I never stopped to consider whether my entire family's life had changed as drastically as mine had. While my mother and Aisha were incredibly grateful for the American victory, they weren't living the sudden utopia that I was. From the beginning, Kandahar had been Mullah Omar's stronghold, and many Kandaharis still believed in his vision of Afghanistan, where women should remain concealed in kitchens and behind veils. Marauding bands of angry, disenfranchised Taliban supporters still posed a threat to any women over the age of thirteen. Ordinary men proved willing to assault women who were behaving in a manner they deemed too liberal or Western.

So Aisha and Moor still wore the blue burqa—even to show their eyes at the bazaar would have been considered shameful, provocative behavior. The pervading culture of conservatism in Kandahar controlled their every move, with the result that the politics of whoever happened to be in power affected their lives only marginally.

IN APRIL 2002, a year after her near-engagement to the thirty-five-year-old, my parents engaged Aisha to another man. Kashif was young, just a few years older than my sister. Most important, he worked in the UK and promised to bring Aisha over in a few years, as soon as he could get her a visa. Even though the future was looking more optimistic for Afghanistan, the country was still stalled by poverty and corruption and an antiquated, traditional belief system. An escape for Aisha to the West was more than my parents could have asked for.

We had her engagement ceremony at our Kandahar compound. She dressed in a long green dress with delicate voile sleeves and draped a thin veil over her head. Aisha was truly happy. She thought Kashif was handsome with his thin-rimmed glasses and contemplative smile. And she was excited to leave Afghanistan, to explore what life could be without the constant interruption of violence.

I was devastated to lose my big sister to a man who had seemingly materialized out of nowhere. Twelve years older than me, Aisha had been like another mother. My younger brother, Javid, and I even used to call her Moor, or Mother, sometimes. But everyone else was rejoicing, exclaiming at Aisha's luck. So I wore the scarlet-red outfit with a matching *dupatta* my mother had made for me, let her tie my hair up in a floppy ponytail, and tried to celebrate.

The rest of us were also moving on to new stages in our lives. My brother Yousef enrolled in school for the first time. The girls' schools wouldn't open for another few months, so Roya and I, along with our younger girl cousins, spent our days at Quran lessons. We no longer attended classes at our neighbor's house. Instead, Ana Bibi enrolled us in classes at the home of a strict middle-aged mother with a sixteen-year-old daughter named Pashtana. Our family believed the mother would be teaching us, but in reality, neither of Pashtana's parents was ever home.

We never knew where they were exactly, but while they were out, Pashtana was watching over us. We soon figured out that Pashtana's father was a part of some illegal business. Their living room was covered in plywood boxes filled with hundreds of blackish lumps. Some of the other students whispered that it was raw opium. I knew what opium smelled like since, as per local tradition, Ana Bibi had once dissolved a small amount in milk and drank it when she fell seriously ill. One day I summoned up the courage to sniff at a box and confirmed the rumors: we were studying the Quran in a home stacked high with illicit drugs.

While we were at Pashtana's house, she spent most of her time embroidering innumerable bedspreads and table-cloths for her future dowry. She instructed us in the Quran only a few hours a week. She rarely did any work around the house and instead made us do all her chores for her. We cleaned the house every day and went out to buy their gro-ceries at the crowded food bazaar. In the evenings, Pashtana's family often had guests who took *naswar*, a green powdered snuff tobacco, then spat the remnants into a nearby bowl. We cleaned out the saliva the next morning, gagging as we carried the vessel outdoors and dumped the slimy liquid away.

Sometimes we even had to sort through the boxes of their opium, restacking the crates to Pashtana's satisfaction. When she grew bored with providing religious instruction, Pashtana forced ten-year-old Roya to teach us Quran les-sons. "If the girls don't listen," Pashtana would tell her, "you can just slap them."

Most of the time when Pashtana interacted with us, it was usually to hurt us. She took a twisted pleasure in beating her mother's students, forcing them to bend over so she could pound her fists into the back of their heads. She burned one girl's forehead with a fire iron. Whenever she quizzed us on the Quran, she slapped anyone who gave a wrong answer. She was more careful with me and my sister be-cause she realized we were wealthy enough for it to matter if our parents found us covered in scrapes and bruises. So instead, she tortured us by grabbing our hair and yanking us around the room.

I cried hard when Pashtana came after me, not only from sheer reaction to the pain but from a desperate anger at my parents for leaving me with her, and a hatred for the girl who could reduce me to tears with her fists and a string of stinging words. But I also sobbed because I knew what would happen if I didn't react. Another girl in Quran lessons simply froze anytime Pashtana beat her, unable to show any emotion or response at all. Pashtana just beat her harder and harder, trying to get her to crack. "Why aren't you crying?" she'd scream wildly as I stared in horror. "Why aren't you crying!" she'd yell again, then push the girl to the ground and pound into her back, leaving red welts above the bruises she'd inflicted just days earlier.

It wasn't until more than a decade had passed that I processed how terribly we'd been treated, how we were being abused in a class that was meant to teach morality and kindness and the virtue of religion. At the time, I thought of Quran lessons as something I had to do but really dreaded, the same way some children think of piano practice or math homework. Aside from their tears in the moment, none of the other girls in my class seemed to complain about the housework and the beatings and the general lack of quality Islamic instruction. It was normal to them, so I assumed that, despite the fact that I was miserable, the happenings at Quran lessons should be normal to me too.

I still tried in vain to get Moor to pull us out of the class by telling her about some of the particularly egregious things Pashtana had forced us to do. But my sister and cousins didn't back me up since they thought complaining would be disrespectful and just get them in trouble. This fact, combined with my growing reputation as the family's most difficult child, meant I failed to convince Moor of anything. "If no one else sees any problem with Quran lessons," she told me over and over again, "then the problem must be with you."

I finally accepted that, no matter how earnest my appeals were, I was never going to get out of the lessons. Once I came to terms with the unending chores and the beatings we continued to receive, I had more mental capacity to focus on the Islamic studies we spent a few hours going over every day. Suddenly, words from Pashtana started ringing in my head. She painted elaborate pictures for us of the abject miseries of hell. "The line between hell and heaven," she would say, "is as thin as a razor blade." I began to worry. With every action I took, I wondered whether I was tipping toward one or the other. Thankfully, I was young enough that the thoughts didn't yet consume me; they just floated in the back of my mind like a persistent insect. Sometimes, though, I got caught in a vicious mental cycle. I worried about what my next life would be like, forgetting that I was only a few years into this one.

IN OCTOBER 2002, EXACTLY one year after we'd first left Kandahar during the American invasion, it came time for Aisha's wedding. It would be the first real marriage ceremony in our family in years. When the Taliban were in control, celebrations had been muted, held in small indoor halls and monitored by Talibs for any sign of forbidden music or fraternization between genders.

The wedding was held in Karachi, where Kashif's parents now lived. As a sign of respect, Kashif's brother came to Kandahar to accompany us to Pakistan. Their family rented a large bus to transport our entire family, including all my cousins and my aunt and uncle. It added up to nearly twenty of us in the bus, singing songs and beating a drum we'd sneaked aboard. We took the entire day to reach Quetta, then drove through the night to Karachi.

In Karachi, Moor shed her burqa and walked around the city in a modest headscarf, orchestrating final wedding preparations. She moved with a boldness I wasn't at all used to. In Kandahar, she always wore a melancholy expression. She spent her days cooking and cleaning, her face rarely breaking into a smile. At night, instead of reading us fairy tales, she'd tell stories of her time in college or teaching at Kabul University, her eyes turning dreamy and distant. But in Karachi, she burst with spirit, enthusiasm, even a hint of silliness.

As we walked together through parks and bazaars, I added a little spring of confidence to my own step. I was allowed to take off the light scarf I often wore in Kandahar to cover my head, and to wear jeans or sleeveless dresses. For the first time in months, I felt the wind sweep across my brow and tangle my hair. The Taliban had banned children's toys in Afghanistan, and most still weren't available for sale in Kandahar, so my father bought me a beautiful doll that I delighted in showing off to all my cousins.

The groom's family rented fancy apartments for us to stay in while we visited Karachi. In the mornings, we awoke to breakfasts prepared by the private chef they'd hired for each residence. The wedding officially began two days after we arrived with the *kheena* ceremony, where the bride and groom's palms are decorated with intricate designs drawn with a reddish-brown paste. A few close male family members attended the event, but the opulent hotel where the *kheena* was being held was mostly filled with women. Aisha, dressed in a golden Afghan outfit and dozens of pieces of jewelry, came to the front of the room and stood beside Kashif. Our family painted the groom's palm, and the groom's family painted paisley patterns on Aisha's.

Over the next few days, a number of dinners and smaller family events took place. I met Kashif properly for the first time when he took me aside with my brothers and Roya to ask us our names and what kinds of things we were interested in. I was only six, and this was the first time any adult I didn't know had spoken to me so seriously. I took an instant liking to my future brother-in-law, even though he was stealing my sister away from me.

Later in the week was the actual wedding. Around eight hundred guests attended, adorned in peak Karachi fashion. Women dressed in shades of bright yellow, scarlet red, and navy filled the hall. Some wore traditional Afghan attire while others came in floor-length gowns with gold-thread embroidery.

The opening notes of "Ahesta bero," the traditional Afghan wedding song, signaled that Aisha and Kashif had arrived. My sister was draped in a dazzling white gown with a gauzy hem that swept the floor. My older cousin walked behind her, lifting a Quran over her head to impart blessings. My parents walked alongside her, beaming. Moor would later tell me that Aisha's wedding was one of her happiest moments. "I couldn't send my daughter to school," she told me. "But at least I could marry her to someone kind and smart, from a family that values education."

After the ceremony, the close family members of the bride and groom danced for hours into the night on a raised stage at the center of the room. The hundreds of guests gathered around, clapping and singing to the beat of the music.

My mother, Roya, and I stayed in Karachi for an entire month tying up loose ends around the wedding. I didn't want to leave the city. I dreamed about our entire family moving to Pakistan. But there was a tacit understanding that Baba would never move. Though Karachi offered liberty for us, it offered no promise of wealth. My father's business was structured around importing goods into Afghanistan. If we moved, he would have no job to support his children.

So in November, we finally left Aisha at the house of her new parents-in-law. She would stay with them for two years while Kashif returned to Birmingham to work and finalize her visa.

BY 2004, THE NOVELTY of post-Taliban life began to fade. Afghanistan devolved into a kind of gray zone. The cities continued to modernize, but there was a sharp uptick in fighting. Taliban members in hiding orchestrated bombings to destabilize the government. Meanwhile foreign aid coming into the country dwindled. Perhaps because Afghans were struggling to make up for their loss of income, huge corruption scandals unfolded within the fledgling democratic government.

The most horrifying of these was a kidnapping-extortion scheme. In 2004, in an attempt to get ransom money, abductors captured at least two hundred children. To demonstrate their intentions, they would deliver the chopped-off fingers of children to parents who didn't pay up. The kidnappings became especially frequent in Kandahar, terrifying my parents.

My childhood was soon punctuated by piercing reminders of the inherently dangerous, unstable place I lived in. At night I heard the thunder of distant suicide bombing attacks. The next day, riding in the back seat through the center of Kandahar, I would see the utter devastation: an entire mosque leveled to the ground, car frames mangled beyond repair, large piles of debris encircled by a clamorous crowd.

We tried our best to live fully the lives we still had, without indulging in fear of a looming violence we deemed both indiscriminate and inevitable. On some summer nights, I asked Baba to take me out for something sweet. I was so committed to getting my dessert that I actually ran to close the windows to muffle the *tsk, tsk, tsk* noise of rapid gunshots outside our courtyard. I wasn't going to let a few stray bullets deprive me of ice cream and a Coca-Cola.

Soon the Western soldiers we'd once welcomed became another dimension of danger in Kandahar. We realized they were deployed to "keep the peace" at truly any cost. They dressed in protective helmets and vests but pointed their long, mounted machine guns threateningly at unassuming targets such as cars with broken windows, gangly teenage boys, and mud-thatched roofs. We heard constant stories of them mistaking civilians for suicide bombers and shooting randomly out of supposed caution. They rode through neighborhoods and markets and busy intersections on monstrous tanks fitted with colossal, cylindrical guns and an intimidating system of huge wheels that resembled a conveyor belt. I had always viewed my father as the strongest authority in my life, but even he was dwarfed by the men atop these terrifying armored vehicles.

Almost as quickly as it had emerged from Taliban rule, Kandahar was becoming a shadow of a city, descending rapidly into poverty and relentless violence.

CHAPTER
SIX

THE AIR GREW UNMISTAKABLY HOT, AND THE SUN BEAMED over mud-walled houses and mustard-colored awnings. The streets seemed to swell with activity as Kandaharis savored the fleeting period of early summer before the onset of ravaging heat. My eighth birthday passed just before the weather turned.

It was 2004, three years after our return to Kandahar. I sported a quasi-pageboy haircut that fell just below my chin. I had an easy grin and wide, jet-black eyes that dominated my face. In pictures from the time, I pose with assurance, my shoulders thrust back and my chin pointed squarely at the camera's lens as though I'm emulating a movie star.

I felt more mature and more evolved now that I wasn't the baby of the family. My younger brother, Javid, was six years old, and I adored him with the fondness and devotion found only in a first-time older sibling. We were bound inextricably by the fact that we were so close in age. I clung to the months that separated us, though, instructing Javid on what games to play and persuading him to join me on my mischievous escapades.

One of my favorite pastimes was to dress him up. I'd

spend hours putting him in my mother's blouses and wrapping him in my girliest dresses, tying the red sashes into a triumphant bow around his waist as he blinked curiously at me with his dewy, affectionate eyes. Then I'd hurry to the mirror to transform myself. I'd balance my father's gray-beige turban atop my head and loop the meters of excess fabric over my shoulder. I'd struggle into his massive *kameez* and, with my mother's eyeshadow, draw a thick mustache and the shadows of a beard onto my smooth face. Parading around the house, we made quite the pair, eliciting uproarious laughter from our cousins and suppressed giggles from Moor and any guests she happened to be entertaining. One afternoon I decided to make Javid's costume even more elaborate. I fitted him in my mother's bra over one of her old off-white blouses. I brought him out for Moor and Ana Bibi to see, but instead of the laughter I expected, I received disapproving glares. "Sola always takes everything too far," said my mother with a sigh, coining a phrase she would repeat innumerable times in the coming years.

A spunky eight-year-old, I relished any opportunity to make decisions on my own or to defy the very people to whom I was expected to show deference and respect. For instance, one afternoon when my aunt came to visit, I entered the room with my hair clipped back, slightly off center. "You should wear your hair down," my aunt scolded me. "But I like it this way!" I insisted. "It doesn't matter what you like!" she responded, exasperated. "You should dress for other people, not yourself." I refused to comply. Even at such a young age, it seemed absurd that I should center my existence on how other people would like me to behave. My slight impertinence in these scenarios must have worried my mother. But still, in most cases, she was content to let me make my own decisions.

Most weeks Moor took me to the bazaar to help her select a new dress or a piece of jewelry to give to someone. I stretched my arm up to grasp her hand, turning my head from side to side to take in the bejeweled, mosaic-like purses, the draped Afghan carpets, and the bustle of other mothers wrapped in veils or burqas, pulling on their child's wrist. The vendors clamored for my mother's attention, lavishing lofty promises of top-quality materials and low prices. Moor never bought anything unless I approved, trusting me to evaluate each vendor's claims on my own. I took my responsibility seriously, sifting through piles of scarves, holding necklaces up to my mother's chest to see how they would look. The shopkeepers quickly grew frustrated. "Why do you listen to this little girl but not to a grown man like me?" they asked. "I'm telling you my products are of the highest quality." I beamed at their grumpiness, proud at how much my mother trusted me.

But these idyllic childhood moments do not live alone in my mind. They're marred by remembrances of the anger I began to develop, the magnitude of which I was too young to understand. My family continued to send me to Pashtana's house even though I came home every afternoon distraught, the images of other beaten-up girls branded into my brain. I tried to convince my parents that Pashtana was hurting me, but there was no evidence to give my words credence. She was careful to never leave any proof of her assaults on me, not even a small bruise or a tiny scrape.

I had to resort to more surreptitious methods to get Moor to see my perspective. One opportunity came on a

sticky summer afternoon, during the season when Kandaharis with thatched roofs mend damages from the winter
rains with a mudlike paste. Pashtana's mother wanted to do
her own repairs that day, but didn't want to pay for a supply
of paste. So she sent me and my cousin out to steal paste
from someone else's house and bring it back to her. We
obeyed her, snatching an unattended bucket from a neighbor who was up on his roof and didn't suspect a thing. I
knew my mother would be horrified that the teachers she
trusted with our moral education had forced us to steal. But
I suspected she wouldn't believe me if I delivered the story
at face value.

So I talked my cousin into joining me in slathering the
muddy paste all over our bodies. I hoped that, confronted
with physical evidence of our deeds, Moor would finally
come over to my side. We tried to sneak out of the Quran
lessons like this, but Pashtana's mother caught us. "You
can't let your parents see you like this!" she cried out.
"They'll think we've done something bad to you, and they
won't let you come back here!" We sulked back into the
house and washed off underneath their spigot. Then, because our pants were especially wet, she made us sit without them on the carpet until we dried off. Pashtana's mother
eventually let us go home, but I convinced my cousin we
needed a victory over the Quran lessons if we were ever
going to escape. "Let's go back to the muddy place and put
it all over ourselves again!" I told her. She agreed begrudg-
ingly.

We ran home looking as though we'd gone swimming
in a pool of sludge. We delivered our story to Moor with
the most tearful, convincing expressions we could muster.

But for whatever reason, Moor didn't take our side. Maybe she didn't want to interfere with Ana Bibi, who had sent us to the school in the first place. Maybe she didn't want to cross Baba, who insisted that Islamic lessons were a rite of passage, something he had endured and we should too. Either way, she seemed thoroughly unaffected by our story.

WHEN MY ATTEMPTS TO quit Quran lessons failed, a deep-seated rage toward my parents and grandmother began to fester. Resentment clawed at my chest and threatened to boil over, suddenly and unpredictably. Sometimes, racked by vexation and dread, I would walk out of Quran lessons altogether, ignoring cries from Pashtana ordering me to stay. I steered myself back home, remembering which turns to take and how to cross a busy intersection, panting from the exertion and the small hope that I might be free.

But after just one or two days, my grandmother would insist that I go back to class. When I turned toward Moor, trying to signal to her with my eyes, she looked at the ground. I was beginning to understand that Ana Bibi had a strong pull on my mother. She berated Moor frequently in our presence, blaming her for raising her daughters to be spoiled and inept. With every passing year, my mother's influence seemed to weaken, as Ana Bibi grabbed the reins and disciplined me with her characteristic severity and harshness.

Every time I ran away from my Quran lessons, Ana Bibi bought a box of expensive truffles for me to give to Pashtana's family. The next day she wrapped her wrinkled, bony fingers tightly around my wrist and dragged me to the school. At the door, she shoved the chocolates into my hands and whispered sharply, "Now go and kiss your teacher's hands and ask for her forgiveness." I was miserable every time, my stomach turning at the thought of the assault I would face once Ana Bibi left and Pashtana's indulgent, forgiving smile quickly disappeared. But there was no way to escape.

Quran lessons were awful, but they weren't the only cause of my discontent. Back in 2002, when I was six, Roya and I had started splitting our time between Quran classes and actual school. The local school, funded by international aid groups, was poorly equipped and didn't even have chairs for us to sit on. Instead, we gathered every morning on an old burnt rug. I hated school, and most mornings I had to be forced out of bed. Our teachers were similarly unmotivated, and most of them lacked even a high school education. Teaching wasn't even their only job. In the evenings, we'd see them on the streets, hawking day-old eggplants and zucchinis to drivers stuck in traffic.

The days passed. It was understood that most girls attended school just for the free food and medical care. Some would come to class only at the end of the month, when handouts were distributed. Girls who did come to school regularly showed up in dirty clothes and often brought lice into the building, which inevitably found its way into our scalps. There was little effort from anyone to teach us a proper curriculum.

Every morning I dragged my feet toward the ramshackle building, alone. When we first enrolled in school, Roya and I would walk there together, dodging motorbikes and rickshaws and drawing deep breaths of air not yet saturated with the day's smog. But soon my sister grew impatient with my loitering. I stayed in bed too long and stumbled down to the breakfast table only minutes before we had to leave, moody at the prospect of another school day. So Roya left earlier than me, and I hurried out the door a half hour later, my uniform askew and my book bag weighing uncomfortably on my shoulder.

I admitted it to no one, but my veneer of irritability toward school was due partly to fear. As the years following the American invasion ticked by, Taliban insurgents regained strength, and life in our city continued to deteriorate.

It was the bombs that frightened me the most. They struck unpredictably—in the mornings as I was getting ready for school, during dinner, and on weekends as I was chasing my brothers around in the courtyard. They usually detonated in the center of Kandahar, but the blasts were so loud that we could hear them easily from our house, a ten-minute drive away. The massive explosions rattled our windows and shook the doors within their frames. My family waited together for the sound to abate, each of us praying that no one we knew would be hurt. Sometimes, unable to take the uncertainty, I'd climb to the top of our roof and look to see which direction the smoke was billowing from, trying to figure out whether the attack was near my father's business or my brother's school. Then I'd return to the living room, and we'd sit in silence, my observations doing nothing to assuage our fears.

Eventually, we would see the damage on TV: images of

bodies submerged in rubble, buildings cracked in two, the naked insides of schools and business centers left without walls and ceilings. Our newly paved streets began to crack, betraying the site of an explosion even after the debris had been cleared.

I turned nine and then ten. All my front teeth came in. I shot up toward Yousef's height, washed teatime dishes with my mother, played card games against my cousins.

And still the violence grew worse. An attack occurred nearly every day, but every time I heard a dull, thundering blast, I experienced the same sweaty fear. Sometimes, in a callous attempt to create a double tragedy, the Taliban would detonate another bomb, aimed at the mourners and rescuers who gathered where an attack had taken place only a few minutes earlier.

A barrage of explosions always echoed in my ears. I grew afraid to leave the house, to venture to the bazaar with my mother. *What if our rickshaw has a car bomb strapped to it?* I wondered, crazy with worry. When I did go out, I recited hundreds of *duas*, a Muslim prayer that promises safety. The verses I spoke softly under my breath were supposed to be repeated only once or twice, but I refused to stop my endless repetitions until we stepped back into our compound, unharmed.

Every time my parents or brothers left the house, I paced by our doorway, my fingers knotted nervously together, convinced that they would never come back. At night sleep evaded me. Visions of a life spent alone, forever mourning the members of my family, kept me awake.

Though this influx of violence was reminiscent of life

prior to the American invasion, the severe conservatism that had marked that earlier time was now noticeably absent. Though many residents of Kandahar were still opposed to modern ways, they couldn't quell the increasing liberalization of their city. Every month women and children avidly consumed new reality television dramas and news programs syndicated from Pakistan and India. When Moor's friends came to visit, they lifted their burqas to reveal straightened hair and sleek makeup in the style of Bollywood stars. Even as suicide bombers destroyed buildings and homes, developers invested in new construction: stylish condos, man-made lakes, paved roads. It was easy to look at all this and take it for progress, forgetting that it was happening against a backdrop of political instability and random attacks.

But I couldn't forget that everyday life in Kandahar was still brutally dangerous. My twenty-minute walks to school were paved with searing fear. Turmeric-orange rickshaws dotted the crowded roads, and I scanned each driver's face as they weaved past, deathly afraid one would suddenly blow himself up. "There aren't enough people to kill here," I tried to reason with myself, to stave off a dizzy panic. "Why would they waste a bomb on us?"

I had other worries, too. As I walked to school, I was terrified of something I didn't yet have a name for but imagined would happen in a shadowy street, beneath the din of rattling vehicles and the hoarse shouts of Pashto that emanated from street vendors.

School was meant to be separate and safe, but it was hardly a physical or an intellectual sanctuary. The dust from

Kandahar's streets settled everywhere. It caked my male teachers' shoes and darkened the bulky *kameez* they shoved into their Western pants. It was plastered on the faces of my classmates as they stood in line for deworming pills and vaccinations. Even the free bread they handed to us was gritty and inedible, tossed aside even by children who were hungry.

The aid school teachers in Kandahar were angry, bitter from a life of poverty. After the American invasion, there had been an immediate need for educators, and so street vendors and snack shop owners who had once served as pre-Taliban government officials were thrust into positions of power. They turned on their new students as a way of releasing their rage. For inconsequential reasons or no reason at all, they doled out beatings. One of my friends later told me he used to wear layers upon layers of clothes to school to soften the inevitable blows.

I was often late to school and often didn't turn in my homework, which made me a regular target for these beatings. Sometimes I was let off with a swift slap across the arm. Other times I was struck with a PVC pipe, a cruel gift from a student's father to the school, decorated in the colors of the Afghan flag. Usually, however, the teachers whipped me with a long, thin pomegranate branch. The pain was blinding. For nearly an hour afterward, I felt the sharp sting of every fiber that had lashed my arm. Scarlet welts rose on my forearms as I gritted my teeth from my seat on the floor, trying to overcome the pain with willpower.

Some girls cried when the teachers beat them. But I just grew hot with embarrassment, angered by their attempt to hurt and humiliate me in front of the class. Every time, I resolved to do even less homework, to arrive even later to school, just to spite my teachers. The harder they hit me, the more I tried to resist them.

The older girls in our school were mostly immune to these beatings. Our male principal was kinder and gentler to them, often sitting so close to them that his hip would touch theirs. In the afternoon, in lieu of lessons, he would gather all the female students around and tell jokes and stories. He sang lilting, romantic melodies to them, an endearing smile plastered on his face as the girls blushed and giggled and whispered excitedly to one another. Every one of them was destined for an arranged marriage, denied the chance to date, to fall in love, to be charmed and courted. Their principal seemed to represent the man of their dreams, dashing and smart and always out of reach.

I was too young to understand any of this. I once overheard the principal tell a story about the time he witnessed a rickshaw accident. "A beautiful girl was trapped under the rubble," he said. "She had seductive blue eyes and skin so fair it almost looked white." He went on to describe in great detail the size and shape of the woman's breasts. "I pulled her out of the wreckage by those breasts," he would say. "I saved her life."

I wondered innocently why our principal hadn't just grabbed the girl by her hands. I thought maybe her arms were injured, or her delicate fingers couldn't grasp on to him. Only many years later did I understand the true intent of his story, and remember the echoes of scandalized laughter and flushed cheeks—and realize there never was a beautiful blue-eyed girl at all.

MY PARENTS SENT MY siblings and me to be educated so we could achieve something more than a bag of rice or a liter of cooking oil, and experience more than flirtatious story-telling or unmitigated lashings. On our first day of school in 2002, our father had gifted us new sparkly pencils and leather-bound notebooks. Our teacher was disdainful. "Your father should not waste his money buying these things for you," he spat, then cracked the pencils in half and sent us to our seats at the back of the classroom.

I belonged to a much more affluent family than my classmates, most of whom returned home to thatched huts or even shacks covered with corrugated metal. It was because of this vast chasm between our family and theirs, I later realized, that I found it difficult to make friends. I felt wronged by the attitude of teachers who clearly thought teaching girls was just a way to pass the time, who believed that nothing could ever come of any of us. But my class-mates didn't see it my way. Marked with the disadvantage of being poor and being daughters, they found it special for someone to even acknowledge their existence. The fact that the teachers noticed them at all was exciting.

The disparities in our perspectives were especially appar-ent one afternoon when our Islamic studies teacher decided to give us a surprise. A teaching conference had been held at the school earlier that day. In honor of the occasion, the administration had brought in a long conference table and expensive black desk chairs. They catered a fancy buffet and ordered small cakes and cookies for dessert. My teacher led us to the room, now a complete mess, filled with half-eaten food and dirty cups and plates. "Eat, eat!" he said, beaming. The other girls picked up dirty plates filled with leftover piles of okra and scraped at the last pieces of meat remaining on discarded chicken bones. They spun around in the swivel chairs, giggling. I watched them quietly. In an attempt to fit in, I picked around the bite marks of a half-eaten cake, a stale, sweet scent drifting up toward my nose.

Meanwhile my brother Yousef was enjoying a far different educational experience. My parents had enrolled him in a prestigious, private all-boys secondary school. They paid five hundred U.S. dollars annually for him to attend, enough money to support an Afghan family for an entire year. Yousef was taught exclusively in English. He followed a rigorous math and science curriculum, wrote poetry, and studied Sufi Islam, the religion of the famed Persian poet Rumi. The goal of the private school was to help Afghans leave their country, to expose them to opportunities and experiences outside their volatile homeland. The school would later fund my brother's travels to international competitions and academic Olympiads, and encourage him to apply to academic programs in Europe.

Baba was so proud of Yousef. He brought home special gifts for his scholarly son: Afghan sweets glazed with sugar syrup, flaky fried breads, glass bottles of soda. Roya, Javid, and I would gather around Yousef, asking for just a few bites of his food. "All we siblings are Yousef's beggars," we would say resignedly, after he placated us with a few chips or a taste of ice cream.

No academy like Yousef's existed for girls. So as he carried his textbooks out the door every morning, I shook the dust out of my white uniform headscarf and walked as quickly as I could to the local school, terrified of the suspicious cars and packs of loitering men. I dreaded each day more than the last.

FOR THE EDUCATED IN Kandahar, the line between contentedness and dissatisfaction was thin, and by the time he turned fourteen, Yousef had crossed it. Before, being educated had made him happy, elicited compliments from his friends and our relatives, and paved the way for his rise through local society. But history lessons and school trips soon gave my brother a glimpse into the lives of non-Afghans. He learned about Apple computers and foreign governments. He saw pictures of breathtaking Roman ruins and bustling Asian metropolises. His English grew strong enough to read the articles published about our country, pieces peppered with phrases like "third world" and "downward spiral" and "war." He realized that the things he'd grown up thinking of as luxuries—electricity, imported clothes, working toilets—paled in comparison to the riches available in countries like Britain and the United States. He felt robbed, cheated out of bigger dreams.

On a winter night in 2006, his dissatisfaction came to a head. The electrical system in Kandahar had become so unreliable that we were forced to create our own power by relying on a generator, which Baba switched off on winter evenings as he prepared for bed. That night Ana Bibi sat in her bedroom upstairs, unbothered by the lack of light. My parents were sound asleep. But the rest of us stayed awake together in the living room, unwilling to let a generator dictate our bedtime.

Sitting together in the dark, we could barely make out each other's silhouettes. The blackness seemed to feed the cold, and we huddled closer to one another.

Yousef let out a lengthy sigh in the darkness. He was angry. "I cannot believe Baba makes us stay here," he suddenly burst out, the acrimony in his voice startling us.

Our father had chosen to stay in a country that was spiraling downhill. He had recently lent money to several of our relatives who had emigrated to Pakistan or Europe, but he never seemed to consider relocating our family. He was indifferent to the fate of his wife and daughters, to their inability to go to school or have careers or even walk freely through the streets.

Baba claimed that if we moved, we would have to live in poverty and start over. His skills as an importer, he said, would be useless in a country with unfettered access to the global market. Our relatives who moved abroad had encountered similar problems. Baba worried that, after leaving everything behind in Afghanistan, he'd be unable to support Moor and the four children who still relied on him.

Baba also maintained an attitude that infected thousands of Kandaharis at that time: he believed that if so many other people were staying in Afghanistan, then it was no problem for our family to stay too. "A problem to everyone," he used to tell us, "is a problem to no one." Even decades later I was unable to grasp my father's logic. But whatever his reasons for staying in the country, they seemed increasingly trivial compared to the real, immediate violence we were enduring every day.

After declaring his anger toward Baba, Yousef went on to denounce the general state of living in Kandahar, the strict culture and the bombs and the poverty. "I'm talking to you without light, with no electricity!" he cried out. "Living here, we have no connection to the rest of the world. We have no internet! We don't even have a mail system!"

Then he began a tirade against Afghans in general. "They are so stupid," he said. "No wonder our country is in this state." At that time Yousef looked European, with his light hair and fair skin and almond eyes. In keeping with this image, he dressed in Western-style collared shirts and pressed, straight-legged pants. He even bought himself some English textbooks and took to practicing new, foreign-sounding phrases upstairs in his room. Relatives and friends began to treat Yousef as though he really were a European or an American, giving deference to his opinions and behaving toward him with an unnatural respect. It seemed to us as though, with all his verbal attacks on the intellectual potential of Afghans, Yousef had forgotten his national identity.

"I will go to America," he declared into the dark. "I will get married and have children who can speak English." Then he settled into a private reverie. Squinting in the blackness, I watched as his brow furrowed in determination.

Until that night, I had never really considered the possibility of leaving Afghanistan. If the thought had crossed my mind at all, I'd probably dreamed of moving back to Pakistan and sharing a room with my cousins. But Yousef was describing a future for himself in a world so far away it was hard to imagine, impossible to picture. When I watched Bollywood movies, it was only the most beautiful protagonists who thought about moving to the West, seeking an upgrade from lives that I thought were already idyllic.

I remembered how the West had changed my sister Aisha. The girl I had grown up with had been quiet, content to fade into the background. But in the spring of 2006, Aisha visited us from Birmingham for the first time, with her two-year-old son, Kamel. She looked older, the lines of her face having settled, making her seem perpetually thoughtful. She sat with Baba and our uncles, volunteering opinions on the Taliban or the problems of corruption in Kandahar's local government. A few weeks after she arrived, Aisha threw a massive birthday party for little Kamel. As guests filled the hallways of the hotel space we'd rented, she stepped deftly among them, passing around plates of heaping food, pausing to admire a newborn baby or shake her head sympathetically as an aunt related stories of joint pain and high blood pressure. Watching her, I'd been struck by how much she stood out from the crowd. "That's my sister!" I had wanted to shout proudly. I wondered if someday that could be me. I wondered what it would be like to be a visitor in my home country.

Yousef's generous vision of his Western future didn't extend to Roya and me. "You will spend your whole life in Afghanistan," he told me gloomily. His prediction for Roya was worse. He described in great detail a future for her in a tiny village with a grumpy husband and six children. "Her children's noses will never be clean. She won't even be able to afford pants for them, so they'll walk around naked."

When Roya wasn't taking care of her children, Yousef surmised that she would pass her hours milking the village cows.

Yousef's prophesying lit my first, halting spark of desire to leave Kandahar. In the months that followed, his outburst would light up my memory. Sometimes, after an assassination in the street or an especially frightening attack, my ears would ring with the aphorism he'd announced that night: "You don't know you're living in dirt until you leave it."

IN THE SUMMER OF 2005, JUST AFTER I TURNED NINE, MY twelve-year-old sister Roya graduated from religious instruction. She had mastered the Arabic alphabet and interpreted enough verses to satisfy our Quran teacher—Pashtana's mother. Moor hosted a Quran finishing ceremony in Roya's honor at our compound, having made her a shimmering midnight-blue dress with long sleeves and a sweeping skirt that was appropriately conservative for the occasion. Fifteen women gathered in our living room to witness Roya's final recitations.

Upon her graduation, Roya was now considered a woman in our household. Her duty was not to better herself but to better others, to concern herself with bedsheets and dirty dishes and the kinds of desserts our brothers liked to eat. She helped my mother to cook three meals every day, arranged biscuits and salty snacks on a platter for teatime, and planned elaborate menus for the constant stream of friends and elderly relatives we entertained. She enjoyed her new lifestyle, reveling in the responsibilities of adulthood.

I thought Roya had been liberated. I was irritated at the

thought of enduring Pashtana's aggressions on my own, knowing that my habit of speaking my mind would provoke her and that my parents and grandmother wouldn't believe a word I said about it.

"Now no one in this family goes to Quran lessons but me," I groaned to my mother, though I expected her, as usual, to do nothing about my complaints. "If Roya can stop attending, then why can't I?" I employed my usual tactics, refused to go, and declared that they would have to drag me to Pashtana if they wanted me to keep taking lessons. Then I switched methods and tried a softer approach, begging Moor to let me quit. I promised her that I would study the Quran diligently at home after school. I would sit quietly in my bedroom and page through the same verses that Roya had learned years earlier.

A few days later, as she bustled in the kitchen preparing dinner, Moor turned to me. "You don't have to take Quran lessons anymore if you don't want to," she said gently. "Just promise me you will study on your own at home."

I was suspended in a state of utter disbelief. For years, I had been asking her every day to quit, and now suddenly she was able to circumvent Ana Bibi, overcome her own objections to me leaving, and withdraw me from lessons? I couldn't understand what had precipitated her decision.

Perhaps Moor had finally come to the conclusion that I would never finish my Quran studies. In my seven years of lessons, I had barely covered the basics, while Roya had finished the entire program. Now that my sister had graduated, there was no risk that my absence from the lessons would discourage her.

"Instead of Quran lessons," Moor told me, "you and

Roya will enroll in English lessons after school with a woman who lives just a few streets down from us." Learning English was unquestionably dangerous in Kandahar, especially as Taliban forces continued to encroach on Afghan government territory, setting off bombs near businesses and civilians that they deemed antithetical to their values. Any lessons other than religious ones were especially risky for girls, since Talibs were still firmly opposed to most female education. The English teacher told my mother that only three other girls were studying with her, hopefully a number small enough not to attract attention. Moor planned to make it look as though we had simply enrolled in new Quran lessons, not that we were forgoing religious instruction to learn the language of Westerners.

Moor was willing to take this risk because she'd been speaking with her father, my grandfather Agha. He no longer lived in Afghanistan—he'd fled to the West decades ago, before the civil war. My grandmother Ana Jana had chosen not to go with him and instead moved to Pakistan to live with their daughter. Agha had come to visit Moor only once since her marriage. Her education had for a time been his greatest pride, and it anguished him to watch it squandered. And he was furious with Baba for keeping the family in Kandahar, effectively condemning his granddaughters to lives devoid of education.

Moor had tried to keep in touch with Agha over the years, but it had been difficult. We didn't have a phone, and Agha refused to open any letters that Moor sent, convinced they'd include details about life under the mujahideen or Taliban that would be too painful to stomach. She did manage to speak to him briefly whenever we visited Pakistan, yelling through the static into her sister's phone, reassuring him that she was fine, that everyone was healthy. The calls were so expensive, though, that she'd have to hang up after just a few minutes.

But in 2004, Baba bought a cellphone. Moor was finally able to talk to Agha—though only briefly, because it still cost nearly two U.S. dollars per minute to place an international call. I watched my mother's attitude shift when she talked to her father. She seemed inspired, more confident in her desire to educate us. "Zahab Jana," Agha told her. "Make your children wear the glasses of education so they can see the world clearly." He reminded Moor that it was her responsibility to provide her children with the highest-quality, most worldly education that she could offer, as he had done for her. His words haunted her until she heard about a young woman living nearby who wanted to make money by teaching English.

From the day I met my English teacher, a young woman in her early twenties I was told to refer to by "Miss," I adored her. She had long sweeping tresses of brown hair. She stood taller than any of us girls or our mothers and had a slender, graceful figure. Her features shone with a sparkling youthfulness rarely seen in Afghan women. Even teenage girls in Kandahar tend to have furrowed brow lines and pale faces not colored by the sun.

Miss was born in Canada to Afghan parents. She attended school there but lived with the knowledge that her future would not be spent there. Upon her birth, her family had promised her to an Afghan man eighteen years her senior. When she was only sixteen, her family pulled her out of school and sent her away to Afghanistan to marry a man who was now almost forty years old. Coincidentally, my family had actually attended her wedding, since my uncle had been friends with her family when they lived in Kandahar. Her new husband was a teacher at our school whom I knew casually from his loud flirtations with my older classmates.

Upon her marriage, Miss's husband stole her Canadian passport and hid it somewhere in the recesses of their large house filled with extended family. He forced her to speak Pashto and allowed her to teach English only for the extra income it would bring in. She stayed at home all day. Our group of five young English students served as her only chance for social interaction.

So after a few lessons on English vocabulary or simple grammar rules, Miss would regale us in Pashto with stories from her childhood. She painted descriptions of the jeans and fitted blouses she wore in Canada, of her short haircut and threaded eyebrows. Her eyes glinted with pride as she told us that she'd been the best in her class at typing. She moved her fingers through the air to demonstrate how rapidly they'd flown across her computer keyboard.

She missed her old life desperately. She told us that she once suggested to her husband that they move back to Canada together. "I could even apply for your Canadian citizenship," she told him, bubbling with nervousness and a slight glimmer of hope. But her husband grew violently angry at this suggestion. "If you go to Canada," he said, "you will never return to me." He had to keep her trapped in Afghanistan, he told her, so she would remain a dutiful wife.

After just a few lessons, the timbre of Miss's stories shifted. In a soft voice, her eyes cast downward, she told us that her husband beat her. Her eyes took on a vacant stare, and her disembodied voice floated through the hushed room. It was as though she were talking to herself. In the weeks that followed, we noticed angry, maroon-colored bruises across her neck and down her arms. The stories kept coming: he'd struck her across the face, he'd hurled a pair of scissors across the room. I watched her as she talked to us, so overcome I couldn't even cry. It was the first I'd ever heard of a man hitting his wife.

Alone at night, though, my tears came. I was watching a woman, practically a girl, disappear. Desperate to halt what was happening, I tried to concoct plans for Miss to escape. I imagined her stealing a phone to call her parents or sneaking out one night to a friendly embassy. But there were always flaws in my plans. Her parents were the ones who had sent her to live with this man in the first place, and how could she get to an embassy without her husband to drive her?

Eventually, a couple of years later, it grew too dangerous for me to attend English classes at Miss's home. My parents withdrew me from lessons, and I never saw her again except for once, around three years later. She had two little girls by her side, daughters who tied her to Afghanistan. Her face was lined with wrinkles, and the sparkle that had enamored her to me was gone. She dressed in traditional clothes that were faded at the seams and worn from use. After we exchanged pleasantries, I watched her step briskly away, and I remember thinking that she was stuck now, that this would be her life forever. I fervently hoped that her fate would never be mine, that I would not have to resign myself to a life so painful and insipid.

———

IN THE SPRING OF 2007, just a few days after my eleventh birthday, a group of men arrived at our compound to speak to my father. It was a windless day, and smog-lined clouds flecked the blue sky. I was upstairs in my bedroom studying for final exams. I craved the upcoming summer, with its promises of no classes and hours upon hours to play with my brothers. My pencil sometimes lagged across the pages of my notebook, but then I'd resume studying with a start, desperate to get my homework over with.

The men approached our door and began speaking in low, urgent tones. I learned later that they served my father a point-blank ultimatum: If you don't stop sending your daughters to school, we will throw acid in their faces. Or we will kidnap them. Or we will do something worse, something you cannot even bear to imagine.

To this day, we don't know who the men were. They could have been Talibs, since the group maintained a growing presence in our neighborhood and had recently committed a high-profile murder just half a mile from our home. Or they could have been angry individuals, unaffiliated but profoundly conservative, united by a desire to turn back the clock in Kandahar. Regardless, their menacing threats were enough to frighten my parents. That night they told Roya and me we wouldn't be returning to school. They pulled us out of English lessons with Miss, as well.

I felt instant relief. No more frightening, frantic walks in the mornings, no more meaningless lectures, no more beatings. I had learned next to nothing in my five years at the local school. I read my native language Pashto at barely a beginner's level. I couldn't even add or subtract.

Even before I was faced with these threats of violence, I'd seen no point in attending school. I was content to give up my education for the freedom to spend my days however I wanted.

But as I looked into my mother's somber eyes, I could see she was devastated. She knew what it was like to laugh under the verdant trees that dotted Kabul University, to graduate, to walk a newborn baby down a street free of rubble. A mother's dream is for her children to see the world, to experience their own beginnings, to be more than she ever was. But mine couldn't even allow her daughters to attend a run-down school for a few hours a day without fearing we wouldn't make it home.

The threat of school no longer loomed over me. I slept soundly in the mornings, right through the noise of my mother preparing breakfast and my brothers slamming the door on their way to school. Initially, I was still too young to help Roya and Moor with household chores, so I started the day by playing with my young cousins or watching a few hours of Indian television. As my mother and sister prepared dinner through the afternoon and early evening, I headed outside to our courtyard. I rode the creaky bicycle that Baba had bought for me earlier that year, in small circles, hugging the walls of our compound. Even then, I wasn't allowed to take it out on the road. I dreamed of accelerating past the bazaar and my father's shop, swerving around street vendors and the groups of boys playing cricket in the alleys.

On summer nights after we finished dinner, Baba would

sometimes take my brothers and me to cool off at the river. I was allowed to join them because I hadn't yet hit puberty, though I was subject to additional rules. I had to walk directly into the water with my clothes on. There was no question of wearing a swimsuit or anything without long sleeves, though my brothers jumped into the river wearing nothing but a shawl tied around their waists. I loved the gentle shock of those first few handfuls of cool water, washing away the sweat and dust on my face.

But after just a few months of these freedoms, the admonishments began, first forgiving, then firm. *Don't jump rope, Sola, your skirt will reach your knees. Cross your legs, Sola. You're too old to swim anymore, Sola.* I was soon forbidden to play with my male cousins or go for day trips and spontaneous excursions. Even at eleven years old, I was considered a temptation to men. Showing my cropped hair or even my ankles would have been an indiscretion. My parents didn't believe in most of the restrictions they imposed on me, but to let me run free would have been culturally unforgivable and dangerous.

I was still permitted to tag behind my mother on infrequent trips to the bazaar, wearing a long white scarf that wrapped around my shoulders. The bustling, chaotic atmosphere grew more precious to me as my freedoms were curbed. I still enjoyed advising my mother as she haggled from beneath her sky-blue burqa, seeking a slightly lower price for a dress or a pair of shoes. One day we walked to the open-air market because I was afraid suicide bombs might be lurking in the rickshaws. A man caught sight of us and decided to follow us the entire day, perhaps as an attempt to intimidate a woman and her daughter out alone.

He lurked in adjacent stalls and nearby buildings, stalking us. Without a word, Moor pulled me into a rickshaw and urged the driver through the market. "If he keeps following us," she whispered to me, "we'll have to turn around and quickly go home." She rested her hand across my knee and glanced uneasily out the back of the rickshaw until the man faded from sight. After that day, whenever my mother offered to take me to the bazaar, I chose to stay home.

The stillness within our compound was tangible and suffocating. I lived in desperate boredom, walking quietly from room to room, waiting for an end I knew would never come.

CHAPTER EIGHT

I BECAME A TEENAGER DURING A SUMMER OF MERCILESS bombings. Four months into my thirteenth year, on a scalding September day, a scarlet mass of flames erupted across the dusky sky.

It was the middle of Ramadan, the Muslim holy month. I was finally old enough to fast with everyone else, and the dull hunger pressing gently on my stomach made me feel grown up. The scent of saffron and cumin and cardamom permeated the air. Moor had spent the entire day preparing our evening meal. She'd been fasting, too, unable to take even a little taste to check if the vegetables had enough salt or the stew needed more spices. We were going to eat on the floor the way we did every night, our backs and legs padded by elaborately embroidered brick-red floor cushions. Roya had already laid out platters of food and plates and sodas in a wide circle on a special dining cloth, accenting the setting with bowls of plump dates.

I sat outside in the compound garden with my siblings and cousins, waiting for the *iftar Azan,* or the call to prayer that would signal the end of our fast. Every evening of Ramadan we waited together for the warbled call, then ran inside to excitedly announce to everyone it was time to eat. But this evening, as the summer breeze swept over us and dusk fell, the *Azan* never came. Instead, a deafening explosion jolted Kandahar, shaking the foundation of our compound and blanketing the city in instant darkness.

The first thing we'd heard was a massive blast, then a series of echoes that rumbled across the city. We ran inside. The bomb was so close to our house that the floor trembled. Thick smoke fell over our neighborhood, followed by the acrid smell of burning buildings. From our downstairs window, I could see orange flames licking the rooftops, spreading rapidly from one to the next.

I remember there was an eerie moment of silence, of disbelieving, before the city erupted in panic. We froze in the living room, listening to the cries of motorists and street vendors and hundreds of Kandaharis who were out for Ramadan, buying final ingredients for dinner or traveling to break their fasts with friends. In the kitchen, my mother's food grew cold.

I heard my father's heavy footsteps coming from the other room and turned around. As I locked eyes with him, he grabbed our phone, and in that instant I remembered that my eldest brother, Nadir, was not home. Thirty minutes before the detonation, he'd left work to buy flatbreads for dinner, and now he was out there amid the havoc.

I turned to Moor and watched her face go slack with horror as she came to the same realization. Baba stood firmly, grasping the cellphone, projecting a strained sense of calm. We held our breath as he dialed Nadir's mobile number. The line went dead. I stared out the window, numb. Behind me, someone started to wail. It seemed impossible for my brother to still be alive.

I was drowning, falling from a great height. The room was cold, the walls blurred around me. I understood nothing, felt my chest sink and my breath leave me as I was overcome with the searing magnitude of loss.

And then there was the sound of tires crunching over debris in the street, the dull hum of an idling engine. We ran to the front door as my brother emerged from the car, bread piled in his arms. Seeing him in the driveway jerked me out of an abyss and left me without words, gasping for breath like a rescued swimmer cast onto solid ground. I took in Nadir's reassuring, sideways smile and felt a cascade of relief. Moor threw her arms around him and didn't let go.

Nadir told us that he had missed the explosion by only five minutes. He'd been driving back toward the house, inhaling the scent of fresh bread and watching throngs of shoppers fill the streets, when the bomb shook his car. Through his rearview mirror, he watched destruction rain down as he sped toward home, maneuvering around the sudden traffic jams and disoriented pedestrians. He hadn't received our phone call because the explosion had disabled the city's communication systems. As he talked, my mother, sister, and I all cried. Moor prayed and thanked Allah. She repeated a well-known Pashto saying: "The evil was there, but its power did not materialize." Later we learned that forty-three people had been killed in the attack.

Nearly losing Nadir forced me into a confrontation with my own mortality. I was old enough now to grapple with the reality that my nationality, my family home, and my city, all integral parts of my identity, exposed me to a level of risk I was powerless to change. In the months that followed, the dangers in Kandahar proliferated, and bombs went off nearly every day. We had too many close calls to keep track of. The hall where just a few weeks earlier my cousin had celebrated her engagement was overrun by Taliban fighters. They stormed and occupied it, then fired recklessly at nearby government buildings from their perches in its windows and atop the roof. Eventually, to stop the barrage of gunfire, the Afghan government dropped a bomb on the hotel that killed everyone inside. The sound of the building's destruction was deafening. One morning around five o'clock, I awoke to hear my father on the telephone, learning that one of his business colleagues had been killed by a land mine. We all felt that the likelihood of one of us dying increased with every day.

Unlike Baba and my brothers, I had plenty of time to sink into a flood of disquietude and worry. My movements were increasingly restricted. I was confined to the house. I toiled away at a never-ending series of household chores in the uneasy silences that seized the late mornings and early afternoons. I jumped at the sounds of gunfire and detonations, even as they melded into a soundtrack for my life.

I watched as my friends and cousins, just a few years older than me, were married off. They left to great fanfare, in opulent, massive weddings that sustained us all during those violent years. But when the wedding halls were silent, I felt alone. I was shrinking into the folds of domesticity. Every day I faced the prospect of two deaths: the death of my body and the death of my personality, my independence, my girlhood.

And so I tried to push these thoughts away. Instead of staying mired in worry and regret, I threw myself into a world of frivolity and tried to fill my mind with gallons of nothingness. I watched hours upon hours of television, silently absorbing tired soap operas and overproduced movies until they actually became interesting to me. To fill more time, I taught myself to sew and embroider. One afternoon my cousins and I smuggled a deck of cards into the house. Another time we dared to venture to the compound gate to buy ice cream from a street vendor. These moments ranked as among the most exciting in my year.

When I tired of these activities, I turned my attention toward something new. Aisha had started sending me pictures of the latest dresses and patterns from Birmingham, and I pored over the images, marveling at the cut of a certain skirt or the bright colors of a blouse. Soon I became obsessed with fashion. Afghan women dress extremely conservatively in front of men, but they often wear elaborate, brightly colored outfits under their burqas for all-female gatherings or weddings, where men and women celebrate in separate rooms. The style of their clothes or the quality of their makeup can determine their social status. In a society where they cannot work and are often forbidden to read, learn, or speak their opinions, looking good shows sophistication. It becomes a purpose, a way to exert authority over other women, to feel the fleeting triumph that comes from wielding power.

My whole life began to revolve around my appearance. I spent far too much time in front of the mirror learning to curl my hair. I applied copious amounts of blush, experimenting every day with new shades and applications. I ordered press-on white nail tips and applied them carefully to every finger. I called Aisha in Birmingham and asked her to send me clothes: a bejeweled pink satin gown, a scarlet dress with black lace sleeves, a sheer cropped jacket adorned with cream-colored daisies. I'd wear these outfits and have fun posing with cousins and friends, tilting my head and smiling boldly into the camera. But after just a few months, I realized that this experiment, too, had no meaning. I was spending hundreds of pounds on clothing that I would wear just once. At the end of Kandahar's wedding season, with no reason to dress up, I was again at a loss for what to do with myself.

In 2009 the internet came to Kandahar. I watched Yousef scroll slowly through search pages on his school computer, waiting patiently as every image took nearly an hour to load. I decided I wanted my own laptop, just like him. One afternoon my mother brought a beautiful pair of bangles home for Roya. She wanted to go back to the bazaar and buy me a set, too. "I want a laptop instead!" I told her eagerly. Later, when Moor told my sister the story, Roya dissolved into a fit of laughter. "When marriage comes, will you just sit and do laptop all day?" she asked, still giggling. "Who will cook while you are on the laptop? Will you tell the matchmakers you want a laptop?"

One afternoon, finding no sympathy in Roya, I lamented my fate to Aisha over the phone. A month later, in a fond gesture to her faraway sister, she actually sent me a laptop. The package traveled from Birmingham to Kabul, and then a friend brought it by car to our house, since Kandahar had no working mail system. It was the most expensive present I had ever received, and I squandered it. I spent hours searching for the Bollywood actors my sister and I thought were most handsome. We giggled over their glamour shots together, fighting over who could scroll to the next page. I made Facebook accounts for all my cousins and posted constantly, refreshing the website to see updates from my tiny circle of friends. Because the internet was so slow, this took hours out of my day.

While I was wasting time on the computer and poring over fashion magazines, Yousef was studying to attend college abroad. His private school education had prepared him for the British college application system. He had a chance to secure a student visa if he scored well on the International English Language Testing System (IELTS) exam, which he planned to take in just a few months. I spent my evenings removing makeup, studying new gown designs, or watching anything that happened to be on television. As the rest of the family slept every night, I would hear my brother in his room on the second floor, quietly practicing English pronunciations, saying the same words over and over. I'd turn off the TV and lie in bed wide awake, my mind empty and my ears catching his whispers in an unfamiliar language: *avarice, predilection, repudiate, zenith.* I would fall asleep feeling empty, longing for a purpose like his. All I had was a social media account, a deck of cards, and a dozen expensive dresses with hems dirtied by dusty floors from last season's wedding celebrations.

CHAPTER NINE

WINTER DESCENDED SLOWLY UPON KANDAHAR. AT A glance, the city's landscape seemed unchanged. Broad rays of sun still bore down on the bazaars, still pierced through tattered storefront awnings. The streets remained crowded with people. But the cooler air cast a pall over everything, quieting the vendors selling trinkets and flatbreads and emptying makeshift soccer fields and cricket pitches. A chill wound through our unheated bedrooms before settling into our icy pipes and onto the tiles lining our kitchen floor. The temperature outdoors danced around freezing.

It was 2010, and I was fourteen years old. Just a few months earlier, during an autumn of warm afternoons and breezy, lingering evenings, marriage season in Kandahar arrived once again. Nearly every week my brothers drove Roya and me to engagement ceremonies and weddings held in palatial halls and manicured gardens. There it was safe for us to let loose and laugh, protected by the walls and shaded hedges that concealed us from the outside world.

When the stream of invitations slowed, our immediate reaction was to exhale, to fold away our embroidered gowns, to tuck away our gold jewelry, and to feel the exhaustion wash over us. But as the weather grew colder, we soon longed for another party. Without any legitimate excuse or obligation to leave our compound, we were stuck there, confined to the drudgery of unabating housework. We soon fell back into our routine of leaving the house only once every two to three months.

But that year Roya and I had a chance to visit our newly-wed friend Huma at her in-laws' house in a different part of Kandahar. She'd gotten married when she was eighteen.

In the years before her wedding, she'd visited us in the compound often, and we'd always thought of her as so much fun, the first to crack a joke or crank on our stereo. She loved Bollywood music and would thrust her hips from side to side and sing the Hindi verses at the top of her voice. She wore jeans around the house while the rest of us were in *salwaar kameez*. In the early evenings, we'd sit together in my room, laughing as we tried to decide whether Salman Khan or Hrithik Roshan was a more handsome movie star.

But now Huma was living with her parents-in-law as she awaited a visa to join her husband in Europe. Her husband's family was extremely traditional, and even when Huma eventually moved to England, she was required to wear a burqa outdoors at all times. No one in the West ever saw any part of her except the bridge of her nose and her chestnut-colored eyes.

We stayed with Huma for three days. I'd expected a change in my cousin's behavior now that she had to conform to a conservative family, but I didn't realize how profoundly her whole personality would have shifted. As we sat together, stirring green tea and snacking on sweets, Huma spoke almost exclusively of religion. She told us stories she'd heard about how her new aunt was possessed by jinns, the mythical spirits from Islamic folklore. She referenced verses of the Quran that even Roya had never heard of. I nodded along listlessly, daydreaming about the girl she used to be.

But once we returned home, Huma's new personality began to gnaw at me. She seemed so assured, so confident in her piety. Did she understand something that I didn't? Like nearly all families in Kandahar, mine was religious. My mother prayed five times a day, and while we were growing up, she emphasized the importance of cleanliness and kindness to being a good Muslim. But beyond that, she'd provided no specific dogmas to govern our spiritual lives. At home, Islam did not permeate our every discussion, it didn't govern every decision we made.

I was much more familiar with the celebratory aspects of Islam. I loved Ramadan, the month of fasting that leads up to the big Muslim holiday of Eid al-Fitr. The novelty of it was invigorating. My sleep patterns changed. My cousins and I stayed up all night eating and chatting and watching TV, then fell into a deep sleep during the day. When we finally woke up around three or four in the afternoon, all the girls gathered in the kitchen to make dinner. We prepared each other's favorite meals, delicacies we rarely ate at any other time in the year: crispy fried pakoras, samosas, lamb korma. The food tasted incredible when darkness finally came. It seemed as though our taste buds had grown more sensitive and discerning after hours of deprivation.

Before sunrise every morning, we all gathered again for morning prayers and another shared meal. Then the men would head off for work or school while we girls fell into our beds, fast asleep within minutes. We had nothing to accomplish besides our cooking responsibilities in the afternoons. It never occurred to me how sad this was, that our days were so empty that we could flip them upside down and be thoroughly unaffected.

For as long as I lived in Kandahar, Eid al-Fitr, the culmination of Ramadan, was my favorite day of the year. Eid is the biggest festival in the Muslim world, a celebration to mark the end of a month of fasting. It is based on the lunar calendar, and so falls on a different day every year. Every Eid, in preparation for the holiday, we'd buy new clothes and display spreads of sweets and expensive nuts.

I loved waking up at the crack of dawn to pray and then perform traditional Eid greetings, where children kiss the hands of their older relatives. After I greeted Baba, he would touch my head affectionately and envelop me in a gentle embrace. As the years ticked by, as I stopped swimming with him in the rivers and driving with him to buy ice cream, my father spent less and less time with me. When I became a teenager, Eid became the only time of the year when Baba touched me. Even now I have only a faint memory of what it feels like to have my father's arms around me, my head nestled into the crevice beneath his chin.

I also loved Eid for the gifts that all the children received. When I was younger, before the political situation in Kandahar changed for the worse, vendors would spill out into the streets on the holiday morning, crowding one another to offer snacks and playthings to children who had just been given more money than they knew what to do with. I used to love running out of our compound toward the market to buy cheap toys and bubbling sodas. But once it became too dangerous for me to leave our compound, I sent my brothers out with a list of what to buy me while I sat at home, waiting.

By Eid nightfall, it was time for the final meal, usually hosted at my aunt's house. We dined on succulent meat and indulgent desserts. When it grew dark enough, we lit sparklers out in the garden and laughed uproariously as the flames danced along every metal wire. I was always clumsy, losing control of the fire, burning the backs of my fancy new Eid clothes, but somehow managed never to get seriously hurt. We left for home in the early hours of the morning, high on excitement from the party.

But after my visit to Huma, this relationship with religion seemed inadequate. I wondered what a closer connection to God would mean, whether my recent state of aimlessness could be fixed by spiritual enlightenment. A few days after returning from our visit, I found a religious textbook propped up in Yousef's room alongside his computer and a pile of notebook paper. I started to turn through the pages of the textbook, but Yousef saw me and rushed to take it out of my hands. "Don't read that, Sola," he said urgently. "I'm only using it to write a paper for school. It's terrible, it's too extreme." But desperate for an understanding that I felt neither he nor I possessed, I snatched the book off the table and continued down the hall to my bedroom.

The book was terrifying. It contained detailed, graphic descriptions of what happens to us after we die. Good people, the textbook said, would proceed immediately to the day of judgment. But sinners would remain trapped in their graves as the walls caved in around them. I imagined myself in a half-alive state, thrashing against mounds of tightly packed dirt as it engulfed me. I worried that just one sin—disrespecting my mother, forgetting a prayer, lifting my veil—would be enough to condemn me to this misery.

Another passage described how, when I died, an angel would come to me and ask me to recite the Kalimas, six fundamental beliefs that all Muslims should know, to secure my passage to heaven. I used to practice the Kalimas over and over again, but I was plagued with worry that, upon seeing the angel, I would be rendered speechless and sentenced to hell.

I knew my parents weren't worried about constricting graves or perfectly memorized verses. But instead of comforting me, this fact made me more uneasy. I began to believe Baba and Moor didn't possess the necessary knowledge, that they were doomed for a wretched afterlife. I was afraid that I might inherit the same fate if I didn't commit myself entirely to becoming a good Muslim.

In 2007 my brother Nadir had married a woman named Shabana, who now lived with us in our compound and shared household responsibilities with Roya and me. Shabana came from a more conservative family than ours, as most of them in Kandahar were. I had no real idea how to begin my search for religious salvation, so one day, as we wrung out the laundry, I asked her, "Shabana, will you teach me the rules I need to follow to be a perfect Muslim?" I wanted a code that I could methodically follow to achieve a religious awakening.

Based on Shabana's advice, I changed the way I dressed. I traded in my short-sleeve cotton *kameez* tops for shapeless dresses that reached to my toes, and I started wearing a scarf around my head at home, even when I was around

just my mother and my sister. During the day, I moved duti-
fully through my household tasks, sweeping and stirring
and folding clothes, stopping only to adjust my heavy hijab
that smelled vaguely of frying oil and cloves. I stopped
dancing.

I began to pray five times a day, waking up and setting
out my prayer rug before the sun even cracked the night
sky. Afterward I stumbled through the Quran, trying to decipher the Arabic script that I had barely learned to read, in
spite of the hours of lessons with Pashtana. When the characters started to blend together, I'd go back to my bedroom
and catch a few more hours of sleep until eight or nine in
the morning.

Moor and Roya could not understand why I was suddenly acting so differently. Just a few years earlier I'd hated
studying the Quran, and now I was spending much of my
day on it. "Sola, you are living on the edge," Moor insisted.
"If you do not learn to balance your life, to live in the middle, you will always be discontented." But I ignored her,
convinced I was on a pathway to ultimate fulfillment.

Only a few weeks earlier, I'd passed my spare time in the
company of swoon-worthy Bollywood stars and rousing Indian dance music. But now I turned off the television.

I even scolded my mother when she tried to turn it back
on to watch an old movie or listen to a traditional Afghan
music concert. The books I was reading insisted that TV
and music were against Islam. The authors instructed that a
good Muslim should spend every waking minute of life in
contemplation of God.

The only show I permitted myself to watch was on an
Indian Muslim channel that broadcast religious lectures.

The show was in Urdu, a language similar enough to the Hindi I'd picked up by watching countless Bollywood dramas. An old white-bearded imam, set against a glass bookshelf filled with religious texts, stared fixedly into the camera. He delivered monologues on Islam, his tone fluctuating between intense passion and a more intimate, gentle persuasion. I sat still in front of the television, tempted to adhere completely to his doctrine, a way of thinking that could glue together my shapeless life. I was struck by how much of Islam I did not know and understand, and I vowed to study the lectures carefully every day.

But Shabana soon informed me that even this was sinful behavior. A true Muslim woman, she told me, never looks into the eyes of a man, even on a television set. She said this with urgent conviction, though the principle had never stopped her from enjoying soap operas and reality shows. But I trusted my sister-in-law, so I flipped the television set on and turned my back to the screen, listening to the imam's voice carry across the room, careful not to catch a glimpse of his face in any reflections.

Shabana wasn't the only one to feed me religious advice that she didn't follow herself. As news of my Islamic journey reached my various distant aunts and cousins in Kandahar, they flocked to our house to advise me on an unending stream of practices that I needed to take up to be the perfect Muslim. One family friend told me that it was sinful for me to laugh with my mouth open. Many aunts talked to me about my future husband, about how as an Islamic woman I should worship him next to God. One even told me that if I were not naked when my husband returned home from work every day, it would be sinful. In service to God, she told me, I should be able to anticipate and fulfill his every desire.

I became consumed by these rules, convinced that adhering perfectly to every restriction was my only option. I longed for the respite of dreamless nights, and I dreaded waking up every morning. What was the point, if the day held only the potential for a hundred sins? The hours of daylight crawled by, but the weeks blurred together. I agonized over every movement I took, analyzed every thought that crossed my mind. I wondered: *Is this what I am living for, to be confined inside a house, trapped in a quest to be perfectly religious?* I wished my life would just end.

THIS WENT ON FOR MONTHS. I was never content with the state of my devotion to religion. I was convinced that my obstacles would be resolved once I read every religious text, watched every religious program, and spent every waking hour contemplating God. But I never considered that this religious devotion might be too intensive, that I would soon exhaust the books, the TV shows, and the advice of my relatives, and be left with only the most soul-wrenching questions. Maybe they didn't realize just how much my religious studies were consuming me, but they did not push hard for me to stop.

I began to question the religion that was taking over my life when I realized that, under Islam, women were subject to a set of additional rules. I was forbidden to be an imam. It was apparently permissible for a man to marry two or three women. I couldn't understand what it was about a husband that made him worthier than his wife.

My anger at these things arose in part from what I was seeing around me. My brothers left every morning and returned every evening with piles of math worksheets and paper plates of half-finished street food. I stayed at home. I now realize I'd studied religion out of a desire to imbue my life with the meaning theirs had. But instead, my readings only justified my inferior status.

A more central contradiction arose one evening as I sat silently, absorbing the words of the TV imam, and it planted itself squarely in the center of my consciousness. *If God created the universe,* I wondered, wide awake in the early hours of the morning, *who created God?* Despite having thrown myself into religious studies for several devoted months, I felt wholly unequipped to answer this foundational question. I now wanted to shake the imam by his shoulders, disrupt his calm demeanor, and demand an answer. I thought briefly about asking my mother or Shabana about this, but it felt sacrilegious. If I admitted my doubts out loud, how would everyone perceive me? People simply didn't ask those kinds of questions in Kandahar. Years later I would read an article that quoted a story about Saint Augustine. "What did God do before he created the universe?" someone asked him. Augustine replied, "He was preparing Hell for people who ask such questions." The story resonated with me, because this was the reaction I feared from my own family.

Perhaps if I had just talked to someone, my doubts would have been resolved. But without anyone to share my worries with, they started to consume me. I floated vacantly through the house, tears streaming down my face. I stopped laughing with my sister as we cooked, and I rarely stepped outside into the courtyard. My skin grew pale. I turned away from my mother as I sobbed involuntarily, clutching the folds of my veil as if that could keep me together.

The central question of who created God took up every ounce of my consciousness. I pondered it so intensely that when someone tapped me on the shoulder or called my name, I jumped. The nights provided brief, sweet relief. But then when I woke up in the early hours of the morning to use the bathroom, I was racked with uncertainty all over again.

I felt a stifling guilt: surely no good Muslim should have these doubts. But I just could not come up with an explanation that satisfied me. *Who created God, who created the person who created God, who created that person . . .* , I wondered in the dark. It felt as if my relationship with religion were tainted. Now I just wanted to get away, to banish these questions from my head for my own sanity.

At first my sisters and cousins teased me. They were convinced I was in love with someone, crying over a boy. Even my mother joined in. "Girls who act this way just want to get married," she said, laughing gently. But weeks passed, and I never smiled. My brother Javid grew worried and brought me little pieces of the bustling, outside world— hot plates of Afghan-style pizza and icy imported energy drinks—to try to cheer me up. My sister phoned me from the UK. "We want our old Sola back, the girl who loved fashion and dancing to Bollywood songs," she said. "I'll buy you any dresses you want. Something with lace? How about a skirt with flowers? Please, Sola?"

When my state of mind still didn't improve after a few months, and I couldn't tell Moor what was troubling me, she guessed it had something to do with my religious obsession. She thought that maybe I was afraid of going to hell. "God is kind," she told me. "He is like a parent, he will forgive you." At night she started sleeping next to me, her arms blanketing me, willing me to be at peace. I lay beside her, feigning sleep as my eyes stayed firmly open and my mind swirled with confusion.

Soon even Baba was begging me to stop acting this way. "People will think you are going mad," he pleaded, a grave look clouding his eyes. His somber words pulled me out of the dizzy fog I was living in, just for a moment. I realized that I was drowning in my own unanswerable questions, losing the very essence of myself.

PART
TWO

CHAPTER TEN

MY GRANDFATHER AGHA USED TO SAY, "PEOPLE WHO know English have no worries." He'd lived the truth of his adage. Born into abject poverty, he taught himself English by reading old dictionaries and tracing unfamiliar letters onto discarded sheets of paper. Once he learned the language, his fortune changed dramatically. He went from being a penniless young father to a financially comfortable intellectual. Money flowed in from his job as a translator for merchants. Even as the American presence in Afghanistan dragged on for years past 2001, Agha never faltered in his praise of the English language.

I saw proof of my grandfather's saying everywhere. In Kandahar, shopkeepers, laborers, and street vendors spoke only Pashto. Those with the keys to English were government officials or soon-to-be expats. In Pakistan, the country I believed to be so much more modern and secure than my own, it was extremely common to hear English. And Yousef was learning English and seemed destined for greatness in the form of a European education and an enviable life abroad.

When my cousins visited from Pakistan, Yousef conversed freely with them in English as I stood beside them, nodding and smiling hesitantly as they burst into laughter. I felt foolish as I strained to understand, trying to make sense of a jumble of unfamiliar consonants and phrasing. "What are you saying?" I'd ask earnestly, but I never received a straight answer. My question always seemed to deflate their animated conversations. Yousef would mumble something at me, and my cousins would eventually scatter from the room. Many years later, when I became closer with my Pakistani cousin, she admitted to me that Yousef had been telling jokes about me and Roya in English, making fun of the fact that all we could do was speak Pashto. "I used to think you were stupid, too," she admitted to me sheepishly. "I wondered, how can someone be so ignorant that they cannot even speak English?" I must have picked up on their disdain, because I started avoiding their conversations entirely.

But I never forgot the power that English could have. It remained a lingering thought, a fuzzy aspiration, especially as I grew older and my problems mounted. Before he passed away in 2008, my grandfather was fond of repeating, "English is the window to the world." By my teenage years, I desperately needed a window, a glance of what lay beyond my own consciousness.

IT WAS 2011, AND I was exhausted by my religious reckoning. Mired in guilt and a disorienting sadness, I was worlds away from the clarity and direction I'd sought through my initial study of Islam. What had begun as a passing interest had now razed me to the ground, robbed me of my spontaneity, my sense of mischief, my happiness. Life had become

a grueling marathon toward a spiritual salvation perenni-
ally out of reach.

My spirit slackened and seemed to ooze out of me. I
wanted to scramble and leap up to salvage my identity, grab
hold of the fading facets of the girl I used to be. But every
time, a kind of sluggish, resigned melancholy stopped me.
I watched passively as my essence wisped away.

But by the spring, after months of this silent agony,
something shifted. I realized I was spiraling downward, and
I grew more afraid of what awaited me at the bottom of
that psychological whirlpool than of whatever hell I might
face for questioning religion. I saw the lives that people
were living around me and remembered when I used to live
like that, too.

I slowly lifted myself out of despair. I tried to push away
the prodding thoughts that followed me everywhere. I
smiled for my parents and watched them beam back at me
with relief. My newfound contentment was intensely fragile and rough around the edges. But I felt as though I was
rebuilding a life I could claim entirely for myself. I was unwilling to fall back into an existence defined by the restrictions and opinions of other people.

I made a conscious effort to change my daily habits,
from what I wore to what I did. I stopped draping a veil
over my hair every morning, I tapped my feet to the music
my cousins played while we cleaned, and I slept through
early morning prayers. I turned my eyes toward the TV
screen again and sank into the comfortable folds of the
couch while watching dramas and Indian comedies. Still,
the depression lurked around me. Sometimes, after bursting into laughter at a joke or a TV scene, I'd be seized by

intense guilt. *What have you done to deserve this fun?* I'd ask myself as the laugh track continued to run. *You have accomplished nothing, and yet you sit here, happy.* But mostly I forced myself to be more positive. I settled into an unsteady, self-propagating sense of comfort, each happy day making the next one a little better.

One afternoon our family friends from Kandahar were to visit for tea. I dreaded their arrival because their daughters, two girls close to my age, walked around with a constant air of superiority. They dressed in expensive clothes with asymmetrical cuts and ornate embroidery, clothes so fashionable they couldn't be found in any Kandahar markets. Their mother boasted constantly about how gorgeous her daughters were, how they were inundated with matchmakers bearing more marriage requests than they could even consider.

As the girls settled atop our fanciest floor pillows and sipped daintily from their teacups, I fell under their spell. I marveled at their swooping earrings and confident postures. I crumpled back into myself and sat by them quietly, my head slightly bowed.

My grandmother Ana Bibi watched it all unfold. A few hours into our friends' visit, she whisked me aside and urged me to drop my deferential attitude. "You are just as good as they are!" she whispered fiercely into my ear, her fingers encircling my wrists tightly. "Do you know who your father is?" I nodded softly. "He is one of the most respected men in this entire city. Actually, he makes you even more important than your friends!" She pushed me back into the living room.

Usually, Ana Bibi got upset at me for being too loud or unruly. She was the one who'd dragged me back to Quran class, who'd often told Moor that I was spoiled and lazy. But that afternoon her vehement lecture shocked me into sudden self-confidence.

At night, though, I reflected more closely on Ana Bibi's words. *"Do you know who your father is?"* she'd asked. She hadn't assured me that I was smarter than those girls. She hadn't even complimented me on my new *salwaar* and freshly curled hair. Instead, she'd essentially explained to me that I was worthy—but solely on the basis of who my father was. And that drove me into another mental spiral, a blinding torment that felt comfortable and familiar, though I wasn't dealing with the hypotheticals of religion anymore. This psychological descent felt grounded in reality, justified by the happenings of my entire existence.

I wondered if Baba's status was the only thing separating me from a life of poverty. Who would I be without the implications of his name supporting me? A slum-dwelling beggar, destined to make a living by tapping on car windows? A servant in a big house, forced to launder and iron someone else's clothes? A faceless wife, burdened with the weight of ten children? I had nothing of my own to stand on besides the ability to fold sheets and prepare enough rice for a dozen people.

I panicked, afraid that my precarious recovery was slipping away from me. I hounded my brain for something I could do to stand out, to rise above my reliance on Baba for my identity. It was then, in a stroke of sudden insight, that my grandfather Agha's words came back to me. *"People who know English have no worries. English is the window to the world."* I decided to try to learn this new language for myself.

I KNEW A SMATTERING of English words, but not enough to hold any semblance of a conversation. When we were little, my mother taught us the English alphabet and numbers. After we'd escaped the Taliban and fled to Pakistan in 2001, my aunt had taught Roya and me how to read and write some basic English sentences. Her singsong voice had lilted over sounds that were jarring and foreign to our ears. She'd given us pencils and pieces of note paper and guided our pudgy fingers across the page to form letters. She explained how, in English, words move from left to right—the opposite of how Pashto is written—and smiled as we recited the phrases she'd taught us: "Hello," "Good morning!" Roya and I had been distracted students, more interested in playing with our cousins or peering out from her dusty apartment window onto the streets of Karachi. But our aunt had insisted we study this new language. She knew she had limited time before we returned to Afghanistan, to a future where we were ensured nothing but uncertainty.

Bits and pieces of what she'd taught us had stayed with me through the remaining years of my childhood. When we enrolled in lessons with Miss, I'd built on that knowledge slightly, though most of the lesson time was consumed by Miss's stories. I memorized sounds like *sh* and *th* and learned what a vowel was. I studied basic grammar, learned to say "I am" not "I is," and "He was" not "He were." Miss read English picture books to us that I still remembered, tales about kids named Harry and Sara who colored with crayons and carted around teddy bears.

So now I could stand in front of a mirror and declare, "Good morning!" at my smiling reflection. I could write simple sentences. But I couldn't understand the telephone conversations that Yousef had with Aisha in English to practice for his upcoming IELTS exam. I couldn't comprehend any English news programs or YouTube videos. I couldn't read words, could only identify letters. If I wanted to study this language, I would essentially be starting from scratch.

Compounding my difficulties, even in my native Pashto I could read and write only at a basic level. I had no access to textbooks, and had I tried to meet with a tutor, my life would have been in danger. So I turned to my brother Yousef.

Yousef bluntly refused to help me. Though he himself had overcome great odds to learn English and get a ticket out of the country, he had no desire to help me do the same. "I just learned one hundred different English adverbs," he bragged to me one evening. "How can you think you will ever be at my level?" The calculus was simple to him, and he laid it out for me: women weren't supposed to learn English, to learn anything really. Over the past few years, in his quest for personal betterment, he had engaged in a great deal of critical thinking and reflection, developing nuanced opinions on politics and ethics, learning complex formulas and scientific theories. Yet he had never questioned his belief that my sisters and I should not do what he had done. He felt no malice, didn't harbor a vendetta against women.

But he accepted the inequality between men and women as easily as he would any law of nature, and he never gave it a second thought.

After Yousef turned me down, I was indignant. All my life I'd been his favorite subject for teasing. He'd always had low expectations for me and had been smug and unsurprised when I hadn't exceeded them. His attitude finally lit a fire under me. I was determined to achieve something concrete, to acquire some skill or knowledge that could be measured against his, to prove that I was his equal.

I loaded a Pashto-to-English dictionary onto my laptop, the same device I'd previously wasted by watching hours of YouTube videos and scrolling through pictures of handsome Bollywood actors. I found a notebook and slowly copied down vocabulary words, making sure to keep two neat columns, one for each language, tracing the curves of the English letter *s*, the tail of the letter *p*. The pages filled steadily until I could flip through half the notebook and watch hundreds of penciled entries fly through my fingers.

My parents were dismissive of my new interests. They weren't concerned about safety since I confined all evidence of my educational pursuits to my upstairs bedroom. At first they thought that I was going through another phase that would pass, just as my obsessions with fashion and religion had. Though initially disappointing, their lack of interest was a blessing. Only a handful of families in Kandahar would have accepted the news that their teenage daughter was studying English the way my parents did. Most would have reacted with horror and forced her to stop, maybe even dealt blows or forced her into marriage to quiet her rebelliousness. But Baba and Moor let me be. They gave me this small freedom when nearly everything else had been taken from me.

I studied at night and between meals. After the final dishes were scrubbed, I dashed upstairs to quiz myself on my growing vocabulary. I spent hours bent over the small desk in the corner of my room, my eyes strained from the dim lighting. But I'd emerge late at night feeling undeniably alive, wishing someone were still awake to share in my excitement. Baba had recently bought me a cellphone, and I recorded myself on it, pronouncing new English words and phrases. I played the tapes back constantly, as I folded laundry and during my late-afternoon bike rides inside the compound walls. I made flash cards and taped them above the kitchen sink so I could review them while washing dishes or soaking the rice to be served at dinner. Soon, spurred by my rapid improvements, I was studying nearly thirty hours a week.

Studying was invigorating but still incredibly difficult. I began watching English coverage on CNN and the BBC to try to improve my comprehension. Two or three segments would go by, and I wouldn't understand a single word. I relied entirely on the news anchor's facial expressions and the images flashing across the screen to figure out what topic was being discussed. I tried to read simple books and newspapers in English that I borrowed from Yousef's room. But most times the words would blur in front of me, an incomprehensible jumble of letters and spaces. My Pashto dictionary started to fail me: its translations were approximate at best and sometimes wrong. So I tried to look up words in an English dictionary, a process that was laborious and frustrating. I'd look up a word like *together* and find a definition reading: "with or in proximity to another person or people." And then I'd have to look up *proximity* and *another* and decipher both of those individual definitions. One time I tried to translate a single sentence from a newspaper article and ended up entering fifty new definitions into my notebook.

Despite these challenges, learning English still seemed within my reach. I felt myself making steady progress, zipping through my flash cards and retaining all the definitions and grammar rules in my notebook. For the first time, I experienced the incredible high that comes from the simple act of learning, something I'd never felt on the crusted floors of my government-aid school or while I was pressed up against Pashtana's fists. For most of my life, I'd needed other people to help me with even the simplest things. My brothers brought me food from outside, my father gave me money, my uncle drove me around to weddings and engagement parties. My life was often at the whim of bombings and shootouts I could not control. The fact that I was finally doing something on my own, that some part of my life was in my hands, was enough to carry me forward.

IN THE SUMMER OF 2011, Yousef prepared to leave Afghanistan. The IELTS exam he had been studying for was notoriously difficult, and two of his friends who took the test failed it. But Yousef passed the exam easily, earning marks far higher than necessary for admission into an English university. After receiving his scores, he applied for and was accepted to an economics program in Birmingham. He planned to fly out of the country in August.

As I watched Yousef pack for his life abroad, pride washed over me. I was drawn back to an afternoon years earlier, when the sunlight had been soft and waning, peeking through our windows. My mother was entertaining Baba's sister, my aunt, who was visiting from her home in Denmark. They were drinking tea and laughing over old memories when Yousef walked in. He was barely a teenager at the time, dressed in traditional Afghan clothes and the black turban that had become obligatory for boys as the Taliban regained influence. My aunt looked him up and down, then remarked, "This boy will become a Talib." She was speaking offhandedly, almost joking, commenting more on the dire political situation than on Yousef's individual prospects. But my mother was deeply wounded. She nearly cried recounting the story to us, so upset that Yousef's own family could believe he was destined for a terrible existence just because of the place he'd been born.

But now Yousef was packing button-down shirts to wear to lectures and pound notes with which to buy cups of coffee and pastries. He'd stared his prescribed destiny in the face and then circumvented it entirely, painting a new chapter for himself. Family members called from abroad to congratulate Baba and Moor on their son's accomplishments. "We cannot believe he's become such a smart boy after spending his whole life in Kandahar," they said.

When it finally came time for Yousef to leave home, I was racked with a sudden sadness. Despite all his teasing and mockery, I shared a unique connection with my middle brother that was different from what I had with my other family members. Yousef and I were rivals and adversaries because we were so similar, both headstrong and stubborn, confident in our own correctness. And he was undoubtedly the smartest person I knew. He inspired me even as he tried to tear me down.

The night before he left for the UK, our sister Aisha called to congratulate all of us on Yousef's success. We talked for an hour, passing the phone around to one another. Before she hung up, Aisha spoke to me. "Sola, you'll be next!" she said. I was startled by how much I wanted to make her words come true.

S TUDYING OPENED UP MY WORLD. I WAS NO LONGER A
girl stuck in our Kandahar compound, stifled by the
smells of yesterday's dinner and the sticky, smoggy air that
filtered in from outside. Instead, I was in Birmingham, sitting next to a news anchor who rounded his vowels just as
my sister Aisha had been doing since she moved to the UK.
I was in our capital of Kabul, standing on the street outside
towering, menacing prisons described in the newspaper
clippings I read. I was in New Delhi following a reporter
into a female-only metro car, squished between women returning home from work, their fingers curled firmly around
their briefcases and smartphones.

I stretched toward these new horizons, allowing myself
to yearn for a life among the people and cities I was reading
about. But eventually, reminders of the growing violence in
Kandahar always pulled me back to reality. The immediacy
of the shootings and bombings that surrounded me demanded attention. They stole even the space in my brain to
dream.

By 2012, as I approached my sixteenth birthday, unrelenting fighting between the Taliban and Afghan government forces was the norm. Our compound was situated just a few streets beyond the front lines of this war, where battles were unfolding in bazaars and schools rather than in open fields. Since I was so confined to the compound, I never saw active fighting or even the remnants of explosions on the streets. But my brother and father told me about the danger they witnessed as they left for school and work, and I watched television coverage of the implacable combat from home.

Though the government still held on to overall command of our city, the Taliban showed undeniable strength. They conducted assaults and attacks boldly, without regard for who they were killing. They were willing to attack as many civilians as necessary to gain control of more territory. They targeted every part of the Afghan government: its buildings, its employees, and anyone who was known to support it.

The Afghan government's main advantage over the Taliban was its ability to conduct aerial warfare. It targeted the insurgents from above, launching airstrikes on Taliban hideouts and strongholds. But the airstrikes were imprecise and often missed their targets, killing civilians instead. Low-flying government planes passed over our house regularly, and we worried they might suddenly release a barrage of bombs. Even years later the roar of an airplane was enough to terrify me, to bring me back to the days when war was unfolding overhead.

One day the Taliban mounted an attack outside Javid's school in downtown Kandahar. From three o'clock in the afternoon until just after midnight, bullets rained down over the school building while the students huddled together in the basement, waiting. When they could no longer hear any shots, they burst through the front door, each boy walking quickly down the street in a different direction, hoping desperately to make it home before the fighting resumed. Javid ran to a relative's house and was finally able to reach us. We crowded around the phone as Baba answered the call, our panic dissipating and our lungs filling with the air of sudden relief.

Life in Kandahar was further complicated by the fact that the Taliban and the Afghan government weren't the only players in the war. NATO troops were a constant presence within our city. In the eleven years since they first invaded Afghanistan, the Americans and their allies had lost their status as heroes. They were now embroiled in the stickiness of war, responsible for both victories and missteps, for many civilian casualties and for firing upon passenger buses and cars with innocent people inside. The NATO forces justified their actions by claiming that the vehicles posed a threat or appeared to be carrying suicide bombers. But like most of our friends and family, we found that difficult to believe. How could a dull green bus crammed with dozens of people look like a threat? Why had the NATO troops' response been to try to kill everyone on board?

In 2010 our family friend had been traveling home from a business trip when his bus approached a NATO convoy. The NATO troops, apparently believing the bus to be filled with suicide bombers, opened fire and killed the bus driver and several other passengers. Our friend was shot in the leg and was unable to walk for weeks.

Despite these incidents, no one I knew ever spoke a word against the Americans. In Kandahar, politics had become a binary game: you were either for the Taliban or against them. People feared that voicing their discontent with American conduct would get them branded as Taliban supporters.

In March 2012, however, popular opinion of the forces occupying Kandahar plummeted. In the early-morning hours of March 11, American Staff Sergeant Robert Bales left his army base in Kandahar province and murdered sixteen Afghan villagers in the Panjwai district, nine of whom were children. Their bodies were found riddled with bullet holes and even partially burned to ashes. Many of the victims were related to one another, families torn apart in one horrific night.

The details of the brutal attack were mired in secrecy. Our family heard reports that American military officials swooped into the Panjwai district after the attack, cordoning off the crime scenes and removing key evidence. They promoted the narrative that Sergeant Bales was irresponsible and evil, a lone wolf who was unrepresentative of the broader American presence in Afghanistan. But the Americans' story ignored the accounts of several villagers, who swore that there had been more than one soldier in the Panjwai villages that night—maybe closer to fifteen or twenty. At the time, this version of events, where several American soldiers embarked on a killing spree, seemed likely closest to reality. How could one man have rounded up sixteen victims entirely on his own?

———

THE ATROCITIES SWIRLING AROUND us produced the kind
of searing, agonizing pain that eventually must turn to
numbness. After the initial shock from each violent attack,
we learned to fold our emotions tightly and tuck them away
so we did not implode from anger and abject sadness. We
lived double-sided lives, existing sometimes in the harsh reality of war and other times in a suspended state of nor-
malcy.

During these pockets of quietude, I actually felt happier
than I had in years. I was learning, finally, to live within
the immovable boundaries I'd previously chafed against. I
cooked dinners and boiled water for tea. After I finished
studying for the day, I played cards with my sister and our
cousins. After teatime in the late afternoons, I danced, spinning to the beat of the latest Bollywood music.

I was happier too, now that Yousef had gone. I missed
my brother, but I had risen to take his place in the family.
Baba now turned to me for simple things, to reset the TV
remote or print out some paperwork for his business. For
Yousef, these tasks had been routine, even slight annoy-
ances. But in my life, Baba had never asked me to do anything for him. I felt I'd faded from his consciousness as I
grew older, becoming a financial burden, stuck living stag-
nantly at home until I could be married. Now I was silently
thrilled that he was choosing me to rely on a little bit, trusting me with small bits of responsibility.

Of course, something else sustained me during this
time: my personal solace, learning. To aid with my studies,
Javid bought me a wooden desk and gifted me his own

chair. "You need something nice to sit on, Sola!" he told me. "I only study at home for a few hours, but you are sitting here learning all day." I placed my new setup in the corner of my room, just across from my bed.

Since Yousef was gone, I took some things from his desk and placed them in my new study area. I loved being surrounded by my brother's thick IELTS textbooks and stacks of old newspaper clippings, by the tattered works of Mark Twain and other Western authors that he'd taken from my grandfather Agha's original collection. They were a physical reminder of why I was spending so much time studying.

I still spent hours every day learning vocabulary and sounding out words in books and newspaper articles. My progress was so rapid, it surprised even me. After just a few months, I was able to understand most of the basic texts I read. I stumbled over words and relied heavily on my dictionary, but I found that I could now get by in English. If I ever had to, I could follow the news or read a short novel, all in a language I was teaching myself.

As I learned more and more, the days that used to drag on interminably flew past. I lost track of time while I was studying, consumed entirely by the passage I was deciphering or the English news show I was watching. And my household duties seemed to move more quickly, too. I played recordings of me reciting English sentences as I swept the floors and folded the covers over my brothers' beds, racing to finish so I could return to my desk.

But though I was progressing quickly with my studies, time eventually caught up with me. I turned sixteen in May 2012. My age was significant because sixteen in Kandahar is considered the right age for a girl to start looking for a husband. Matchmaking was the one aspect of life in Kandahar that I wanted to lose to the war but that everyone else refused to let go of, even in the face of extreme violence. I was only a teenager, finally standing on my own, secure in the fact that I was providing for myself intellectually, building up to be my own person. It would have been a stunning defeat to crawl back into someone's shadow, to fall into an existence defined by my husband. And beyond any logical reasons not to get married, the thought just repulsed me. I wasn't ready to be thrust into the roles of wife and then mother.

My sister Roya was nineteen at this point, with luscious brown hair, large round eyes, and a slim figure. So many matchmakers wanted to meet with her, to introduce her to the mothers of various sons who might be interested. When potential mothers-in-law came over to evaluate Roya, they also wanted to see any other girls in the house. So I'd reluctantly walk into the living room after my sister, my head draped demurely in a scarf, counting the minutes until our guests left. I relied on the fact that my sister was more beautiful than me, my relative unattractiveness protecting me from a slew of unwanted proposals.

One afternoon when Roya was meeting with a pair of matchmakers, Moor called for me and my younger cousin Mojdeh to get ready and join them. We got dressed, and then I gestured to Mojdeh to go ahead of me, indicating that I would follow. But instead, as soon as she entered the room, I bolted. I ran into my room, leaving Mojdeh and Roya fumbling to explain my absence. I knew it looked bad, but I didn't care.

———

EIGHT MONTHS EARLIER, in the fall of 2011, Javid had been driving a motorbike in downtown Kandahar when he crashed and broke his femur. Soon afterward Baba received a call from a strange number. "Your son has been in an accident," the voice began. "You must come and get him."

The threat of kidnappings in Kandahar had not abated from the time I was a young girl. Since we didn't hear from any doctors or from Javid himself, my parents began to fear someone had abducted him to obtain a ransom from my father. They thought the kidnappers had concocted the accident as a ruse. Eventually, Baba decided to go to where the caller claimed the accident had occurred. Moor and I stood at the front door as he left, shaking with worry.

Half an hour later Baba called to tell us that Javid was alive, that he actually had been in a motorbike accident. Javid was in so much pain that Baba rushed him to the local hospital. Over the past few decades, the quality of medical care in Kandahar had deteriorated to a point where only a handful of qualified doctors remained in the city. They managed to find one who would perform an emergency operation on Javid's leg. He returned home days later, exhausted and grimacing with pain.

Over the next several months, Javid went to the hospital for more operations. The doctors in Kandahar made mistakes, inserting rods that prevented his bone from growing and failing to set his bone fragments properly. After one surgery, Javid exited the operating room with one leg shorter than the other. The doctor then performed another operation to try to fix the damage, but afterward Baba decided Javid should go to Pakistan to see a doctor there and make sure the leg healed correctly.

In 2012, at the end of May, my uncle agreed to take Javid across the border with him on one of his regularly scheduled business trips. The morning of his departure, I asked my brother if he would bring me back some interesting English-language reading material. Yousef had left behind some novels in his room, but most of them were very old and used words like *betwixt* and *thou* that made them difficult to understand. The English newspapers I read at home were unsuitable in a different way. They covered the most upsetting news stories in Afghanistan. I found myself working through paragraphs about brutal prisons and asking Yousef for help translating words like *prostitution*. When I wasn't reading, I was watching news coverage on the TV that was equally depressing, following stories like the Syrian Civil War and Delhi gang rapes.

Javid finally returned to Kandahar in early June 2012. The Pakistani doctors had confirmed his leg was healing properly, and my brother was in great spirits. I was thrilled to find that he had brought me an entire stack of books and magazines and English newspapers. The first thing I picked up from the pile was *Time* magazine's "100 Most Influential People of the Year" issue. I slowly worked my way through it, sometimes stopping to translate a word I didn't understand. Flipping through the pages, I came across an entry for Sal Khan, the founder of a free online educational nonprofit called Khan Academy. The article, written by Bill Gates, explained that Khan Academy was a revolutionary website featuring over three thousand bite-size videos on all academic subjects. Students could watch Khan Academy videos taught by Sal Khan to learn new concepts. Then they could work on practice problems and return to the videos to review any ideas they still struggled with. "The aspiration of khanacademy.org is to give every kid a chance at a free, world-class education," Gates wrote. Khan Academy was a new kind of school, one without overbearing teachers or exams or judgment from peers. It was just the student and the teacher, moving through content together at any pace they desired.

I paused. I had never considered that my new English skills might give me the ability to return to school, to make up for so much lost time.

That evening I pulled my laptop close and visited the Khan Academy website. The first thing I saw was a bright advertisement for algebra lessons. I'd studied only basic addition and subtraction in school, and that had been over five years ago. I closed the computer firmly. Khan Academy, I thought, was for students more advanced than me.

I continued my English studies, paging through the other books and magazines my brother had brought me back from Karachi. But the idea of teaching myself all the school material I had missed out on was deeply tempting, even if it seemed slightly fantastical. At the end of the week, after a long day of cooking and ironing and scrubbing, I opened the laptop again and surveyed the courses they had to offer. The single-digit addition and subtraction I was comfortable with was marked on the platform as "Kindergarten Math." Alone in my bedroom, I blushed. Here I was at sixteen, at the same intellectual level as an American five-year-old.

I was too embarrassed to begin working on the arithmetic problem sets, even though I needed help in that basic area. So I asked Javid what math topic came after subtraction. "Fractions," he told me. The next day I logged on and started watching videos. They buffered often, bogged down by our sluggish cable internet. Somehow I managed to start doing problems. I was delighted by the bright green check mark that flashed on the screen every time I got something right. However, every problem that required addition or subtraction I still got wrong.

One day I started on a fractions concept that seemed familiar. I remembered one of my cousins trying to teach it to me a few years earlier, as a way to pass the time. But after watching several Khan Academy videos, I realized he had been doing the problems incorrectly. I couldn't believe that he had gone to school for almost his entire childhood and still made such a basic mistake. Proving my cousin wrong, even many years later, gave me the confidence to start my mathematics journey over properly. I knew that in order to go any further, I would need to master basic arithmetic. So I began watching videos on how to add and subtract. Each short video built on the one before it, making it easy to follow along. I copied down the numbers and symbols that appeared on the black virtual chalkboard. Sal Khan drew dots on the screen and counted them out loud. I paused the videos often to calculate slowly on my fingers.

Eventually, after I conquered basic arithmetic and fractions, Khan Academy's software told me I was ready to move on to percentages. My parents and cousins suddenly looked impressed and told me that this level of math was quite difficult to learn. I was delighted—it felt like magic to be able to do the things others had thought I couldn't. Studying on Khan Academy was one of the first times I was able to defy expectations, to do something my brothers could without fear of immediate, dangerous retribution from Taliban sympathizers.

I set a schedule for myself. My sister-in-law, my sister, and I still took turns cooking and cleaning the house, so I spent every third day doing chores, and I studied nonstop on the other two. On those days I wanted to spend all my time on Khan Academy. But my brothers needed access to the internet for their schooling, and our connection was too weak to support more than one user at a time. I had to give them priority. So late at night, after everyone else fell asleep, I would download Khan Academy videos onto my computer. During the day, I would watch them all, and the next evening I would take quizzes.

My progress was rapid from the start. Despite the fact that I lacked a sturdy educational foundation, I found I was able to move through an entire year's worth of math material in just a few months.

At first this progress was exhilarating, but I soon began to have doubts. My brothers had attended one of the fanciest schools in Afghanistan, and they had taken triple the time to master concepts I was moving through in only a few weeks. Maybe, I thought, this Khan Academy website is a scam. These math problems can't be as difficult as the ones everyone else has to solve. I imagined large, fake, loud advertisements reading TAKE THIS COURSE AND BECOME A MILLIONAIRE! and FINISH A YEAR OF SCHOOL IN JUST ONE MONTH WITH KHAN ACADEMY!!

In the summer of 2012, my cousins from Pakistan and Denmark came to visit Kandahar. As our families sat together on our sapphire-red woven rugs, my father issued a fun math challenge to all the children based on decimal division. I had just studied the concept a few days earlier and was the first to deliver the answer. Baba glanced at me in surprise, then recovered and declared me the winner. My uncle broke into a mischievous grin. "You cheated, didn't you, Sola?" "No! I promise!" I said with a laugh, pleased at the widespread astonishment. I was thrilled at how far online learning was taking me and felt a little sheepish for ever doubting Khan Academy.

I continued to study diligently. Every day I went through more videos than I had been able to download the night before, so Javid started smuggling me Khan Academy DVDs from the private school he attended. I soon discovered that Khan Academy featured other subjects, like genetics, physics, and ancient history. I moved as quickly as I could through the math curriculum and continued to work on my English, thrilled by the possibility of all the knowledge that was waiting for me.

EVEN AS I MOVED through Khan Academy at an electrifying speed, even as I proved to my family that I was as serious about my studies as Yousef and Javid, the threat of marriage continued to haunt me. In October 2012, when she was just nineteen, Roya got engaged to a young man from Norway. As Aisha had done ten years earlier, Roya would escape the throes of Afghanistan's instability by marrying a man with a European visa. Roya had attended just a few years of school and spoke only Pashto. She spent most of her time preparing for her inevitable role as a wife and a mother. By most measures, this match seemed like the best possible outcome for her, and she was happy with the arrangement.

Her engagement ceremony was held on a freezing autumn day, hosted by her husband's family in a tiny run-down hotel with peeling wallpaper and layers of dust carpeting the floors. I woke up early to dress for the event. The morning was so cold that our water heater stopped working and my cousin Mojdeh and I had to take ice-cold showers. Our uncle then drove us to a nearby salon to get our hair done. I usually enjoyed the rare outing in the early morning before a big event, but that day I was grumpy, snapping at the stylist and making her redo my updo over and over. "Who do you think you are, some movie star?" the woman asked, irritated. I was ignoring her by then, consumed by the thought that my wedding would be next. I had no more unmarried older sisters to point at to deflect questions of my own marriage.

By the time I arrived at the hotel, Roya was already there, tugging unhappily at her bulky dress, which looked out of place on her slim figure. It was a cheap approximation of the styles she'd dreamed of since her preteen years. Her makeup had been applied heavily and unevenly, distorting the youthful glimmer of her fresh face. "Oh, that bride looks so old," I heard a woman whisper to her friend. I felt a rush of hot anger, that someone could speak of my sister that way on what was supposed to be one of the happiest moments of her life. It seemed to me like a bad omen for us all.

A few weeks later my cousin Mojdeh, younger than me by four months, was engaged too. She was only sixteen. My grumpiness grew to terror at the prospect looming before me. I was certain in my mind that I just could not get married. But I lacked the audacity to stand before my mother and ask her to stop her discussions with the various match-makers who approached us. And I couldn't bring myself to risk my fragile new relationship with Baba and beg him to help delay my wedding.

Still, Moor must have sensed my hesitation and discontent. "There are so many unmarried Kandahari women who are forced to live with their brothers," she told me one afternoon. In Kandahar, it was impossible for a woman to live alone. "Their sisters-in-law hate them, and they are treated for the rest of their lives as unworthy." She then repeated what had become a common refrain: "Baba and I will die someday. My greatest fear is that there will be no one left to take care of you when I am gone." She tried to convince me that marriage was necessary for my survival, that no matter what husband I ended up with, he would be better than the alternative of being left alone.

Moor's prophecies weakened my resolve. As I drifted off to sleep at night, I thought, *What if I become a person with no world of my own, with no place to turn to?* Would I realize one day that I'd wasted all my time on studying, that I had accumulated reams of useless knowledge that I couldn't turn into any opportunity? By then, it would be too late to get married—what Afghan man would marry a woman who'd reached her mid-twenties? I'd be stuck with a bundle of unrealized dreams, wishing I'd just listened to my mother and forgotten all about my foolish aspirations.

I only doubted my convictions more when I saw how easily academic dreams could be shattered. In December 2012, about a year after he'd left, Yousef returned home from the UK discouraged. At first he'd reveled in his new lifestyle there. He'd cracked open brand-new textbooks for his economics degree, aced his exams, and spent late nights and weekends with new friends. But soon the whole endeavor became too expensive. From the beginning, we'd barely been able to afford the program since afghanis don't translate well to pounds. Since he didn't have enough money to afford a dorm room, Yousef lived with Aisha, Kashif, and their kids in a tiny, cramped Birmingham apartment. The price of food was astronomical compared to what he was used to at home, as was the price of transportation. Many of Yousef's new friends and professors, when they heard about his financial situation, told him he would likely never get a job high-paying enough to justify what our family was spending on his education. Their words weighed on him as he watched his supply of money rapidly disappear. Eventually, he booked a flight back to the country he'd planned never to live in again, exchanging the stimulating lifestyle and bustling, paved streets of Birmingham for Kandahar, a city crumbling to pieces.

Yousef was miserable at home, and we diligently tried to avoid the implication hanging in the air, that he'd failed at the one thing he'd wanted to achieve his entire life. One afternoon Baba made the mistake of suggesting to Yousef that he enroll at Kandahar University, the local college—a far cry from the prestigious international education he'd been receiving just a few weeks earlier. Yousef grew angry and silent, enduring the painful emotions that would live within him for months.

I proved an easy outlet for my brother's frustrations. At the time when Yousef had left for Birmingham, I'd barely been able to string together a sentence in English. But now I was proficient in the language, able to hold basic conversations and read increasingly complex texts. I was studying math topics on my own that he'd learned from a teacher. He'd been branded a disappointment, while my trajectory was pointed upward—just tempting him to bring it down.

Yousef teased me constantly. Though he himself had embarked on a similar academic journey, he disparaged mine as a waste of time, proof of some kind of abnormality. When I asked to use the General Certificate of Secondary Education (GCSE) preparatory books he'd brought home from England, he stared at me pointedly and declared, "These are for Javid." One day I was working on some Khan Academy algebra problems when he sauntered up to me. "Is this what you will do when you get married?" he mocked me. "When your mother-in-law asks you to cook, will you just say 'I cannot cook, but I can find x and y!"

Suddenly I'd had enough. I slapped Yousef hard across the face, so hard that my own hand stung. But he just walked away calmly, as though even with a welt spreading across his face, he'd gotten what he wanted.

Moor always took Yousef's side in these arguments. No matter what he did, he was always her beloved son. My mother had come from a family of all girls, and whenever I complained about Yousef, she used to tell me, "I wish I had a brother. If I had one, I would never treat him the way you do." Often when Yousef asked me to cook for him or to clean up a mess he'd made, I'd refuse and insist he do it himself. But then my mother would come and start doing whatever he asked for, and I'd have to take over out of respect for her. I'd bubble up with frustration as I mopped the floors or prepared my brother's meal, angry at a situation that I was confident Yousef had engineered precisely to his specifications.

One day Yousef stayed out all afternoon repairing his broken sedan, then returned home after everyone else had eaten lunch. It had been my turn to cook that day, so I'd prepared a massive spread and then cleaned up afterward, washing the dishes and drying every last platter. I was dying to run upstairs and log on to Khan Academy, but just then Yousef walked through our front door. His hands were smeared with black oil from fixing his car. He wanted something to eat, but I refused to prepare anything for him. "This is my time to study," I told him. "My turn for cooking is over." So Yousef went and woke up my mother from her nap to cook for him, and she did. But afterward she was furious with me. "I studied, and look what my life became," she told me, her words tinged with sour regret. Her father, she told me, had kept her naïve. Because Agha had told her every day that women could do anything in Afghanistan, she had grown up believing it. Perhaps it had been too painful for Agha to expose his young daughter to the realities of the outside world—Moor couldn't fault him for that. But she believed her upbringing had set her up for a lifetime of disappointment. The moment she left university, her unblemished vision of the world began to shatter, taking with it her confidence and spirit. She transformed into the wife and mother I would come to know: uncomplaining and re-signed, crushed by a pervading melancholy about what could have been. "You need to stop this and focus on your actual duties," she told me, before walking out of the room.

M Y STUDYING UNEARTHED REGRETS, INSECURITIES, and prejudices within my family, but it also brought me an unexpected cheerleader: my grandmother Ana Bibi. She was older now, her face lined with deep ridges, splotches, and a set of sunken bags under her eyes that gave the appearance of a mottled rock face. Her hands had grown even thinner over the years; bones and deep blue veins protruded prominently through her crepelike skin. Her hair was thin and wispy, a few grayish-white strands barely visible at her temples beneath the gossamer white headscarf she wore nearly every day.

Ana Bibi's face betrayed elements of her former personality. Her eyebrows, still colored a dark brown, angled sharply inward and projected the severity she was known for. When she smiled, she almost looked as if she were grimacing. It seemed to take tremendous effort to just barely turn up the corners of her mouth. But I noticed something new in her eyes too, a tenderness.

When I was younger, Ana Bibi used to exile my sisters and me from her room—she allowed only the boys of the family to sit and talk with her. When she saw a group of her grandsons, she'd smile and urge Moor to bestow a traditional Afghan blessing on them to ensure their safety and prosperity. But when she saw us girls sitting together, she'd grow angry, slap her palms over her ears, and screech at us to stop being so noisy and lazy. "Why don't you stop your useless talk of fashion and movies?" she'd yell at my female cousins who'd been forced to drop out of school. "Just pick up a pen and do something—it is not so difficult." She was exasperated by our ignorance, unwilling to accept it was something we didn't ask for.

But as I eschewed gossip and television for studying, Ana Bibi softened toward me. She started asking me to come talk with her or just to sit with her in silence. She could read only basic Pashto, so she asked me to read aloud to her from books like *One Thousand and One Nights*. As she grew increasingly ill with cancer, she was confined to her bed. She gradually lost her ability to walk and perform basic functions for herself, so she'd call out for me. I sat alongside her, atop her wrinkled covers, spooning thin broths through her pursed lips. At night I slept in her room, waking up intermittently to make sure she was still breathing. She never told me that she was proud of me, never wrapped me in a hug or even revealed a smile. But in her sudden acceptance, I found a tacit approval that fueled me even as she withered.

In her old age, Ana Bibi was rejecting the woman she'd become, the woman who bemoaned the birth of girls, who'd valued women only for their ability to cook and bear sons and stay silent, who'd wanted my mother to have a college degree but never use it. Instead, she was turning backward, reverting to the kind of woman she'd been fifty years earlier: a young mother filled with so much hope for her daughters that she'd educated them all covertly behind her husband's back, a widow forced to make her own living to support her children. She saw something in me—a toughness, a sense of discipline, a hunger—that she'd relied on within herself to survive her former life. It awakened something in her that made us unlikely kindred spirits, bound by ambition of years present and years past.

BY THE END OF 2012, I had learned enough English to read young adult books, stopping only a few times each chapter to look up unfamiliar vocabulary in my online dictionary. After racing through basic arithmetic and algebra on Khan Academy, I was now studying trigonometry, calculating angles and committing theorems to memory. It was the purest kind of learning, not driven by tests or grades or even other people's expectations. I was engaged in a pursuit of knowledge simply for the sake of it.

Reflecting on the immense progress I had made was never an option. For one, I didn't want to dwell on what I had already done rather than what I could do. And I couldn't bear to think of all the hours and hours I'd spent studying and wonder what the point of it all was. I was still stuck in Kandahar, hurtling toward a life where all my newfound knowledge would be rendered useless. Maybe I was just grabbing on to extra weight as I fell toward the same life as all the women around me.

I tried to push these thoughts from my head, but they

persisted, fueled by the avalanche of weddings occurring among our family and friends. After her engagement in 2012, Roya was married in the spring of 2013. As is traditional for Afghan weddings, the groom's family paid for and organized the entire event. Roya had no control over where the ceremony was held or even the final guest list. But she managed to assert herself in little ways, like rejecting the dress they chose for her in favor of one she'd picked out for Aisha to bring from Birmingham. I watched with deep unhappiness as Roya carried out constant tiptoed negotiations with her in-laws, anticipating my own eventual misery.

The morning of Roya's wedding arrived. I woke up early to get dressed in an Indian-style outfit with a heavy teal skirt, a long-sleeve sea-blue blouse with silver detailing, and an embroidered scarf draped over my right shoulder. The fabric was unexpectedly uncomfortable, tenting over my legs and plastering to my lower back. The unfamiliar material itched, too. I squirmed trying to find a comfortable position. In the early morning, the air was already oppressive and warm. I was sweating even before we arrived at the venue.

The wedding was held in the same sort of small, shabby hotel where Roya's engagement ceremony had taken place. The same thin carpets lined the hall, covered in dust, and the corners of the room were caked in dirt. A horrible smell permeated the venue, a grimy mix of stalled sewage pipes and rancid stuffiness. It was even warmer inside than out on the streets, since the hotel had extremely poor ventilation, and as guests filed into the room, the heat grew unbearable. Sweat stains bloomed from bejeweled outfits and a veneer of perspiration glistened on everyone's faces. Little children tugged grumpily on their sticky clothes, their faces red and bunched up in irritation.

My sister Roya was the sole bright spot that day. She looked stunning in her white gown, which shimmered under the fluorescent lights. Her hair was pulled back, leaving only a few wavy locks to cascade over her shoulders. She wore a delicate tiara and fastened a tulle veil at the back of her head. In her hands she held a small bouquet of violet blossoms and white lilies, tied together with a purple ribbon. She maintained a dignified smile throughout the whole affair, betraying her true emotions to no one. I guessed that she was happy, proud to be marrying a European.

I stuck to my sister during the party, trying to absorb her serene, unaffected attitude and admiring her beauty up close. But apparently not everyone shared my opinions about Roya. As the rest of the family was dancing, the mother of the groom came up to Aisha and let out a massive sigh. "My daughter told me that I must be blind," she said to her, leaning in close. "I must be blind to choose your sister for my son. That girl is not even pretty." I grew so angry when Aisha told me about her remark, furious that my sister was giving up her whole life for a family who wished they'd chosen someone else.

A few months later my younger cousin Mojdeh was married as well. She had turned eighteen just a few weeks earlier. Her wedding was a miserable affair, made a disaster by her parents-in-law. From the beginning of the wedding, they criticized Mojdeh, unveiling the same spiteful attitude that Roya's mother-in-law had revealed to Aisha. "We thought she had fairer skin," the groom's mother complained. "We even thought she had blue eyes." Mojdeh was a bargain gone wrong, they seemed to be saying. They were going through with the marriage only because it was too late to back out.

At one point in the wedding, I found Mojdeh in a back room, sitting alone. She was upset because her new husband's family had forced her to use a special makeup artist who had done a terrible job. Her eyes looked wide and uneven, and her cheeks were saturated with blush. I went and grabbed some of my other cousins, and we tried to cheer her up, while I fought my own anger toward her parents-in-law. "Just let some of us redo it," we told her. "Then you can go back out there and enjoy the rest of your wedding!" With glee, we began to wipe off her face but stopped abruptly when her new mother-in-law walked in. She berated Mojdeh, screaming loudly about how much the makeup artist had cost and how Mojdeh was such an ungrateful daughter-in-law. We all started to cry. Everyone else was wounded and shamed by the insults this woman hurled at us. But I brushed off hot, indignant tears. I was angry that this would be Mojdeh's life from now on, that she wouldn't be able to make any decisions, no matter how small or personal, unless her husband and his family approved.

THE WOMEN IN OUR FAMILY weren't the only ones tied to prescribed destinies. Yousef remained at home for months after he'd returned from Birmingham. It seemed he might never find an opportunity to leave the country he hated so desperately. He struggled to adapt to life in Kandahar, bruised by memories of his more glamorous life abroad.

That same year, in the summer of 2013, Yousef tried to leave Kandahar for the second time. He discovered a college called Sharda University in Uttar Pradesh, India. The school advertised on TV in a short commercial that featured sweeping views of the school's campus and videos of students laughing and studying together in romanticized slow motion. "The world is here," a woman's voice narrated enticingly. "Where are you?"

Yousef applied and was accepted. He believed the university would provide a legitimate path to a degree in engineering, which would help him make more money than would an economics degree. Baba gave him the money he needed for tuition and booked him on a flight to Uttar Pradesh. But after he landed, Yousef was confronted with a rude reality. Sharda University, he realized, was a private school with a dubious reputation. He worried his degree would be worthless upon graduation. Within two weeks he flew back home, even more bitter than he'd been after returning from Birmingham. But his obvious discontent didn't stop me from taking the opportunity to tease him. "The world is here," I said, laughing. "Where were you?"

Upon his second humbling return home, Yousef tried to resign himself to the fact that he would be unable to leave Afghanistan. In an attempt to make a career in Kandahar, he took Baba's advice and enrolled in the local medical school. But the quality of academic instruction was atrocious. It was impossible to find a good doctor in Kandahar and even more difficult to find a decent medical professor.

The teachers barely spoke English, and the students didn't even have textbooks—instead they relied on hundreds of photocopied loose sheets of paper that billowed across their desks and fell out of their bursting backpacks.

But finally Yousef got lucky. He found a special program offered by the government of Austria, designed especially for Afghan students. If accepted, he would travel there and spend a year in intensive language courses before enrolling in medical school. He would receive a living stipend and be licensed to practice medicine anywhere in the European Union upon graduation. He would have the chance to take semesters abroad in countries like Turkey and England. The program was relatively new—Yousef had found it by chance after dozens of nights of endless Google searches. His possible acceptance was enough to give him a spark of renewed hope.

A few months after he sent in his application, Yousef received an invitation to join the program in September 2013. He was thrilled, his confidence restored, his eyes set firmly on his future. But not even this spate of good luck made Yousef more merciful toward me. He told me I would never get the chance that he was getting, that even if I was ever accepted into a university, Baba would never let me go. "You know Baba cares too much about what people think," he insisted, almost gleefully. "Have you ever seen a girl leave home to go to university? In this city, girls only leave home to get married." I stammered back something indignant and projected a practiced nonchalance, but his words stung. Yousef was crushing desires I hadn't even had the chance to dream up yet.

In the weeks after he arrived in Austria, Yousef called home, complaining about how his quality of life was nowhere near what he'd experienced in the UK. I listened to him quietly, perched behind my mother as she peppered him with questions and lauded even his smallest achievements. *Don't complain anymore,* I begged him silently. I didn't want Yousef to return home again, angry and rancorous, looking to start a fight. But more than my concerns about the way he would treat me, I worried about what one more failed return might signify for my own future. If my stubborn, driven brother—who had all the disadvantages of being an Afghan but all the advantages of being a man— couldn't escape his destiny, then I feared there was no chance for a girl like me.

AT THE END OF 2014, Ana Bibi died. Her illness had progressed rapidly enough in her final days that her death was not unexpected. But up until the hours before she died, she'd been conscious, lucid. She'd taken a bath the evening before, declaring that when she died, she wanted to be clean. I avoided my grandmother in her final hours, terrified by the prospect of her imminent passing. Though we'd lost family and friends and innumerable fellow Afghans to the violence of war, I had never experienced a personal loss before. I was afraid to see what it looked like when someone was dying.

I did manage to venture once to Ana Bibi's side the afternoon before she passed away. In Birmingham, Aisha had just given birth to her second child, a girl named Fatima. I showed my grandmother pictures of her surrounded by a crowd of cousins and friends. "I like this girl," Ana Bibi whispered to me, pointing at her great-granddaughter. "I like her." I remembered then the stories Moor had told me about Ana Bibi's horrified reaction to Aisha's birth, and how she'd refused to hold me when I was born because I was not a grandson. In her final hours, my grandmother seemed to have relented.

After the burial, our compound was flooded with cousins and aunts and uncles who'd come to pay their respects. As per Muslim tradition, women gathered in our living room to pray together for Ana Bibi, their fingers dancing over handfuls of holy beads. I stayed sheltered in the kitchen, busying myself by boiling dozens of cups of milky tea and drying dishes. When the food was packed away and the tea glasses laid to dry, I skirted around the crowds of mourners and took my young cousins by their hands, leading them upstairs to distract them from the grief unfolding around them. As I taught them games and talked with them about their school friends, I pushed a nagging sadness from my mind, trying to escape my sorrow at losing a grandmother I'd finally come to love.

We lived the following weeks and months quickly and breathlessly, as though we were trying to outrun the sentiments of grief and realities of mortality that came with Ana Bibi's death. But we also felt guiltily freer without her, unplagued by her domineering, exacting personality.

In the spring of 2015, Aisha visited Kandahar with her two children. She slept in her old bed on the second floor of our house, nudged her daughter toward Moor and Baba,

and encouraged her son to play games with me in the afternoons. Their presence was a welcome distraction, a chance
to turn our focus toward the beauty of burgeoning life instead of the sadness that comes with its ending.

But a few weeks into Aisha's visit, the mood changed. At
five o'clock one evening, as the sun still lit the cerulean sky,
the sound of gunshots exploded across our neighborhood.
In a cruel irony, four Taliban members had overrun my former school building and were using it as a base to attack
nearby government buildings. They'd chosen the school because it was located in a densely populated area filled with
tightly packed houses and businesses. The Afghan government was forced to be conservative in their defense, to scru-
pulously avoid any civilian or even property damages. But
the Talib fighters were driven by desperation and an utter
indifference to human life. They were willing to spray bullets in any direction, to use up every last piece of their
weaponry in pursuit of victory.

I was paralyzed by fear. A cold sweat enveloped me like
an unwelcome blanket, and my chest tightened until I
struggled to draw every breath. I remembered my walks to
the school so many years ago. Even with my short legs, it
had taken me only twenty minutes to reach there in the
mornings. I realized that the fighting was barely a mile away
from our home.

That night I begged my parents and siblings to sleep in
the living room with me. "If we are going to die tonight," I
told them, my voice unexpectedly raspy from the threat of
tears, "at least we will die together."

I managed to keep my emotions contained, worried that
if I started crying or hyperventilating, I would never stop.

But Aisha was unable to stay calm. The ricochet of gunfire recalled her memories of being trapped in mujahideen crossfire as a little girl. Her body was overcome after every shot or explosion, dissolving into unmitigated waves of trembling. Her teeth chattered loudly, and her eyes panicked. She grasped her children's wrists tightly and brought them to the center of our living room, away from the windows and any mirrors that might shatter. She remained on the phone with her husband in Birmingham the entire night, assuring him that everything was fine, even as the hand she held to her ear shook with terror.

My sister-in-law Shabana joined Aisha and me in the living room. She quieted all the children, whispering stories to them as she tried to control her own shaking. Javid lay on the living room floor in a bundle of sheets and pillows. Eventually, as the night turned to early morning, I fell into a fitful sleep beside him. I was jolted awake every hour or so by massive explosions and made a quick, harried survey of the room, making sure everyone was still alive.

Despite my entreaties, Baba and Moor had gone upstairs to their own bedroom, my father even popping a sleeping pill to get him through the noise. I was angry at them, unable to fathom their nonchalance as gunfire rained down just minutes from us. Weren't they worried something would happen to us as they slept upstairs, blissfully unaware? Weren't they afraid at all, the way we were?

It took me many years to understand what my parents were trying to do that night, that they were projecting calm for us and retreating upstairs to conceal their own terror. Had my self-possessed mother and forceful, stoic father shown their fear, the whole household would have crumbled. Someone had to keep up the illusion that everything was okay.

We woke the next morning to piercing sunrays and a breezy silence. We learned from a news broadcast that the Talibs holed up in the school had fought to the end, unwilling to capitulate except in death.

CHAPTER THIRTEEN

I WAS EIGHTEEN, AND A SENSE OF DREAD BURNED INSIDE me. It lurched against the walls of my stomach so that I couldn't eat, coiled sharply around my ribs so I couldn't breathe. It flared when I heard a report of gunshots, filled me with the horrible certainty that this time I wouldn't survive. But it surged in the moments of quiet too, when I had time to contemplate my impending marriage. The thought of losing everything to a man I didn't know terrified me. At times, the prospect of a physical death seemed better than the symbolic one I'd face at my wedding.

Moor tried to assuage my fears. She never explicitly promised me anything, but she hinted that she wanted to marry me to a European Afghan so I could live abroad, like Aisha and Roya. "It is enough that I live here," she told me gently. "I do not want my daughters to live here, too."

But I knew marriage would rob me of my independence, erase the reasons I'd created for myself to keep living. Sometimes I tried to imagine my existence under a husband, picture washing his dishes or raising his children. But all I saw was a mangled darkness that stretched on forever, gradually incorporating me into its void.

I endured horrible nightmares that left me breathless. I dreamed that it was the morning of my wedding, and I was running frantically through empty corridors and crowded halls, trying to find a way out. Then suddenly I was living in a cramped apartment in Europe with a taxi driver or construction worker, my head swirling from loneliness and stifling silence. And then I was back at home, at the door of our compound, my feet covered in the rising dust, begging and begging my parents to take me back, until they slammed the door in my face. Waking up provided a sweet relief that vanished as I contemplated the ways my nightmare could turn to reality.

I was left with a hardened resolve to get out of Kandahar, to escape somehow on my own terms. It was a crazy proposition, the stuff of fantasies. I didn't know of any Afghan girls who'd escaped on a scholarship. It was nearly impossible to get a visa out of the country without a sponsor. And in any case my parents would likely never let me leave.

I tried to let go of my aspirations, to convince myself that I could never cast off the looming threat of marriage. But once I tasted the dream in my imagination, glimpsed for a moment a life of liberty, I was insatiable. I lost myself for hours, picturing myself riding in elevators, sitting in a classroom, living alone in an apartment. I wanted that life so badly that I had to believe it was possible for me to achieve. Otherwise I'd be crushed under the weight of my own longing.

AMID MY DREAD AND my nightmares, my wild, improbable goal still lived within me. I was charged with purpose. A light beckoned to me, if only I could figure out how to get to it.

Yet I felt wholly unprepared to fall into an eddy of visas and passports and applications. I needed to fortify myself first, to build up enough strength to carry me through the journey ahead. I watched inspirational speeches on You-Tube, scribbled quotes onto loose sheets of paper as the video buffered. I even gained inspiration from Bollywood movies. My favorite quote was from the movie *Yeh Jawaani Hai Deewani*, or *This Youth Is Crazy*: "I want to fly, run. I am not even afraid of falling down. I just don't want to stop." I woke up at five every morning, throwing off the blankets quickly to shake off my tiredness. Sustained by a tall cup of instant coffee, I pored over books about philosophers like Democritus and Socrates. Their ideas on nature and existence inspired me to study a new topic on Khan Academy: physics. As the sun rose, I watched videos on projectile motion and linear dynamics. I downloaded an online textbook and completed hundreds of physics problems. I cherished my total absorption in my work, against the lingering quiet, interrupted only by my mother's soft footsteps as she unfurled her mat for morning prayers.

That year I found an online copy of *The Autobiography of Benjamin Franklin*. I lost myself in the story of this man who'd also left traditional school as a child. Franklin embarked on a self-education and eventually went on to become an incredibly important figure in American history. At that time, Yousef was fond of telling me, "If you don't have a paper to show, no matter how educated you are, it is worth nothing." I realized that Franklin's story proved my brother wrong. Seized by a rush of inspiration, I decided to start looking for more practical ways out of Afghanistan, ways that didn't require an official diploma.

Initially, I maintained a naïve belief that I could follow the same path as Yousef had to get out of the country. I'd simply score well on a set of exams and apply for the same Austrian scholarship for Afghan students. I imagined us together in Vienna as equals, living in our own apartments, meeting occasionally to have dinner together or call home. Javid would join us a few years later, and we'd help him adjust, advising him on which university classes to enroll in and buying him a coat to insulate against the biting cold. But I was mistaken in thinking the path out could be so simple for an Afghan girl.

The first obstacle I faced was bureaucratic. The Austrian scholarship program required proof that I was at a twelfth-grade academic level. This had been easy for Yousef to prove when he was applying. He had simply obtained copies of his high school final examination scores and sent them along. But I hadn't taken any formal exam in nearly ten years. I didn't have the necessary certification. I searched for other opportunities, amending my daydreams to take place in France or Morocco or even the United States. But all those scholarships required academic certification, too.

I was undeterred. One day I ran downstairs and found my mother in the kitchen. "If I can pass the twelfth-grade exam, I can apply to scholarship programs," I told her excitedly. "I know I will score well if someone will just administer it to me. All I have to do is go to the government offices and try to take it!" This was an absurd suggestion. An eighteen-year-old woman in Kandahar couldn't just walk into someone's office and demand an examination. Except to attend weddings, I hadn't left the house at all in almost a decade.

To my amazement, Moor responded immediately, "Okay. I will come with you to the ministry. We will ask your uncle to drive us there." I was shocked. Moor had been so focused on my marriage, I couldn't believe she might consider a different way for me to get out. But first she had to talk to my uncle and then inform my father what we were doing. "I will not go with her," Baba told Moor. "But if you want to, that is fine with me."

Every other hour I checked again with my mother: "Moor, are you going with me for real?" After a full day of my questioning, Moor finally turned to me and laughed. "If you keep bothering me like this, I will say no!" I went instantly silent, and felt an excited grin spreading across my face.

On a hot, arid afternoon a few days later, my uncle drove me and Moor to the Kandahar Ministry of Education, in the hope that an official there would proctor the test for me. We pulled up to the small, pale yellow government building. Its arched windows were framed by scarlet paint, and a periwinkle circular fountain marked the front entrance. An Afghan flag fluttered on a pole low to the ground. Though my mother was fully covered by her burqa, I was wearing a black niqab with more netting around the face than was usually allowed. The two men at the front desk threw lingering gazes at my extra two inches of exposed skin. As my mother asked if I would be allowed to take the exam, the officials were distracted, their eyes roaming crudely up and down my body. This was common behavior in Kandahar, men mistreating women who tried to rise above their "proper places." I shrank into the folds of my veil and turned my face toward my mother. Finally, after they tired of leering at me, the men refused to administer the exam. "It would be unfair to the other children who attended twelve years of school for the chance to take this test," they snapped.

WITHOUT SOME FORM OF a high school certificate, it would be impossible to get into any foreign universities. My plan was cracking. The feeling of dread returned, and I struggled to draw deep breaths. Even my sleep was restless. I awoke every morning to a tangle of blankets at my feet. Once again I was plagued by burning anxiety. The more I contemplated my desired future, the more impossible it seemed to achieve. I felt an incredible urgency to do something, but lacked any ideas as to what my next steps could be.

One morning I googled "What exam do you take when you haven't finished school?" The search results loaded at an excruciating pace. It took me hours to click through various links and find out about the GED, the American version of the high school proficiency exam. It seemed that passing this test would definitely prove my mastery of Afghan graduation requirements. Later that week I called Aisha and asked her to ship me some preparation books from the UK. Since the GED is an American exam, she first had to ship the books to her house from the United States. Since Kandahar had no mail system, she then had to send them to a locker at a shopping mall in Kabul. Several weeks later a relative brought the books to Kandahar. By the time

I cracked them open, it had been almost a year since my visit to the Ministry of Education.

I began taking practice tests and filling out bubble answer sheets, happy to spend days on problems with answers that waited for me in the back of the book. But reality soon caught up with me again. When I tried to sign up for a test administration, I found out that the GED wasn't offered anywhere in Afghanistan. I typed *Pakistan* into the search box, wondering if I might be able to travel across the border quietly with my father or uncle. But the exam wasn't administered there either. A cavernous ache spread through my body. When I'd discovered the GED, I'd been so thrilled to find another way out. It hadn't even occurred to me that, unlike the IELTS exam Yousef had taken, this test wouldn't be available anywhere near me.

After this second failure, I gave up researching new tests and paths out of the country. I had been studying English for four years. In math, I'd begun by solving problems in addition and subtraction and now only three years later I was learning calculus. I'd read hundreds of English newspaper articles and books by Oliver Sacks, Walter Isaacson, and Nelson Mandela. What was the point of all this?

Over the next few months, I studied occasionally for the IELTS exam on the chance I'd have to suddenly prove my English proficiency. But otherwise I simply waited.

I FELT THE WEIGHT of every moment that passed that year, as time rolled over me with excruciating slowness. I was nineteen when I stood at the door as Javid loaded three massive suitcases into a waiting car and left for the airport. While I'd been consumed with studying for exams, my younger brother had applied for the same scholarship that Yousef had won. He was accepted into a bachelor's program in Austria and left for Europe just a month after receiving the acceptance letter. Plane tickets back to Kandahar were prohibitively expensive, so he planned to visit only every few years.

I was surprised by the bitterness that gathered in my stomach when we found out he'd won the scholarship, and by the effort it took me to plaster a smile on my face and wrap him in a hug. I hated the searing envy that latched on to me whenever I heard Moor laud his accomplishment to her friends or when I watched Baba glance at him with unrestrained pride as we all ate dinner. I wanted to shout that Javid was younger than me, that by leaving before me, he was disrupting a natural order. It was my turn to go, but I'd been cast aside.

Throughout his time at private school in Kandahar, Javid had had the chance to travel to Kabul and even Nigeria to compete in academic Olympiad events. He'd returned home with boxes full of medals, proof of his excellence in mathematics and recitations. I knew that, if given the chance, I could have achieved the same things he did. One night I even peeked through his math notebook, confirming that I knew how to solve every one of his competition-level practice problems. But, of course, I'd never have the chance to do it on a stage, surrounded by other fierce competitors, strict officiants, and nervous teachers. I'd never return home with a medal around my neck, laughing excitedly as I told my parents what I'd won. And I began to realize that leaving Kandahar was another thing that Javid would do that I couldn't. The thought scorched me from within. I couldn't decide whether to cry out in pain or scream with rage.

MY EMOTIONS CONSUMED ME SO THAT I couldn't think straight. I didn't have time to contemplate that I was losing my best friend until after he was gone. When he was just a baby, Javid would clasp my hand, his tiny fingers barely able to encircle my palm, clinging tighter if I ever tried to let go. I held few childhood memories in which he wasn't by my side. We got into unbelievable amounts of trouble together and made it worse for ourselves by giggling when we were supposed to be repentant. As he grew older, Javid remained my partner in crime. He seemed the only one in the family not resigned to the inevitability of my fate, the only one who still felt indignant at what he could do and I could not. Sometimes, late at night, he'd take me for drives into Aino Mena, a new high-end neighborhood in Kandahar adorned with sprawling greenery, dancing fountains, and multicolored pavilions inspired by traditional Afghan architecture. Javid had a friend there who owned a small American-style restaurant, and he occasionally let us sneak inside when the place was empty. Furtively, we'd devour slices of spicy vegetable pizza and juicy burgers. Within an hour we'd drive home again, and for days I'd walk around in a dreamlike state, still relishing my taste of freedom.

Once when I was a young teenager, I'd asked Javid what he thought about the lives of women in Kandahar. "When I was still a kid," he told me, "I was jealous that you were staying home while I had to wake up early to go to school. But later I realized how confining your lives are. I said to myself, 'Sola has the same brain as I do, but she is stuck at home.'" He told me he would go crazy if he were forced to live the life I did. It was the first time I'd ever heard someone else articulate that my life was unjust, that I deserved something greater.

It was not that the rest of my family believed I deserved less because I was a woman. Moor wanted desperately for me to escape Afghanistan, to live my life fully instead of just existing for someone else. In her dreams, I was a doctor, a politician. When she was forced to pull me out of school, a part of her was irretrievably broken.

But my mother was ultimately governed by her fears. She couldn't bear to watch me live as she had, beginning with blind hope and ending in searing disappointment. To support me fully in my studies and my attempts to leave the country would have been to mislead me to believe that I could lead a life that she knew was unobtainable.

Still, Moor couldn't commit herself entirely to this painful, practical mindset. Sometimes in my lowest moments, she could sense how much I feared marriage, how badly I wanted to burst out of the confines of our home. Her eyes would grow teary, and she'd place her right hand gently on my head. "Be someone who can leave this place," she'd say finally, her voice thick with sadness and solemnity.

My father surprised me, too. Sometimes in the early hours of the morning, when he'd find me studying in my room, he'd come in and say abruptly, "Sola, let's go outside." He'd take me walking down the unlit alleys behind our house. We were protected by the cover of the starless, smoggy sky, so I'd walk with my hair uncovered, smiling as a sudden gust of wind waltzed across my scalp. The only sound would come from the lone howl of a stray dog.

I moved tentatively, as though I were walking on borrowed pavement. Like someone regaining the ability to walk, I stumbled, startled by loose stones and divots in the road. I'd forgotten what it felt like to live without inhibition.

Baba never told me why he took me on these brief, risky adventures. I imagined he didn't want me to forget that the world held more than existed within our compound doors.

THE MOST BEAUTIFUL GIRLS IN KANDAHAR ARE MARRIED off first. Matchmakers and prospective mothers-in-law swarm their homes, admiring their dewy eyes and sweet smiles. When these girls are fourteen or fifteen, their mothers make a selection from the wealth of suitors. They consider rich men looking for a young wife or European Afghans who can secure their daughter a visa. At their weddings, the girls drape themselves in pounds of gold jewelry and gilded dresses, line their eyes with kohl, and dot their cheeks with blush. At first glance, the makeup makes them look older than they are. But their small feet, swimming in a pair of heels, or their nervous glance toward their mother shows them to be mere children.

Within a few weeks, a girl learns her husband's favorite vegetable dishes and how sweet he likes his desserts. She learns to cook every night for his entire family, to adjust the salt and spice levels to their tastes. Within a few years, she learns how to swaddle a newborn baby, how to calm a crying toddler.

As the girls grow quickly into women, they cling fiercely

to their past, the days when they were so stunning that men and mothers clamored for them. They take pride in the brevity of their youth. "I was so young at my wedding, I didn't even know what marriage was," they tell their friends. "I cried and cried, I was just a baby."

And so this idea spreads, that it is a virtue to be married young. Those who wait until sixteen or seventeen are deemed flawed, less appealing. Mothers scramble to find their daughters a suitable match, becoming frantic as they approach the fatal age of eighteen. Girls become desperate as they grow older, more willing to take any offer that comes their way. And unmarried girls become the stuff of cruel gossip, casting shame upon themselves and their families.

BY THE END OF 2015, I was approaching the last months of my teenage years. Moor was consumed with heightened pressure, worried she'd waited too long, that with every passing day my prospects of a good match dimmed. There was never any question of letting me remain unmarried. A single girl would be a permanent, painful blemish on my family's name. Beyond that, Moor feared that after she and Baba died, I'd be left to fend for myself, alone and in infamy. As a woman, I'd be unable to get a job or rent an apartment. Without a man to depend on, I'd have no means of staying alive.

The intense pressure that Moor inflicted on herself was only compounded by the women around her. Family and friends alternately berated and teased her about her unmarried daughter. Could she not control her wayward girl, force her into a marriage? Was there something wrong with Sola, was that why she was still unmarried? What kind of mother lets her daughter languish away without a husband?

My father's sister, my aunt Gulpari, was especially persistent. She admonished Moor, "My fourteen-year-old daughters are more interested in marriage than your daughter is!" Eventually, she turned her attention to me too and declared it her personal mission to get me engaged. She tried to find me potential husbands. She constantly suggested local men from Kandahar who might be a suitable fit, describing at length their good family backgrounds and career prospects.

It is Afghan tradition for a bride's parents-in-law to send boxes of *falooda*, a cold vermicelli-based dessert, to her house upon her engagement to their son. Whenever Aunt Gulpari encountered me, she would mull, "I really feel like eating *falooda*. When do you think I can eat *falooda*?" The implication was painfully obvious.

Soon Aunt Gulpari grew even more aggressive. Mothers with matchmakers in hand began showing up at our house, unannounced. They demanded to see me, wanted to assess whether I would be suitable for their sons.

Upon their arrival, I'd rush upstairs to change into *salwaar kameez* and a tightly wrapped headscarf that didn't reveal a single strand of hair. Then I'd walk into the living room demurely, my eyes cast downward. I went to my potential mother-in-law and kissed her hands respectfully, then whispered *salaam alaikum*. I'd back quietly toward my mother and wait silently for someone else to speak.

I tried to remember the host of rules Moor had pressed

upon me. *"Don't smile,"* she'd said. I was to appear gentle and sweet and speak so quietly they had to strain to hear me. I wasn't allowed to ask them even a single question. Instead, I was to sit still as they looked me over, determining whether I met their son's specifications.

Though I'd watched my sisters go through the same process with nervous anticipation and excitement, I found the experience humiliating. By the time the women arrived, Aunt Gulpari had already told them about my family's reputation, my level of education, and my ability to cook and clean. She lied to them about my age, saying I was younger than I actually was.

The only reason the women visited was to assess my looks, to estimate the size of my waist, or to determine whether their son would like the shape of my eyes. I felt like a piece of fabric at a bazaar, a mere commodity to be inspected carefully to see if I was good enough to stand beside their flawless sons.

AFTER A FEW OF these visits, I simply refused to come downstairs and talk to any more mothers. Moor grew angry with me. "What am I supposed to tell these women?" she demanded. "You are humiliating me!" But my mother was much more petite than I was—she couldn't make me come downstairs. I made up my mind that Moor would eventually forgive me for my insolence, but I would never forgive myself if I acquiesced and agreed to a marriage I dreaded. By this point, I considered my refusal a matter of survival.

But the women kept coming, clamoring to see the

daughter-in-law Aunt Gulpari had promised them. One mother even went so far as to climb our stairs and throw open my bedroom door, demanding I submit to an interview. We stared at each other awkwardly before I turned back to the philosophy text I was reading. She left, exasperated.

One day Aunt Gulpari was so angry with me for refusing to meet these women that she tried to physically drag me out of my room and down the stairs. But I was stronger than any of them and literally fought her, pushing and kicking until she let me go. "You are not my daughter," Moor said to me that day, after she'd tried to explain to the waiting mother and matchmaker why she could not just demand her daughter come downstairs and join them. Her words stung. I'd never known Moor to be so angry. Even when I was a child, she'd reprimanded me softly, her hand resting gently atop my head. I knew that I was pushing her too far, that I was causing her sleepless nights. Beneath her anger was powerful, debilitating worry. But I was adamant, driven by a fear even more potent than hers. "If you don't tell my aunt to stop sending marriage proposals," I told her, "then I will."

It would have been a massive scandal if I had confronted my aunt directly and demanded she give up on trying to get me married. Moor had no choice but to agree to my demand. She took my aunt aside quietly and asked her to stop the slew of potential mothers-in-law from coming to our home. "Ohh . . ." my aunt began, embittered by the rejection. "Sola is probably disgracing herself and seeing some man on the internet—this is why you want me to stop looking for honorable matches for her." When the news got out that I wasn't looking for a husband anymore, women flailed insults at Moor. Vicious, whispered gossip followed her in family gatherings, religious celebrations, and other girls' weddings. My mother was overcome with humiliation, but I was too relieved to care.

WHEN AUNT GULPARI STOPPED LOOKING FOR MY husband, the threat of marriage was deferred, at least for a few months. I filled my extra time studying for the IELTS examination. I still had no idea whether I'd be able to apply for a scholarship without my twelfth-grade proficiency exam. But I believed that proof of my English-language skills would be useful to me at some point, so I prepared for the test. Just the way Yousef had years earlier, I pored over exam preparation books, whispering English conjugations under my breath long after everyone else in the house had fallen asleep.

I scored well on the practice IELTS sections focused on writing and listening comprehension, but it was impossible to practice conversational English alone in an entirely Pashto-speaking household. If I eventually took the test, dialogue evaluations would make up one full day of the examination. In an attempt to solve this problem, I placed Google Hangout calls to a cousin in Canada. Before, when I had called long distance on Baba's cellphone, it had been too expensive for us to talk for more than a few minutes.

But now, through the power of the internet, we could talk for as long as we wanted. We spoke for an hour every week about food and movies and current events, all in English. But the minutes ticked by too quickly, and I decided that to have any chance of passing my exam, I needed to practice far more regularly.

I signed up for an online language-learning platform that matches language learners with native speakers. I first connected with a humanitarian worker from the Red Cross, who listened to every story I told with a look of dismay on his face. The questions he asked me were wrapped in apologies and sorrowful glances. When my mother found out about my late-night calls with this man, she asked me to switch to a female conversation partner. She was afraid this would only bolster the rumors that I was having an online romantic relationship. "I trust you completely," she told me, softened by my dedication to learning English. "But what will people think?" I was secretly glad to bid the man goodbye, to shake off his smothering pity.

In September 2015 I connected with a young woman named Emily who had signed up for the website after reading a book on Afghanistan that inspired her to learn Pashto. While I had some European Afghan cousins, I'd never actually met an American apart from the soldiers Baba used to stop and talk with in the early days of the invasion. I read U.S. newspapers and watched videos from their news sites, read memoirs and textbooks by American authors. But I had no conception of the everyday people, of girls who dressed up for prom or couples who lived in suburban houses or toddlers who attended preschool.

So Emily was my first real introduction to America. She had waves of dark blond hair and an easy smile. She leaned into her webcam as I introduced myself. She repeated my name softly and asked me which part of Afghanistan I lived in. I learned she was four years older than me, that she was an undergraduate at the University of Iowa. I was secretly pleased to discover she barely knew any Pashto beyond what she had googled—I hoped that we'd speak English instead so I could learn faster. Almost immediately we began calling each other regularly. I learned to quickly calculate the ten-hour time difference between Kandahar and Iowa before dialing her on Skype.

The time passed easily. Emily was content to chat for hours with me in English, to tell me all about her boyfriend and her schoolwork and her family. We talked about me, too. She was amazed by every small story I told her, about leaving school and wearing a burqa and teaching myself to add and subtract. It was the first time I'd ever considered I might be doing something others would consider impressive.

Emily had the kind of sunny personality that I was unused to, an innate cheeriness that had been calloused over in almost everyone else I knew. I luxuriated in her carefree attitude. Our calls became a respite from the harsher realities that awaited me once I hung up. But sometimes the distance between us felt immense. Occasionally, in telling her about my day, I described dangers that had become routine to me: suicide bombs, bullets, rogue Talibs. Emily's eyes grew wide as I moved on with my story, oblivious to her visceral reaction. I struggled to understand what a peaceful world she lived in. It had never occurred to me that stories of my daily life could elicit such shock.

Despite our differences, it was clear that Emily was deeply affected by my situation. She asked about my life, and I slowly opened up to her, describing the compound walls I never left, the suicide bomb attacks, and the books on philosophy and physics that lay on my desk.

One evening while talking to Aisha in Birmingham, I mentioned Emily. "I met an American online!" I told her. "She's been helping me with English, and we talk almost every day!"

"Ask her if there's a way for you to get out of Kandahar!" Aisha responded excitedly. "She'll know if it's possible. Maybe she can help you get to America." That night Aisha's words echoed in my ears. For just a few minutes, I imagined walking through an American college, studying on a campus green, and eating American-style pizza with a group of friends. But I quickly snapped back to reality. I'd been crushed by unfulfilled dreams before.

During our next Skype call, I casually asked Emily if she knew of a path for me to immigrate to the United States. "I'll look into it," she said, and I didn't push her any further. We spent the next hour chatting about recent novels we'd read and her plans for the upcoming weekend.

The next time Emily called me, she told me she'd spent hours reading documents and government websites to see what I should do next. With excitement in her voice, she hinted that she'd discovered a kind of solution. I grew hot with embarrassment, convinced she had wasted her time. I'd spent years trying to find a legitimate path out of Kandahar. How could she have figured it out in just a few days? I didn't believe she fully grasped the barriers that Afghan girls faced.

But before I could interject, Emily began speaking about something called the SAT. I swiftly typed the name into a search bar. The Scholastic Aptitude Test, used for college admissions in the United States. With sections in math, reading comprehension, and writing, it was scored with a possible top mark of 2400. The closest testing site was Karachi, Pakistan—the city where my cousins lived. Emily told me that if I scored high enough on the test, I could be admitted to an American university. "If you bring your acceptance letter to the U.S. embassy in Kabul," she said with infectious confidence, "you'll be granted a visa." I began to cautiously believe the SAT could be my ticket out of Afghanistan.

Later that night I tried to register for the exam. I wanted to see if there was even room for me in the next administration and to secure a spot, even though I knew the likelihood of me making it to Karachi was slim. I'd have to persuade my parents to let me travel for an exam they'd think was pointless. I'd have to find a male relative to drive me through Kandahar, accompany me across the border, and deliver me safely to my cousins' house in Karachi.

As I read the instructions for the SAT, I realized I would not be allowed to take the test without a passport as a proof of identity. I'd never owned a passport. Most Kandaharis, especially women, do not have official documents. There are few occasions to leave the country, and many women routinely make it across the land border with Pakistan without papers, as my female relatives and I had done in the past. Besides my sisters, who lived abroad, I didn't know a single Kandahari woman with a passport.

I TOLD MOOR ABOUT the SAT. Surprisingly, in the past few weeks, her attitude had continued to soften toward my opposition to marriage and my insistence on getting out of Afghanistan on my own, through education. I believed she wanted badly for me to leave the country but finally understood that I wouldn't follow the same path my sisters had.

Moor had seen her own sister, Yasmin, leave Afghanistan on her university scholarship to the Soviet Union. Decades later she finally started to believe that maybe I could, too. "In every prayer I pray for you," she told me one day. "I pray that you reach your goals and do what is in your heart."

My mother agreed to help me get to the passport office, located inside Kandahar's police headquarters. From her experience helping my sisters get documents to travel to Europe, she knew that the men at the police station would act even more inappropriately than those at the education ministry had. If I didn't bring a man to accompany me, they'd harass me, crack crude jokes, and stare suggestively before finally refusing to deliver my documents.

When Moor asked one of my cousins to drive me, he stopped returning her calls. Weeks later I found out that another cousin who lived in our family compound was planning to visit the police station to get passports made for himself and his mother. "Can you tell me when you leave for the office?" I asked him. "I want to come and get a passport for myself, too." But days passed, and I discovered he had gone alone, without telling me. I wondered if he thought my pursuit was frivolous, even wasteful. What was the point in helping me jump through all these bureaucratic hurdles if all I would eventually amount to was being someone's wife?

Finally, my mother asked my father's clerk to help me. He drove me to the office, helped me organize the pictures and documents that I needed, and sat next to me during the appointment. A weight lifted off me. Now all I had to do was to study and wait for my passport to arrive.

But in December 2015, as we ate dinner together on the floor of our living room, reaching across each other for bowls of vegetables and pieces of flatbread, my uncle announced he would soon be going to Pakistan on business. These trips out of Afghanistan were exceptionally rare, especially now that the violence in Kandahar was worsening. My stomach grew tight with nervousness. I knew that if I didn't accompany my uncle now, I might not be able to take the exam for another year or two. As the rest of the family moved on to discuss an upcoming engagement ceremony, I stopped eating. The prospect of my imagined future loomed so close, and I was suddenly panicky that I wouldn't be able to pass the test, that I'd squander my final chance to leave the country. And then I felt a greater fear: that I wouldn't get to go at all. Why would my parents let me make the dangerous crossing into Pakistan and take an exam all by myself in an unfamiliar city, in pursuit of a dream they just barely believed in?

"I WANT TO GO with Uncle to Pakistan," I told Moor a few days later, leaning casually over the sink as she boiled a pot of water for tea. "It would just be for ten days." She looked at me in surprise, and I froze, worried she knew I was crafting a lie. "I'll come back when he does," I added hurriedly, to fill the silence.

After my uncle had announced his plan to go to Pakistan, I spent days agonizing over how to ask my parents for permission to go with him so I could take the SAT. I wondered whether to approach Baba first, or whether Moor would be more acquiescent. I practiced speeches in my head, impassioned ones demanding my right to go, and gentle ones begging for their consent. But finally, I realized I lacked the courage to do it. I knew they would say no. My uncle needed to return to Kandahar within ten days, but I would need to stay in Pakistan for three months, shuttling between Quetta and Karachi to take both the IELTS and the SAT exams. I knew this was likely my last chance to leave Afghanistan. I was old enough now that I might not even be able to get married to an eligible Afghan man living abroad.

So, burdened with a suffocating guilt, I lied to my parents. I told them I wanted to travel with my uncle to Quetta and that I'd visit my cousins, quickly take my exams, and return in ten days. In reality, I'd have to coordinate my exam registration, move between the two cities, and find family members to stay with—all completely on my own. And I'd somehow have to placate my parents in Afghanistan and prevent them from forcing a Pakistani relative to take me home before I'd completed both exams.

It pained me to lie to my mother. I was ashamed by how naturally the falsehood slid off my tongue, how I could easily make up details and flash a convincing smile. I was making a desperate gamble. I thought if I scored well on the exams, Moor might be proud, but then after she discovered my ruse, she'd be overcome with worry and even feel betrayed. I packed a suitcase with too many clothes for a ten-day trip, hoping no one would ask any questions.

On the morning of our departure, my passport still hadn't arrived. I probably wouldn't need it to cross into Pakistan, as the border police rarely checked women's documentation. But without a legitimate passport, I'd be unable to take the SAT or register for the IELTS exam. I decided to take the risk anyway, since I didn't know when I'd be able to travel to Pakistan again. Baba knew I needed a passport for my exams, and laughed incredulously when he heard I was planning to go to Pakistan without it. He then repeated a Pashto saying that roughly translates to "You are trying to glue things together with just your saliva."

Due to laws prohibiting Afghan vehicles in Pakistan, my uncle and I planned to drive from Kandahar to the border, then walk across by foot and take a different car to Quetta. For the first leg of the journey, we sat in silence, broken only by the soft Afghan music emanating from the car radio. Within two and a half hours, we arrived at the Afghanistan-Pakistan border. My uncle explained carefully that I'd have to cross without him, as there were separate male- and female-only security lines. We agreed to meet again on Pakistani soil.

As I stepped through the rusted checkpoint, a chaotic crowd of Afghans and Pakistanis swirled around me, a hurricane of blue burqas against a backdrop of barbed wire and dusty roads. I clung to the brand-new suitcase Moor had bought me for my travels, its polished exterior an anomaly amid a sea of torn and dusty bags.

An Afghan policeman unzipped my suitcase roughly
and prodded through its contents with the butt of his rifle.
He stared at me for what seemed like an eternity until I
grew frightened and my breathing became labored. Finally,
he grunted his assent for me to move on.

When I emerged on the Pakistani side of the border,
however, I was greeted with an entirely different experience. A young woman patted me down gently before peering into my bag. "Books," she murmured in Urdu, upon
seeing the titles hidden under my clothes and toiletries. She
looked at me with a sense of awe, and her eyes grew moist.
After a moment, she recovered herself and urged me on, a
soft smile lingering on her face.

I reunited with my uncle as he stepped out from the
men's security line. He broke into a relieved smile as I
walked toward him, gesturing with a little wave that everything had gone smoothly. He hoisted my bag across his back
to keep it off the dusty road. I walked beside him, lifting the
bottom hem of my burqa to keep it clean. As we settled
into the car to drive to the city, a quiet exhilaration spread
within me. Most girls I knew traveled to Pakistan only to
shop for their weddings. They visited large stores with shining glass fronts and bought bright green bridal gowns and
delicate shoes that couldn't be found anywhere in Afghanistan. I was privately proud to be visiting for an entirely different reason.

WE ARRIVED IN QUETTA that afternoon. My uncle dropped
me at my aunt Khadija's house and continued into the city
to make his business arrangements. I was thrilled to reunite

with her daughter, my seventeen-year-old cousin Leela. We screamed and jumped into each other's arms before collapsing into peals of laughter. At dinner we talked hurriedly in between bites of my aunt's rice and lamb *dupiaza,* interrupting each other to share our news.

Later that night I connected my computer to Leela's internet and logged on to the College Board website to register for the SAT. I hadn't had time to register before—I'd left Kandahar only four days after my uncle announced he was traveling to Pakistan. And I hadn't wanted to register before arriving in Quetta, in case my uncle's plans changed.

But when I typed *Pakistan* into the College Board search bar, I found that the January 2016 exam registration was full. There were no spots available. I sat still, unable to process my total devastation. I had come all this way and overcome innumerable hurdles. I couldn't believe I wouldn't be able to take this test, my only chance at a ticket out of Afghanistan on my own terms.

I dialed Emily, willing the call to connect, barely able to keep it together. Shattered by a seemingly unending series of *almosts,* I was furious at myself for not registering earlier. But Emily was still hopeful and said she would try to get someone to open up a spot from the United States. I had little faith that her efforts would change anything. I'd lied to my parents, crossed the border without any documentation, and undergone a grueling journey into Quetta, all for nothing.

Regardless, the next week I decided to join my uncle on a crowded bus to Karachi, where the SAT would be administered on January 23, just in case a spot opened up at the last moment. My uncle was confused when I told him I would be staying in Karachi instead of returning with him to Afghanistan. He had believed me when I told my family I was going to Quetta only for ten days. But I explained to him that I needed more time to take my exams, all of which were only offered in Karachi. To my surprise, he quietly agreed and left for home without me.

When my uncle returned home alone, my sister Aisha was furious at me for staying in Pakistan. She called me from Birmingham. "Did you know that people are calling Moor to talk about you?" she asked me. "They tell her that she has no shame, letting her daughter stay in someone else's house when, at this age, she should be married." My mother was upset with me too, for making her endure another barrage of insults about her inability to raise her daughter. When Baba called, I lied to him. "I didn't realize my exams were this late," I told him, though I'd known all along. "Now I just have to stay and finish them." He believed my excuse and allowed me to remain in Pakistan.

I stayed with Moor's close friend Perveena in Karachi. Perveena was in her sixties, with graying hair. Her daughter Shazia, who lived with her, was in her forties. Shazia was married to a man named Kamal who worked in Afghanistan and commuted to Karachi every few months to visit her and their two children. Kamal arrived in Karachi around the same time I did. He took us all out every weekend, to parks and malls and even a horseback riding ring. As I chased the children around a playground, running freely, my scarf slipping off the back of my head, Shazia would exclaim, "I cannot believe you live in Kandahar! Look at how confident you are."

Perveena was impressed with me too. "I wish you lived

in Pakistan like my daughter," she would say to me on some afternoons, her wrinkled hand resting atop mine. "Look how much you love to study, and look how difficult it is for you."

My passport arrived in Kandahar a month after I made it to Karachi. Baba gave the passport to a friend who was crossing the border into Quetta. From there, the friend mailed it to me in Karachi. Now that I had the necessary document, I began studying seriously for my exams. I discovered that Khan Academy had an entire section dedicated to SAT preparation. The test administration that Emily was trying to get me into was a month and a half away, and between applying for my passport and packing for the trip, I hadn't yet had time to study. I started spending my late nights and early mornings learning statistics, the one concept on the exam that I had never encountered before. Though I was almost fluent in English, I found it challenging to decipher the verbose word problems that made up the math section. When I explained my challenges to Emily, she offered to buy me access to an online SAT math course. I told her Aisha would let me use her credit card to buy it, that she didn't need to pay with her own money. "It's my gift to you, Sola," she replied simply. I couldn't believe how invested she was in my success.

The reading comprehension questions were equally difficult, phrased so circuitously that I often didn't understand what they were really asking. I couldn't understand half the vocabulary words I needed to memorize. But I still studied diligently every night, flipping through the prep book as Shazia and her children watched Bollywood movies in the other room. I pushed my practice score higher and higher, hoping desperately that I'd get a chance to take the real test.

As I waited in Karachi, Aisha called to tell me I had received a marriage proposal from an Afghan man living in Birmingham. My sister pleaded with me to take the offer. "You need to come home and get married. This has gone too far!" she told me. She felt my academic plans were tenuous at best, that even if I could take the SAT, there was no guarantee I would ever get a visa out of the country. If I married the man in Birmingham, I could live in Europe for as long as I wanted. I could attend school and maybe even get a job. To her, it wasn't a difficult choice.

I was shocked at how quickly my life had turned around. Just a few days prior, I had been planning a solo life abroad, courtesy of the scholarships and university acceptance letters I hoped to get with a good SAT score. Now I was seriously considering marriage. As I clutched the phone against my ear, a wave of resignation washed over me. "If I can't take the SAT this month," I told my sister, "I'll accept the proposal."

CHAPTER SIXTEEN

Languid heat accompanied Karachi's winter, threatening to subsume me, to pull me down into pits of passive submission. I struggled to hold on to my waning motivation, to sustain myself with a blind, irrational faith that my chance to take the SAT wasn't gone forever.

Shazia peeked into my room as I scanned my prep books, my hair tied in a loose bun that flopped every time I leaned over to solve a math problem or annotate a reading passage. She and her kids tried to cheer me up with jokes and little dances. But it wasn't enough.

Almost every night, as everyone else in the house fell comfortably asleep, I stared at the equations in my textbook, tormenting myself once again about what the point of it all was. Maybe I could manage life with a man in Birmingham whom I'd never met; maybe I could sacrifice my individuality just to get out of Afghanistan. Many times I resolved to give up on the SAT, to let go of the debilitating hope I forced myself to maintain. I nearly dialed Aisha a dozen times, imagined the relief spreading across her face as I told her to accept the proposal. I wondered listlessly what I'd wear to the wedding, whether my new husband would let me move around Birmingham freely. But then I'd wake up the next morning with a tiny glimmer of motivation, enough to carry me forward for a few more hours.

Two weeks before the SAT administration, the familiar Skype ringtone came from my phone, buried beneath a stack of papers on my desk. "Sola, I have good news," Emily began on the other end. "I managed to contact the College Board, and they've opened up a spot for you!" I froze, shocked. "You can take the SAT!"

It took me a moment to recover and understand the full story. Several weeks earlier Emily had contacted a few high-level College Board officials via LinkedIn and explained to them how much I had gone through to study for the SAT and get to Karachi. If I didn't take this SAT administration, she wrote, I might never be able to enter Pakistan again to take it. She'd given up on them responding, but after nearly a month, someone had messaged her back.

I broke into triumphant, disbelieving laughter as I gripped my cellphone in my sweaty palm. My face cracked into a smile so wide, I couldn't say anything coherent. "Wow," I finally managed, my head spinning with shock. "Wow, wow!" After she hung up, I couldn't catch my breath for what seemed like hours. I finally ran out of my bedroom and called to Perveena. "I got it, it's going to happen!" I told her. "I'm going to take the SAT!"

The test center was nearly an hour away from Perveena's house. Shazia's husband, Kamal, offered to drive me so I wouldn't have to navigate through Karachi's chaos on my own. When the day arrived, I was silent in the car, nervously adjusting my headscarf, reviewing vocabulary words in my head, and trying not to think about what could happen if I scored poorly on the test. With even more effort, I suppressed any thoughts about what could happen if I scored well. The aspirations I had harbored for so many years bubbled furiously. I worried I'd be distracted by the very dreams I was trying to achieve.

I entered the testing center hesitantly, looking for a place to check in. Almost at once I was surrounded by a group of Pakistani girls in makeup and designer clothes, who lamented to me that this was their third or fourth time taking the exam. I gathered from their conversation that they were from a fancy neighborhood in south Karachi. They regaled me with stories of the SAT tutoring schools they'd attended, and they complained about how long they'd had to study.

I suddenly felt extremely nervous. What if I'd underestimated the difficulty of this exam? If these tutored girls found it difficult on their third try, there was no way I could score well on my first. I worried that I would be flustered by the bubble sheet and input my answers in the wrong rows and columns. Maybe I would get every single question wrong.

But when I emerged after three hours, blinking furiously in the glaring sun, I was cautiously confident that I had scored well. I indulged in a careful hope that things might finally be proceeding according to plan.

I STILL HAD THE other major test to take, the two-day IELTS exam, which I needed as proof of English proficiency so I could apply to U.S. universities.

Even in Pakistan, a country I'd always associated with modernity, it would be extremely dangerous for me to travel to the testing center alone. Both days I would need a man to drive me, someone whose word would hold weight at any checkpoints, whose glance could deflect leering glances and vulgar whistles. Kamal wouldn't be in Karachi the weekend of the exam, so I called Baba to ask if his cousins, who also lived in Pakistan, would take me there. I remembered that these relatives had always been willing to drive my mother around to shops and markets when she visited Karachi. I derived comfort from the idea of them driving me to and from the exam, two familiar faces on those incredibly stressful two days. But my father refused to ask them. In Afghan culture, asking for a favor is often seen as demeaning. Although he hadn't forbidden me to take the exam, Baba still thought it was a waste of time, and he did not want to beg someone for my foolishness. "You have come this far on your own," he told me. "You should be able to do this on your own, too."

Perveena offered to call Baba's cousins for me since he wouldn't. But when they finally picked up, they insisted they didn't have time to drop me at the test center. "We can send a hired driver for her instead," they offered noncommittally. I remembered all the stores they'd taken Moor to in Karachi, all the times they'd waited as she picked out scarves and tried on jewelry. It was as if they were saying that shopping was more worthy of their time than my studies.

I was terrified of being kidnapped. I was alone in a foreign country, letting a complete stranger drive me to the IELTS exam. I sat close to the window and clasped the door handle tightly with both hands. In my lap, I held a borrowed phone with GPS capabilities. As our car swerved through

Karachi traffic, I watched the dot on the screen, checking every few minutes to ensure the driver wasn't deviating from the path to the testing center. During that drive, the content of the major exam I was about to take was the last thing on my mind.

But I somehow made it through the two days of testing. I was relieved to be finished but wasn't sure if I'd passed. While the speaking test had gone surprisingly well, the writing and listening tests had been quite challenging.

The morning after the IELTS exam, I traveled back to Quetta with a distant relative. My taking the exam had delayed his travel plans, and now he would arrive in Quetta several days later than he had initially planned. He was angry and scolded me fiercely for most of the twelve-hour bus ride home. I sat quietly beside him as the sun sank into the sky and the roads dissolved into inky darkness. Staring out the window, I was furious that I had to depend on this man for my freedom. In an instant, he'd reduced my studies and tribulations in Karachi to nothingness, to a mere inconvenience. It made me so angry to think that whatever I did with my life, he'd always see me as worthless, just because I was a woman.

I stayed in Quetta for a few days with my aunt Khadija and Leela. Leela and I had a fantastic time together, browsing all day through dazzling, fancy shopping malls, recording silly dance videos on our phones, and watching one Bollywood movie after another. One night we held a big celebration for the end of my exams, with spicy pizzas, Coke, and sparkling apple cider. My aunt let us stay up late, blasting music and dancing together in the living room.

One morning a week later my relative arrived to take me

back to Kandahar. We reached the Pakistan-Afghanistan border that afternoon. Pakistan had arbitrarily closed a part of the checkpoint, and the Afghan agents manning the crossing were furious that the Pakistanis had the authority to shut the border while they did not. They directed their anger toward Afghan citizens, hurling deeply offensive epithets at drivers and cursing their mothers and sisters. Afghan culture is predicated on honor, and I worried someone would get out of his car to fight. The line crept forward steadily. My relative reminded me that we would again cross the border by foot, leaving this car in Pakistan and boarding another one in Afghanistan. Just as I was about to open my back-seat door, a patrol agent marched toward us and angrily smashed our car's side mirror with his nightstick. The glass shattered, casting a momentary sparkle across the dusty, barren border crossing.

I RETURNED HOME TO a surprise: my mother was brimming with pride in me. I'd lied straight to her face and sneaked away to a foreign country for three months! I expected her to be furious. But instead, she seemed to bask in relief that I'd taken my exams successfully. She escaped her cloak of worry for an instant and reveled in the joy of my achievement. Many other mothers in Kandahar wouldn't have understood what it meant to take an exam. But Moor, though she drank tea with those women and visited their homes and played with their children, was different from them. Every year at Kabul University, she'd spent weeks studying for final exams, rereading the highlighted passages in her textbooks over and over again, scribbling practice problems late into the night as her roommates slept. The fact that I'd taken the SAT and the IELTS exams meant something to her.

My three-month stay in Karachi was the longest I'd ever been separated from my mother, and upon my return, we tried to make up for lost time. In the early mornings, after she finished her first prayers, I'd stand next to her at the stove as she boiled milk tea for us. We'd take steaming cups into the garden and sit in the royal-blue chairs Javid had bought for us one day at the bazaar. The birds chirped loudly, and hawkers' yells for someone to buy their fried snacks or ice cream carried over the compound walls.

We never tried to talk over street noise—we were content to be together in silence. I stared out at the coral roses I hadn't seen in months while my mother read an Arabic religious text translated into Pashto, her fingers tracing every character. Sometimes I studied beside her, reading philosophy and novels and physics textbooks, grateful to be finished with test preparation. The hours passed easily. In the evenings, after cooking and cleaning all day, we'd sit in front of the television and watch a national singing competition called Afghan Star.

A few days after I returned home, I was sitting on my bed reading a book I'd bought in Pakistan. Moor walked into my room, and I laid the book down gently, careful not to crack the spine. She sat down beside me. "From your childhood, Sola, you have always been different," she began. "Even as a little girl, you always stood up for yourself. When some other kid slapped you, you would slap him back. No child could dare to take something from you."

She reached behind her and brought out a beautiful ring, a gold band adorned with a twinkling blue stone meant to ward off evil. It was a small joke between us, since as a young teenager I'd always adamantly refused any jewelry she bought for me, urging her instead to buy me a computer or a stack of books. As I grew older, I'd become even more opposed to jewelry, since that was when, in accordance with Afghan tradition, Moor began purchasing necklaces and earrings for my wedding. I wanted nothing to do with the delicate silver work or dangling emerald stones.

But as I looked at this new present, I realized it represented something different. I slid the ring over my finger, and a lightness came over me, a sudden buoyancy. I threw my arms around my mother and pulled her close to me, refusing to let go.

WHILE I WAS STILL in Karachi, I'd received my SAT results. I had scored high enough to apply to U.S. universities. After I returned to Kandahar, my IELTS scores came in: 6.5 out of 9. I was only half a point below what Yousef had scored after years of studying. I'd scored as high as he did on the speaking portion of the exam, but I'd had more trouble with the writing portion since I'd never had any formal language instruction.

So I began sending in applications to various American colleges. I did not apply to private ones because afghanis translated horribly into U.S. dollars, and my father would be unable to pay the tuition. I refused to let myself feel any excitement throughout the application process, divorcing myself as usual from the implications of what I was attempting. I treated the paperwork and personal essays like another chore, a set of tasks devoid of any greater meaning.

In April 2016 I found out I had been accepted into a few community colleges in Iowa, where Emily lived. It was a significant step, but my admission was no guarantee that I would be able to go to the United States. I would still have to overcome visa hurdles and figure out a way to become a student legally. And I had to convince my parents that living in a tiny town in Iowa, with no husband or backup plan, was a better option than marrying a working, established Afghan man in Europe.

When I told her about the acceptances, Moor said, "That's good news, Sola, but don't get too excited. Let's wait until you get the visa." My father was less hopeful about my prospects for making it to America, convinced by his childhood and war and Yousef's tribulations that it would be impossible for me to make it out of Afghanistan.

I combed the house for the paperwork I would need to apply for a student visa: my birth certificate, my new passport. I conferred anxiously over the phone with Emily, discussing how to answer interview questions and how best to prove my college acceptances. Despite Baba's pessimism, I found myself cautiously hopeful. I couldn't see a logical reason for the embassy to turn me down. I had all the documents I needed to prove my qualifications.

Over Skype, Emily helped me book a visa appointment online at the U.S. embassy in Kabul. But Baba refused to accompany me there. "They will reject you," he said bluntly. "It's a waste of money." But I begged him. "Please, Baba? I am so close—please don't say no now."

Eventually, my father decided to plan a spring vacation to Kabul for Moor, Nadir's young kids Hamid and Ayan, and me. It would be safe for my mother to take us alone since Kabul was a much more progressive city than Kandahar. Baba would let me attend my interview in between sightseeing trips and visits with family. If I didn't get the visa, as Baba suspected would be the case, the entire trip wouldn't be a waste.

Moor was excited to give my cousins the experience of their first plane ride. As the plane took off, she smiled as eight-year-old Hamid and five-year old Ayan craned to see mountains and cities out of the tiny rounded window. I couldn't help but feel that she was indulging me, too. This trip to Kabul was just a way to make us all happy. She didn't actually believe that anything real would come of it. I watched my cousins giggle together at their inside jokes, dwarfed by the navy-colored airplane seats, and hoped fervently that she would be proved wrong, that I would get a visa.

AS THE PLANE LANDED in Kabul, all the women on the flight removed their niqabs and burqas. They chatted loudly, laughing above the noise of the airplane's engines. I felt as though I were arriving in a different country.

Moor was a new person in Kabul. Like the other women, she immediately took off her niqab upon landing. As she disembarked the plane, I could see her pleasure in feeling the fresh air brush against her face. She grasped our hands tightly and walked off the steps leading to the runway, her movements unencumbered and assured.

Moor still remembered Farsi, the dominant language in Kabul, from her days at university. The language flew off her tongue as she asked airport staff for directions. I walked alongside her quickly, struggling to keep pace with her swift steps.

Our relatives picked us up outside the airport and drove us around the city. It was my first visit, and I stared out the car window at dazzling wedding halls and murals and women who walked down the street wearing only light scarves over their hair. But I knew the peace and modernity I observed were not a constant in Kabul. Suicide attacks and large-scale bombings were extremely common, and to most Kabulis, they had become a fact of life.

The next day Moor took us to see Kabul University. She hadn't been back since her days as a lecturer, and she seemed instantly transported. She took us on a tour and was almost giddy as she peeked into classrooms and admired the sprawling tree-lined grounds. "We used to study here!" she told us, pointing to a long classroom building with orange-framed windows. When we stumbled upon a stunning garden, she exclaimed, "We'd listen to concerts at these steps!"

But it was clear that her memories were bittersweet. "This is such a beautiful place," she told us, "but now it is like a prison." The trees that lined the campus used to simply mark its borders. Now they were the only barrier protecting students from the indiscriminate violence that occurred throughout the city.

A FEW DAYS LATER I entered the waiting room of the U.S. embassy in Kabul, my heart pounding furiously. The building was striking, with a large, pillared facade the color of golden sand, accented by blue-green windowpanes and an American flag that swung slowly through the hot thick breeze. But once I entered the interview room, clutching my exam scores and university acceptance letter firmly to my chest, the atmosphere of grandeur slipped away. It was just me and a bald, expressionless man in a white shirt wrinkled by the heat. A glass window separated us from each other. "Where is your $180?" the interviewer barked. I was startled—I hadn't known that I would need to pay a fee. "I can't evaluate your application without the money!" he spat impatiently.

So I darted back out into the waiting room—and as I stood before the crowd of people waiting for their own interviews, a desperate boldness took hold of me. "Does anyone have money I can borrow?" I shouted, a little too loudly. A few people looked up, startled. "I need $180 for this interview. I can return it to you later, I promise."

Unbelievably, an older man stood up and quietly handed me the money. I thanked him profusely, incredulously. I reentered the interview room, trying to hide how flustered I was. The interviewer took my money and filed it away, and then, without even looking at my documents, he told me he was rejecting my application. The floor fell out from under me. "Why?" I managed to ask, fighting back a cascade of tears I hadn't known was within me. He answered that he didn't believe I was really going to America to study. His eyes betrayed no emotion. Seized by a sudden fury, I grabbed my college acceptance letter and waved it at him, willing him to read the words through the smudged glass wall. Instead of reading it, he asked me to leave the room.

Faced with this wrenching defeat, I called Emily. She was furious. "We are going to launch a campaign! We have to get people to care, to see this injustice!" she cried into the phone. She helped me book another visa appointment for a few months later, even though I was convinced my parents wouldn't let me come back to Kabul.

A few days later she called again to tell me she'd emailed a slew of reporters and professors and activists to see if they could raise awareness about my case. A week after that, she launched a GoFundMe crowdfunding page to raise money for me, with paragraphs explaining my story. "Sola was forced to end her formal education at the age of 11 after men threatened to burn her face with acid," she wrote. "Sola's journey of self-education is a testament to the power of marginalized women with access to the internet, but also an embodiment of the challenges of a higher education system with admission based on high school transcripts and standardized test scores." She described how difficult it had been to get prep books and official documents across the Afghanistan-Pakistan border. She included pictures of the shapeless burqa I had to wear every time I left the compound.

But I couldn't share Emily's energy. My visa rejection had sucked all the enthusiasm I'd had out of me. I cried constantly.

The day after, Moor took Hamid and Ayan to a shopping mall in an attempt to salvage their vacation. I stayed behind and sat listlessly, my mind filled with nothing at all. Later that evening our relatives took us to go boating and eat kebabs in an open-air stall. Hamid and Ayan grinned with delight. As they splashed me with water, I smiled halfheartedly. Inside, I was devastated.

When we returned home, I was in a terrible mood. I was afraid that my parents would point to this rejection as proof that I would never be able to escape Afghanistan. They'd force me into marriage, and I would simply dissolve. Years would pass, and only I would remember who I could have been.

CHAPTER
SEVENTEEN

A FEW WEEKS EARLIER, BEFORE I'D LEFT FOR KABUL, Emily had put me in touch with a physics professor at Arizona State University. I'd been reading his book on astrophysics and told Emily about it during one of our Skype calls. "Let me email him!" she said, as I grew animated explaining new theories about the formation of the universe. "Maybe he'll write back, and you can chat about all this with him!" I hadn't been able to discuss any of the science concepts I was learning with anyone, since Emily majored in business in college, and none of my family in Afghanistan had ever studied physics. I grew excited at the prospect of long discussions with an American professor. But as usual, I tempered my expectations, again guarding against the pain I knew would accompany disappointment.

To my surprise, the professor wrote back to Emily almost immediately and offered to meet me on Skype. He was warm and effusive, discussing astrophysics concepts like the Big Bang and dark matter.

Now weeks later Emily wrote to him again to explain my visa situation. He responded promptly, saying he would do what he could to help.

As Emily scrambled to get me out of Afghanistan, I was overcome with a stifling lack of purpose. I sat on my bed, the door closed, my back barely supported by a stack of thin pillows. I scanned the shelves above my desk, populated with books like *Sapiens* and *The Story of Philosophy*. I remembered the risks I'd taken to obtain them, how I'd sneaked some back from Pakistan. The texts had seemed worth it then, filled with essential, almost sacred knowledge. Now I noticed the creases and tears they'd sustained in the journey to Kandahar. I saw them for what they were: compilations of mass-produced information, a perennial reminder of my failures. I imagined stepping into the courtyard to cut the books loose at the spine, watching thousands of pointless pages flutter away before crumbling to the ground, defeated by Kandahar's powerful dry heat.

Back at home and drained of motivation, I easily fell into the routine I'd had years earlier, before I'd started studying. I spent my days in the kitchen. My hands lingered too long in vats of soapy water as I scrubbed dinner plates, my mind occupied by nothing at all. I avoided my mother's concerned looks and my father's impassive countenance, ashamed of what they must have thought of me. I was the last daughter at home, unfit for the life I'd dreamed of in America, forced to settle for the remnants of what lay around me in Kandahar. My failure haunted me.

TWO WEEKS LATER I woke up to a shocking email in my inbox. A well-known *New York Times* reporter wanted to interview me for his upcoming column. The professor from

Arizona State University, who also happened to write for the *Times,* had emailed him on a whim, in an attempt to drum up support for my story. Unexpectedly, the reporter had written back and wanted to speak with me as soon as I was available.

After scanning the email breathlessly, I immediately wrote back, agreeing to speak with him, hoping that his column might raise enough awareness to get me a visa. A sense of strength pulsed through me, invigorating me for the first time since my rejection at the U.S. embassy in Kabul.

Just a few minutes after I responded, the reporter wrote back. We agreed to talk later that night via Skype. That evening, as I waited for him to call, I scrolled through our brief email thread, trying to understand why such a high-powered journalist had found my case of interest. For so long, I'd been consumed by one goal: to get out of Afghanistan. I'd never reflected on whether my story was unique or exciting. Without access to much of the outside world, it had never occurred to me that my experiences might be something others would marvel at. Everyone surrounding me had overcome great obstacles. Baba had risen from abject poverty, and Moor had survived in the face of unimaginable disappointment. My neighbors had lived through wars, and my relatives had lost their limbs or their lives in bomb attacks. I was just another Afghan girl, living in her parents' home, scrambling unsuccessfully to leave the country. Once the reporter realized that my story was relatively unremarkable and marred by failure, I thought, he'd take back his offer to feature me in his column.

That night when we spoke, time flew by. We talked for nearly thirty minutes. The reporter asked me why I'd stopped going to school, what kind of house I lived in, and how long I'd been studying. He told me I spoke great English and complimented me on my accent.

I hadn't told anyone in the house about the article, worried I'd be dissuaded by their concerns about our safety. When the reporter hung up, I stared into the void above my computer, trying to figure out what he might write about me. Had I said enough? I worried the article might come and go, and I still wouldn't receive a visa.

Another email from *The New York Times* a few hours later compounded my fears. It was from a photographer, who told me he needed to come to Kandahar to take my picture for the piece. He wasn't Afghan by birth, but he assured me he could blend in by dressing in local clothes.

I refused immediately. I imagined the chaos that would ensue if this American man walked up to our front door, in full view of the gossips, distant relatives, and Taliban sympathizers that lined our street. I imagined explaining to Baba that this man was here for me, that I wanted to meet him alone so he could take a picture of me to be distributed across the world. I imagined my father's workplace being bombed. I feared attacks targeted at me, the girl who had challenged the customs and traditions of the Taliban, who'd let her photograph and full name appear in the paper, making it easy for anyone to find her. Instead, I managed to convince the *Times* to take a picture of me remotely via Skype, my face obscured by a barely transparent curtain.

The article was published on June 4, 2016, a few days

after my twentieth birthday. It was released in the early morning in New York, late afternoon in Kandahar. After a day of refreshing the *Times*'s home page, I finally located the piece. My name, featured in the headline, stared back at me in bold, clear lettering.

I had expected to feel a mix of nervousness and unbridled excitement, but instead I felt sick. I hadn't expected my name to be part of the title. The reporter included the date of my upcoming visa interview in Kabul in the piece, which I worried would help potential attackers find me. I rescheduled my appointment immediately.

As I scanned through the text, I quickly realized how the reporter had portrayed me. He'd written about me as one would a hero, a champion for education and women's rights. I had no mental space to devote to feelings of pride or flattery. Instead, I was racked with worry that *The New York Times* had portrayed me as a greater threat than I really was, that together we'd created a public behemoth that the Taliban would have to respond to.

As panic overtook me, I confided in Yousef and Javid, in the hope they could help me contain any fallout from the piece. My brothers offered me little sympathy. "Where did you get the courage to do this?" Yousef asked incredulously. "We are men, and we wouldn't dare to do something like this." He was upset that I'd jeopardized the family's safety. "How could you be so selfish?" he demanded. "What have you done?"

AND YET AS THE days passed, all remained calm in Kandahar. My father came home safely every evening, and my

parents stayed unaware that hundreds of people were reading about me with every passing day. At night I shut the
door and logged on to the *Times* website, scrolling through
hundreds of comments left by readers, many addressed to
me. People called me a "brave and indomitable soul" and
"an asset to the world's intellectual community." One
reader wrote, "Sola, if you are reading this . . . know that
many ordinary Americans like myself support giving you a
chance here in the United States." Sitting in the dark, a pile
of blankets at my feet, lit by the white light of my computer, I was buoyed by the unexpected support from these
strangers.

Soon I received more emails from the *Times* reporter,
asking if it was okay to put me in touch with politicians,
lawyers, and others who wanted to express their support for
me. A lawyer wrote with an offer to advise me pro bono on
my next visa application. I read email exchanges between
high-profile U.S. senators and aides offering to coordinate
with the State Department to help secure me a visa.

I had other, less positive exchanges too. One man emailed
the *Times* reporter about a scholarship program he was running for young women around the world. He hinted he
might be able to help me financially and even get me a student visa. I scheduled a Skype call with him, adjusted my
hair in the video feed, and practiced a few points that I
wanted to make. I pressed "accept call" and expected to see
a dignified interviewer on the other end, poised with questions about physics texts and my future ambitions.

Instead, the man who answered was brash and loud,
framed by an unruly mop of white hair. "Why do you want
to go to the United States?" he demanded after I'd intro-

duced myself. As I began to explain, he quickly interrupted. "You should just go to Bangladesh instead! Have your parents even given you permission to leave the country? I need to talk to them to see if they are even allowing you to go— I can speak Farsi." Stunned, I managed to respond coldly that my parents would not speak to him.

"I heard you were funny," he told me, upon seeing that I was upset, trying to lighten the mood. "I'm not in a joking mood," I replied. Later Emily would tell me he'd called her too, ranting about how all women who leave Afghanistan just end up going shopping in America. He assured her I'd never follow through on my plans to attend school. But I'd encountered men like him before, men who'd laughed or even cursed at me when I told them about my learning aspirations. I was set on proving them wrong. Driven by the column and all the support I'd received, I was even more indignant at the men who had thought they could get in my way. I started planning a second trip to Kabul.

MY BROTHERS WERE NO longer angry at me once they realized the *Times* column hadn't harmed our family. But I thought it was still too risky to tell my parents. So Yousef and Javid, knowing the article would improve my chances of getting a visa, persuaded Moor and Baba to allow me to interview at the U.S. embassy one last time.

Moor traveled with me to Kabul that summer. The morning we planned to fly out of Kandahar's airport, I casually checked my email and saw a letter from Arizona State University, a college I'd applied to after returning from the exams in Karachi. "Dear Sola," the message began, "In recognition of your extraordinary achievement, we would like to offer you the New American University Scholarship to support your academic goal of earning an undergraduate degree at Arizona State University. This award . . . will cover the cost of attendance through the completion of your undergraduate degree at ASU." I boarded the flight bursting with happiness, squeezing Moor's hand and grinning underneath my burqa as the plane tipped into the sky.

We stepped off the plane directly onto the tarmac, the heat from the concrete rising up around us. The car ride into the city with our relatives was unruly and exciting. We shouted between the front and back seats, catching up and teasing and laughing uncontrollably. When we arrived at their house, I checked my email again. This time a message from the U.S. embassy informed me that they had made a clerical error. They had to cancel my appointment and promised to be in touch shortly with a new date. I wasn't worried and assumed they'd reschedule for a few days later. Moor agreed that I could extend my trip and even arranged for Javid to come stay with me after she left five days later to commence Eid preparations in Kandahar.

A few days later an email from the *Times* reporter indicated that, based on his conversations with some State Department officials, he didn't believe I would get a student visa to the United States. Instead, he suggested I reapply for something called a humanitarian parole visa, a temporary document to allow me one-way entry into the country. He believed the U.S. government would expedite my approval process, and I might even be able to start college in the fall.

My brimming disappointment was tempered by the reporter's assured tone. Javid and I made plans to return home the next morning. During our last night in Kabul, he and I went to dinner at a family member's restaurant in the center of the city. Because Kabul was more modern than Kandahar, protected against Talib culture by intellectuals, liberals, and American officials, I was able to sit outside among men and women. My head was barely covered by a sheer scarf that billowed in the wind. We broke our Ramadan fasts seated on an outdoor patio, under strings of twinkling lights, as soft instrumental music danced on the evening breeze. I forgot entirely that I was in Afghanistan. I'd never been free like this in my own country.

At that moment, as we snacked on fried okra and gulped down cold glasses of soda, none of Baba's explanations for why we'd stayed in Kandahar instead of moving to Kabul made any sense. I realized then how much easier life would have been in Afghanistan's capital, how I would have been able to go to school and walk freely across the paved sidewalks. Even as things finally began to fall into place for my future, a part of me would never be able to forgive Baba for keeping me from the freedom I could have had during the first part of my life—years I would never get back.

ONE MONTH AFTER THE *Times* article was published, my phone rang early in the morning. It was the U.S. embassy. My new visa application had been approved—I was being granted temporary asylum status in the United States. The only major condition of this visa was that I not leave the United States after entering the country. By traveling to Kabul and picking up my visa, I would open up the real possibility of never seeing my family again.

I knew I had to leave Afghanistan right away. I was afraid that if I didn't get out quickly, someone might revoke my visa at any moment. And if I chose to delay my departure, the countdown would kill me. With every passing day, the idea of leaving my family and my hometown would grow increasingly unbearable. I closed my eyes and drew in a breath. Then, without thinking any longer, I ran to wake up Javid, who was home from Austria for summer vacation. "I got the visa!" I whispered. "I'm going to America!"

I had no way to buy an airline ticket. In Kandahar, there are no credit cards and so no way to purchase tickets online. It would be too dangerous for me to leave home and get a ticket myself, so Javid had to arrange my travel. He told Baba that I needed to go to Kabul to pick up my visa but not that I planned to fly to America immediately afterward. Baba handed Javid some money and told him to buy me a ticket for that evening, so I could fly out with some Kabuli relatives who were in town. He expected me to return home a few days later. At the same time, Emily bought me a ticket from Kabul to the United States with the money she had raised on GoFundMe.

That day we were expecting guests from Pakistan. I spent the morning in the kitchen, cutting vegetables and scrubbing pans, unsure how to announce my plans. Finally, as we laid out plates and napkins on the table, I paused. I told both my parents that this would be my last day in Kandahar. I was leaving for Kabul and then, one week later, for America.

Moor stumbled under the weight of my words. I had never seen her cry the way she did that afternoon, silent racking sobs, tears falling down her face so fast. A searing pain rose in my chest, and I struggled to breathe as I held her, trying not to think of the incomprehensible loss we both would soon face. She begged me to wait just a few weeks. I wept uncontrollably, even as I told her Javid and Emily had already bought my tickets.

That night as I hastily packed my bags, Baba stepped into my bedroom. He'd been silent when I told him I was leaving home. My announcement had barely elicited a reaction.

Now he walked wordlessly past the clothes and books strewn across my floor. He knelt over my suitcase and pulled a carton of my favorite tea from underneath his arm. He tucked the box beneath a pile of folded *salwaar kameez,* and I felt a catch in my throat. I wanted to say something to him, but I couldn't find any words. In an instant he was gone again, his footsteps receding down the staircase.

I left for my uncle's house in Kabul the next morning.

A WEEK AFTER I ARRIVED, I visited the U.S. embassy with my uncle. The building felt different from the first time, somehow less grand and shiny. Everyone there knew my name, and excited whispers echoed across the room as I approached wearing a dress and a loose headscarf. A man at the front desk took my passport for processing. As I turned around, the sounds of clicking pens and bureaucratic chatter and local traffic seemed to vanish. I walked back to the waiting room and into the street. My uncle had parked a few streets away. I was wearing new shoes that dug into my feet, leaving scarlet-red cuts on my heels, so I removed them and walked barefoot across the road, my toes lightly gripping the hot, rough pavement.

That night there was a rocket attack in Kabul. The next day the streets were empty, and then they weren't. People flooded out of their homes, desensitized to the violence and eager to resume their lives. Miraculously, the U.S. embassy was still open, and my uncle drove me there to pick up my passport, with my new visa stamped into it. I let my eyes linger on this piece of paper, the thing I'd wanted so desperately for so many years.

As we drove home, I peered cautiously out my uncle's car window. Every pothole we hit felt like the beginning of another detonation. I was afraid that our car would explode, just as I was about to leave the deadly Afghan roads forever.

The next evening, as night fell over Kabul, my aunt, uncle, and cousin drove me to the airport. We barely spoke during the car ride, silently processing the immensity of what lay before me. My uncle slowed and turned toward the airport. The headlights from buses and cars danced across the building's facade, briefly illuminating the rectangular windows. As I stepped from the car, my bags felt so much heavier than when I'd packed them. But I was pulled ahead by an indefatigable hope, a deeply held excitement for the new life that awaited me.

Late that night my flight finally boarded. As I fell into my worn, turquoise-colored seat, I held back tears and turned to look down on the bustling Kabul evening. At that moment, I couldn't imagine what awaited me in America. Instead, I closed my eyes firmly, exhausted. I fell asleep to the din of quiet whispers and droning engines as the plane tilted higher, climbing toward the hazy night sky.

CHAPTER EIGHTEEN

WHEN I AWOKE AN HOUR AFTER MY PLANE LEFT
Afghanistan, my throat was dry and my neck
throbbed from the way I'd leaned against the plastic cover
over the airplane window. I noticed for the first time two
Indian men sitting to my left, one absorbed in a movie and
the other snoring lightly, his mouth hanging open.

The stale air in the airplane cabin was tainted with unidentifiable smells that made my stomach turn. As I straightened up in my seat, the rush of the plane's engines drowned
out any coherent thoughts about what I'd just undertaken.
I felt a sense of displacement and an overwhelming feeling
that something was different. But perhaps because I was be-
wildered by the magnitude of my journey, the true extent
of my loss didn't sink in.

An hour later the plane skidded across the runway in
Delhi. I snapped to attention at the sound of seatbelts un-
buckling, heaved my suitcase out of the overhead compart-
ment, and followed the throngs of people into the crowded
airport. At least the familiar sight of smog outside the airport windows was a kind of comfort.

I managed to find the gate for my next flight, to Chicago.

As I waited in line to board, my eyes locked on a large screen that read: "Departing to O'Hare International Airport." I suddenly realized I would arrive in America in a matter of hours. I read the phrase over and over again, and my stomach fluttered with excitement.

Emily had told me she would pick me up at the airport. Over the summer, she was working at a camp in the woods for English-language learners. Since she was the only American I knew, I planned to stay at the camp with her for the rest of July until it was over, and then we'd drive to Iowa, where she'd graciously agreed to host me until I could find my bearings.

On the plane ride to the United States, I met another Afghan who told me he was traveling with a humanitarian parole visa. He looked as though he had left the country in a rush. He was dressed in a rumpled *kurta* and the kind of open-toed sandals that Afghans wear around the house. He carried his passport and wallet in a plastic bag that lay haphazardly at his feet. In Pashto, the man said to me, "My brother served as a translator for the American military, and now my life is in danger." This man, however, couldn't speak English, and so I helped to translate, guiding him to the lavatories and ordering him a cup of soda. These tasks distracted me from my own problems and boosted my confidence. Pride washed over me. In Afghanistan, I would have been the one relying on this man, asking him to accompany me to places and buy me things from the shops and markets that women couldn't go to on their own. But already, before I'd even reached the United States, my relationship to men had changed.

By the time we landed in Chicago, I was even more exhausted, thrown by the time change. Half asleep, I drifted in limbo, tugged alternately into the fading past and the looming future. I pulled my bags through the airport and then was pulled aside and asked to wait in a back room for an immigration official to come in and question me. I wondered for a moment if they might send me home, if my visa had been an accident, a bureaucratic mistake. What would it feel like to watch Chicago's skyline slip away through an airplane window?

But when he came, the immigration official glanced at my passport and smiled. "I know you!" he said. "You're Sola from *The New York Times!*" The interview went smoothly after that, and within minutes someone stamped my passport, certifying that I had entered the United States. That was when I removed my headscarf and wrapped the fabric around my neck instead. It was my own private acknowledgment that I had finally made it to America.

AS I WALKED THROUGH the airport's grayish hallways that morning, it seemed as though I were gliding. My mind moved slowly as I struggled to process the rows of gates and duty-free shops and blinking, brightly lettered advertisements surrounding me. When I finally made it out onto the street, pulling my bags onto a concrete sidewalk, I surveyed America for the first time: impeccably paved streets, cars that glistened in each other's headlights, unveiled mothers hauling their children into waiting cars. A man dressed in a neon-green vest directed traffic and helped families find taxis. Large, concrete planters spilled with green vines and persimmon-colored flowers.

Suddenly, I spotted a familiar figure with blond hair and a wide grin. As Emily came bounding toward me, all I could do was laugh in disbelief, unable to process that the woman I'd Skyped with almost daily for a year was actually in front of me, enveloping me in a massive hug. I stood on the sidewalk in a kind of trance as she grabbed my bags and loaded them into the trunk of her car. Then she turned back to me. "We have so much to talk about!" she remarked gleefully. "Jump in the front seat, and we can chat!"

My hand hovered over the passenger door handle. I'd never sat in the front seat of a car before and never been in a car driven by a woman. In Kandahar, our brothers and uncles and fathers sat up front, their legs stretched out comfortably as they changed the radio station or helped the driver navigate traffic. A woman's place was always in the back seat, where our faces and bodies could be hidden, blending together into a clump of fabric.

Emily slid into the driver's seat and grasped the steering wheel with both hands. She looked at me expectantly through the window, and taking a deep breath, I opened the door and sat next to her. I clasped my seatbelt tightly as she pulled into traffic. The expansive windshield and large side windows gave me the frightening impression that we were racing along the freeway. But within a few minutes I relaxed and began to marvel at the view. Emily talked about the buildings we were passing and the weather and what we would eat for dinner. I found myself unable to respond in more than a few words, overwhelmed by the newness around me.

An hour later Emily pulled into the driveway of her father's house—her parents are divorced—in suburban Illinois. His neighborhood, made up of large homes with manicured lawns and jet-black mailboxes, looked like a scene out of a movie. The symmetry was striking compared to the chaos of walled compounds and slums and thatched-roof houses I was used to in Afghanistan. I stepped out of the car and was struck immediately by the presence of serenity. Though it was warm outside, the air felt crisp and gentle. Everything appeared clear, almost sparkling, in stark contrast to the dust that plagued all of Kandahar. The late-morning sky was so blue, it didn't look real. Even as I strained my ears, I couldn't hear any horns or screeching engines. Instead, a light summer breeze whistled through the dozens of trees that lined the block. The few trees I'd seen in Afghanistan were small, a collection of sparse branches stuck atop thin, wavering trunks. I marveled at their piney smell. It was a scent I'd never known existed.

Emily rang her father's doorbell, and he appeared a few seconds later, a look of unadulterated joy spreading across his face at the sight of Emily and me together. He introduced himself and hugged me gently, then lifted my suitcase and gestured for me to come inside. Emily showed me to their guest bedroom, where a set of towels and a new bar of soap were set out on the bed, waiting for me. I wanted to hurry back downstairs, but once I stepped into the shower, I couldn't bear to get out. I stood there for long minutes, perfectly still, as a stream of steamy water washed away the grime from my journey. I remembered how, in Kandahar, oftentimes we had to boil water for our baths, taking cupfuls of water from a small bucket to wash ourselves. I kept being struck by how vastly different America was from the world I was used to.

I dressed in a black *salwaar kameez* and flowing white pants. Downstairs, I was surprised to find that Emily's father had prepared a pot of boiled rice for me. I was so used to the men in Afghanistan who ordered their wives and daughters to bring them everything they needed and never even set foot in the kitchen. I watched in a kind of awe as Emily's father brought me silverware and scrubbed the dishes once I was finished with them.

I sat at the kitchen table, talking about my plans for the next few months and sipping a mug of herbal tea that tasted completely different from the strong black milk tea I was used to at home. I added heaping spoonfuls of sugar, trying to mask the unfamiliar taste. Finally, the conversation slowed, and my English faltered. I admitted to Emily that I needed a short nap. I'd been too overwhelmed by my first sight of America to fall asleep during the long car ride from the airport. I shut off the lights in my room and slid between the soft bedsheets, marveling at the quiet and peacefulness of my new surroundings.

Early that evening Emily took me driving again. We went shopping for American clothes at a local department store, squeezed into a fitting room as I tried on sweaters and T-shirts and jeans, and paid for our purchases with the money Emily had raised on GoFundMe. I'd never seen anything like the store, with its huge fluorescent lights and uniformed employees and private changing rooms. I couldn't even think of what to compare it to.

WE LEFT THE STORE and settled back into the car. Emily gave me a driving tour of her small hometown, even took me to her local elementary school and introduced me to some of her old teachers. On the drive back to her father's house, she blasted a song called "All About That Bass" and laughed at my scandalized reaction as Meghan Trainor sang that she could "shake it, shake it / like I'm supposed to do."

We planned to drive to Emily's camp in Michigan for English learners the next day. Before we left, she brought me to her father's garage and showed me a sleek black bicycle. Admiring its cushioned seat and gears brought to mind how much I'd loved to ride my bike as a little girl. I'd mount the bare gray frame almost every day and ride around the compound courtyard, cutting between rose bushes and across patches of grass. The humidity might bear down on me or the icy winter might seize my *salwaar,* but still I'd pedal, giggling as I wobbled precariously around the yard.

As I grew older, confined within the compound walls, biking became an outlet for my desperation. In between stacks of dishes or hours of cleaning, I'd jump onto the bicycle, turning around and around the small courtyard, sometimes practicing new English vocabulary under my breath, other times simply reveling in the fresh air. But as the years passed, biking became insufficient to counteract the crushing forces that surrounded me. I'd pedal furiously in circles that seemed to grow smaller and smaller. The walls of the compound appeared to fall in toward me, and the sounds of vendors and car horns from the street outside grew muffled and faint. Still, I turned and turned, willing the creaky gears to propel me someplace different.

Emily began to speak, jerking me from my memories. She told me to take the bicycle out for a ride on the nearby tree-lined path and to come back whenever I wanted to. I wheeled the bike out into her wide suburban street. I pedaled lightly at first, finding my balance. I'd never before ridden in a straight line, but soon I was soaring past rows of brick houses and uniform mailboxes. I turned onto the bike path and breathed in the scent of evergreens. The wind whistled past my ears and crept through my hair, blowing loose strands of my curls in front of my eyes. I laughed and pedaled as fast as I could before lifting my feet off the pedals, coasting at a speed I'd only dreamed of.

THE NEXT DAY WE loaded my bags back into the car and drove to Michigan.

THE CAMPSITE WAS LIKE nothing I had ever seen before. We were surrounded by a forest that soared toward the sky. I marveled at the scenery as Emily walked me toward the cabin where I'd be sleeping with her and a few of her friends. She paced around the room, gesturing to the adjoining bathroom, describing her plans for a campfire that evening. Her voice faded in and out as I lay on the hard, lumpy mattress she'd indicated would be mine for the next few weeks. Within minutes I was sleeping soundly, oblivious to her fading footsteps or the campfire songs that floated in later that night from the open window.

I awoke the next morning bleary-eyed and disoriented, still overwhelmed by jetlag and a lingering heaviness. I pulled some of my new clothes out of my suitcase and went to find Emily, who greeted me cheerily. For lunch, she offered me a hamburger that one of the campers had cooked on an outdoor grill. In Kandahar, we'd sometimes cook burgers at home, with juicy patties made of lamb and roasted spices. I crunched into Emily's offering expectantly, but this hamburger was tasteless and dry and crumbled in my mouth.

And it wasn't just hamburgers. I took an instant dislike to American foods like hot dogs and brothy canned soup. Instead, I ate salad for every meal. I avoided the thick, sickly sweet salad dressing that other campers poured generously over their lettuce, instead downing naked forkfuls of raw greens. I spoke very little, nodding at other campers who smiled at me, my thoughts drifting to another world that already seemed irretrievably behind me.

As I adjusted to the Michigan time zone, my grogginess was soon replaced by a powerful homesickness. I knew Moor cried every day that I was away. I remembered our last moments together before I told her I was leaving, the way her arms draped around me as we stood together in the kitchen. Her face, blanketed with sorrow, haunted me as I listened to nonsensical campfire songs. I mourned over what would happen to my mother now, the only one of our family left with unrealized dreams.

A few days into my stay at the campsite, my cousins, aunt, and uncle drove down from Canada to meet me. I rested my head on my aunt's shoulder, willing whatever remnants of home she carried to rub off on me. Later that evening we all went out to eat at a Middle Eastern restaurant. I reveled in the Pashto we spoke, pleased to discover that I hadn't lost my vocabulary of slang and idioms in the week I'd been away from Afghanistan.

My cousins waved furiously at me from the back seat as they drove home to Canada a few days later. The hole they left, compounded by my feelings of displacement, were too much to bear in this rugged campsite. That afternoon I told Emily I wanted to leave the wilderness for a city or suburb.

She understood. "You can drive to Iowa with my friend!" she told me brightly. "You can stay with some people I know, and I'll join you in a few weeks."

The day before I left Michigan, I wandered through the woods for a few hours to take in the unfamiliar beauty of my new home. I marveled at the silence that draped around me, sweet and calming, broken every few minutes by a chirping bird or the crunch of leaves beneath a gray-furred squirrel. Soon I stumbled upon a delightful clearing, a break in the small path that looked out onto a glistening lake and clear sapphire sky. I'd never seen anything so beautiful. I took out a book by Oliver Sacks that my aunt had brought me from Canada and read there for hours, only making the trek back to the campsite once the sunset peeked through the trees and the shadows around me slowly merged together, turning to dark.

CHAPTER NINETEEN

B Y THE TIME I GOT A RIDE TO IOWA WITH EMILY'S FRIEND,
it was August. As the car whizzed down the highway, I
said little and mostly just rested my head against the passenger window and gazed out at alternating patches of
farmland and freeway. That evening, as the sun dipped beneath the roofs of two-story houses, offering a welcome
coolness, we pulled into a neat suburban neighborhood.

I stayed the night at the home of another friend of Emily's, a Pakistani American, along with his wife and two
young children. The next morning they dropped me off at
the local community college, where I planned to complete
one year of study before transferring to Arizona State. But
on my first day, the college proved a resounding disappointment. The orientation I attended was bland. Professors and
administrators droned for hours about credits and course
requirements and behavioral standards. The other students
fidgeted next to me, their eyes glued to their phone screens.
The administration served us limp sandwiches and took us
on a tour of the campus, which felt as small as the elementary school Emily had shown me a few weeks earlier. I

couldn't help wondering, *Is this what I came all the way from Afghanistan for?*

After a few days of uninspiring orientation events, I realized that a year at this place would be a waste of time. I still planned to enroll at ASU, but I decided to devote this year to acclimating to America and studying much the way I had at home, through online courses. When Emily arrived in Iowa a few days later, I announced my intentions to her, and soon after that I made another decision: I'd start living by myself in Cedar Rapids. I planned to use some of the money from the fundraiser to stay in an inexpensive bed-and-breakfast hotel. Though I was incredibly grateful to have Emily nearby, I didn't want to grow dependent on her. I knew I'd have to discover America for myself.

In some ways, I was able to adjust quickly to life in Iowa. My first night in the hotel room was the first night I'd ever spent alone in my life, and I instantly fell in love with the freedom of solitude. Once or twice a week I walked to the secondhand bookstore a block from where I was staying, immersing myself in tales set in nineteenth-century St. Petersburg or the rural English countryside. Emily stayed a constant presence in my life, meeting me for lunch several times a week and bringing me along to dozens of events and dinner parties that she'd been invited to. That September I met a group of Indian immigrants at a housewarming party, and within hours we were gathered in the living room together, dancing to Bollywood songs and belting out the lyrics. I impressed them with the Hindi I'd learned from Indian movies back in Kandahar. After that night, I received an invitation from them almost every weekend to go kayaking or meet at someone's house for dinner.

But moments of culture shock hit me unexpectedly. The first time I went shopping by myself, the cashier at the Target checkout line smiled at me and said, "Have a nice day!" as he loaded my bags into my cart. I balked, horrified, and hurried out of the store. I thought the man was flirting aggressively with me, because in Kandahar, even a stray look from a man has romantic implications. It took me weeks to realize, somewhat sheepishly, that this was how all cashiers acted in America.

Another afternoon I was out for a walk and landed upon a sandwich shop. "Your order will be ready in twenty minutes," the man behind the counter told me. I wandered outside to wait in the sun. "I cannot *believe* this!" I suddenly heard. A man had stormed inside the shop and was screaming at the owner. "How can a sandwich take twenty minutes?? This *sucks!*" I didn't immediately understand what the word *sucks* meant, but I could clearly see how furious the customer was. In Afghanistan, my family stayed calm through bombings and gunfire. How, I wondered, could this man be losing his mind over a sandwich?

I was also shocked by the casual interactions between men and women. In Afghanistan, I'd never even seen my parents, or any other couple, touch. I watched Bollywood movies where men and women fell in love, but they expressed their attraction subtly, through the lingering of a *dupatta* scarf on a lover's lips or the light brushing of two hands. At parties with Emily, guests spoke so freely about who they'd been with and everything they'd done that I wanted to cover my ears. In listening to these conversations, I realized that actions I'd considered wildly immoral in Afghanistan were allowed here, even if they weren't always condoned.

One night I called Moor. When I heard her voice on the other end of the line, strained with days of pent-up worry, I felt everything I'd given up in painful clarity. My throat seized, and I couldn't talk at first. I willed myself not to cry. "I feel lost, Moor," I finally managed, my words weak with sadness. The line went quiet. All I could hear was my mother breathing on the other end.

"I was lost, too, when I first went to university in Kabul," she told me. "Soon you will get used to the rhythm of your new life. You will make new friends. And you will come back like your brothers, to visit in the summer!"

"That's true," I said quietly. But I knew that on a humanitarian parole visa, you can never return home. I just couldn't bring myself to tell her.

BY OCTOBER, MY DAYS began to blend together. I moved through Khan Academy modules and problem sets from physics textbooks I'd bought. The weather turned colder, and I mostly stayed in my tiny room, waiting for something to happen.

One afternoon I got an idea. "Do you think we can email ASU and ask if I can start there a year early, in the middle of the term?" I asked Emily. We sent the email right away. I expected them to refuse, citing scheduling or budgetary problems. Instead, they wrote back almost instantly, agreeing.

Emily was thrilled for me. The night before I was set to leave for Arizona, she threw a goodbye party, and all the friends I'd met in Iowa attended. I wore an Afghan outfit, draped a yellow-and-blue scarf across my shoulder, and curled my hair. I boiled Afghan milk tea and passed out steaming mugs as everyone sat perched in her living room. The din of a dozen conversations filled the house, and guests wandered up to me, enveloping me in hugs and wishing me luck. Hours later, after everyone went home and the dishes sat drying next to the sink, I left for a final night in my Cedar Rapids hotel. I lay awake into the early morning, brimming with excitement, my eyes wide with sleeplessness and anticipation.

Emily offered to fly with me to Arizona and help me move into my new dorm room. As we flew into Phoenix together, I was surprised by how nervous I was. I sat upright, clasping my hands together tightly and staring resolutely ahead, trying to steady my breathing. As soon as we were under way and the seatbelt sign clicked off, Emily turned to me and began to describe in detail everything she thought I needed to know about college. She explained what a fraternity was and cautioned me that my roommate might use our room for a rendezvous with her boyfriend. She painted pictures of drunken parties with flashing lights and sticky floors and music too loud to even talk over. She warned me to be careful of leering upperclassmen and to walk away whenever I saw drugs.

I was horrified. The campus Emily depicted was permeated with more scandal than I'd ever even been allowed to imagine. My entire life, I'd never seen anyone consume a drop of alcohol. Except in movies, I'd never even seen a man and a woman hold hands. My visions of college included large classes, intimate seminars, quiet, studious dormitories, and the occasional late-night gathering. Never once had it occurred to me that I'd have to navigate a wild party scene. More than English essay assignments or cavernous lecture halls, it was this thought that began to terrify me.

We landed in Phoenix late at night. It was too dark for me to make out more than the rows of white and red lights lining the tarmac. I pulled my bag through the airport, and Emily called us an Uber. We sat silently in the back seat as the driver wove through traffic and eventually pulled into the downtown area. I peered out the window as we passed dozens of restaurants and bars. Pulsing crowds spilled onto the street, groups of men with their arms draped casually around women in cropped tank tops and miniskirts. Strings of lights lined every block, and neon signs flickered atop outdoor patios stuffed with throngs of people. Our driver picked up speed, and I turned to look out the back windshield, mesmerized by this wildly unfamiliar display.

A few minutes later we arrived at my dorm, a tall modern building made up of broad windows. I hauled my suitcase upstairs as Emily searched on her phone for an email from the university containing my floor and room number. I pulled my bag to a stop in front of a room just off the staircase and cautiously jiggled the doorknob. The room was unlocked, and I peered inside. I gestured for Emily to come in and then turned again to survey the room I'd be living in for the next year. The floors and walls were bare, and a wooden desk sat squarely in the corner. There were two beds, and as I turned to look at one of them, I jumped. A girl was splayed across a navy-blue mattress, her hair matted and her clothes rumpled. Her face looked ashen, and she jerked unsteadily, as though racked with uneasy dreams. I stared at her, trying to process exactly what was happening.

I soon realized that my room was connected to the one next door with an adjoining bathroom. Emily and I walked past the stained toilet and cluttered basin and knocked loudly on the other room's door. It opened, and three girls appeared, dressed in minidresses and adorned with charm necklaces. They surveyed our unfamiliar faces until suddenly they realized what was happening and began to apologize hastily. "We went to a party tonight, and our friend wasn't feeling well," one girl began. Another finished: "Our room connects with yours, so we let her sleep on your bed since no one else lives here. . . . We didn't know you were coming tonight!" They rushed toward my bed and shook the sleeping girl until she awoke, stumbled out of my room, and abruptly vomited all over the carpeted hallway. I recoiled, disgusted. Emily shut the door firmly, and we stared at each other, too startled for words. I slept fitfully that night, distracted by dreams of stumbling, slurring intruders.

Emily generously stayed with me in my dorm for a few days, sleeping on the extra twin bed across from mine. But on Monday she was on a plane back to Iowa, and I was alone, studying the syllabi for my classes, trying to drown out the raucous hollering outside my door with my headphones, and waiting for my college life to begin.

MY STARTLING INTRODUCTION TO ASU proved indicative of how my first year at the school would unfold. Most nights I sat nervously on my bed as music blared through the halls. On nights when there were football games, I could hear screaming from the stadium across campus. I jumped when the team set off celebratory fireworks after a touchdown, thinking for a moment I was back in Kandahar amid deadly fighting.

In the morning, as I walked down the dorm hallways, I'd hold my breath to avoid inhaling the rancid smells of spilled beer and sweat lingering from the night before. I took occasional walks outside in an attempt to orient myself amid the striking, mountainous scene. I even began swimming in ASU's giant athletic pool every morning, reteaching myself the strokes I'd learned as a little girl in Kandahar's rivers. But unsettled by the throbbing beats emanating from clubs and by the broken bottles that lined the sidewalks, I grew too afraid to leave my dorm after dark. I still spent most of my time alone, the door to my single pulled firmly closed.

I talked to Moor over Skype or WhatsApp almost every day for hours at a time. We spoke in the early mornings or late evenings to account for the time difference. I tried at first to explain life in America to her—the unblemished roads, the trash collection system, the classes I was enrolled in, the friends I'd made in Iowa with master's degrees and PhDs. But I faltered in my explanations, unable to bridge the nearly eight-thousand-mile divide. My parents had never studied the subjects I was learning. They had almost no exposure to American culture. They didn't even have a reference point from which to interpret my experiences. Instead, we talked about life in Kandahar: deaths, engagements, visiting relatives. I clung to details I would have dismissed before as trite and irrelevant, like the color of my cousin's reception gown, the new recipes my mother was trying for breakfast. I was starved for a taste of home. The buffering video calls were a poor substitute for the mornings we used to spend drinking tea together or the evenings we'd spent watching her favorite musicians perform on TV. I missed Moor desperately.

At night I had a recurring dream that my mother was in my dorm room. I'd grow so happy and reach out toward her, then wake up suddenly and realize she wasn't there. I'd try to fall asleep again, to bring the dream back, but it was always too late, I couldn't recapture it.

I bought the same jasmine perfume Moor used to wear when I was a child and sprayed it in my room. If I closed my eyes, I could imagine she was standing beside me, that she was about to wrap her arms around me. I printed a photo of the two of us and looked at it for hours as I listened to old Pashto music recordings, trying to remember every detail of the moments before we snapped the picture.

Sometimes the separation became too heavy to bear. I'd call Yousef or Javid late at night crying. For minutes at a time, the line would be silent as I struggled to rein in my sobs and form some kind of a sentence. Thankfully, I didn't need to explain the stabbing pains of loneliness I felt in my dorm room, away from my language, my country, my mother. They too had lived through holiday breaks spent without family. They'd celebrated Eid alone, with a plate of boiled potatoes and chicken breast from the school cafeteria. They'd watched the same videos I had of our cousins' weddings and our baby niece's first steps, wishing they could simply board a plane and be home to see it all for themselves.

In Afghanistan, Javid had often been the one to comfort me when I fell into an enveloping sadness. But when I called from America, I was surprised to find that Yousef was often the one who made me feel better. "Why do I have to choose between my education and my family?" I sobbed on the line.

"Whatever you are going through," he'd tell me softly, "it would be far worse in Afghanistan." I'd suddenly remember the burqa still hanging in my closet in Kandahar, the endless cooking and cleaning that took countless hours from my days, and the ever-present question of marriage that had caused me so much dread. I would murmur my agreement, still fighting tears. Yousef would tease me then, trying to elicit a smile. "Do you wish you had taken Aunt Gulpari's marriage proposal instead?" I'd laugh, remembering how badly my aunt had wanted me to find a husband. Yousef would hang up a few minutes later, and I'd sleep, relieved of grief for a few days.

INITIALLY, I EXPECTED THAT the classrooms at ASU would provide a welcome respite from the glaring newness that otherwise surrounded me. I'd devoted the past few years of my life to academics, and the first time I stepped into a lecture hall for my introductory physics class, I felt prepared, a weighty textbook jostling against my laptop in my backpack. But almost immediately, I struggled to maintain motivation in my classes. It had been over a decade since I'd stepped into a formal classroom, and life at my Kandahari primary school could hardly be compared to the lectures and homework assignments I faced at ASU. I wasn't used to watching lectures, taking copious notes, or finishing weekly problem sets. Though the classes on writing, calculus, and physics interested me at first, they eventually felt slow and laborious. At home, I'd traversed years' worth of math and physics content in a matter of months. Here I squirmed in classrooms as the professors drew and redrew concepts on the whiteboard in brightly colored markers. It often seemed as if I were stuck in an endless loop of review. My homework was tedious and took hours to complete, even though I already understood the concepts.

In class, when a professor bellowed at us to pay attention and warned us our grades would suffer if we didn't complete the assigned homework, I was transported to Pashtana's house in Kandahar, her fists closing around clumps of my hair, demanding I do what she'd asked. It was an irrational comparison, but it haunted me. I yearned to be in control again, to spearhead my own learning. I neglected some of my schoolwork, instead spending hours in my room studying the way I used to, taking free online classes on physics and world history hosted by MIT.

But eventually, I found an outlet at ASU. In the winter of 2017, I enrolled in a seminar taught by Frank Wilczek, an ASU professor and the 2004 recipient of the Nobel Prize in Physics. The class was titled "Workshop in Perception Technology," and I struggled from the beginning to understand everything Professor Wilczek lectured about. But I found myself infected with the same exhilaration I'd felt years earlier as a teenager in Kandahar, stumbling through English vocabulary and arithmetic problems on Khan Academy, driven to grasp answers that lay just beyond my fingertips.

A few weeks into my physics seminar, I received an email from the school administration informing me that Professor Wilczek's wife, Betsy Devine, had heard about my story. She thought Professor Wilczek would be a great physics mentor for me and invited me out to lunch with them both that Saturday. There's a picture from that day that I often look at. The three of us are sitting inside a yellow-walled ice cream shop. Frank is wearing a beige bucket hat and a green vest, while Betsy sits in a black-and-white dress. I'm in a yellow blouse, a grin spreading across my face. My eyes are wide, almost dazed. I look as though I cannot quite believe what is happening to me.

That afternoon as we walked along the downtown Tempe streets, Frank suggested we take a hike the next day and continue our conversation. Over the next two months, until Frank had to return to his primary residence outside Boston, these hikes became a regular occurrence. We talked for hours together, discussing a sweeping range of intellectual subjects. I was especially fascinated by Frank's descriptions of quantum physics, a subject I had never explored before. "Quantum physics is a beautiful, profound science," he told me. "It allows us to see the fundamental building blocks of our reality." He told me I should read about quantum computers, devices built on the laws of quantum physics that can do some computations at previously unachievable speeds.

I was drawn immediately to this new field that had the potential to explain the most basic foundations of our uni-

verse. I later realized that, throughout my life in Afghanistan, I had been longing for something like this: a set of
principles that could explain and give meaning to my existence.

I was surprised to find that Frank shared my love of
books, too. He had read almost every text I had and could
analyze each one in detail with me. We spent hours discussing European novels like Mann's *Buddenbrooks* and Tur-
genev's *Fathers and Sons,* whose self-assured, commanding
characters spoke to me. In Kandahar, I'd become interested
in philosophy after listening to an English-learning podcast
produced by the British Council, which defined the word as
literally meaning "love of wisdom." Frank furthered my interest, encouraging me to read Plato and Bertrand Russell's
History of Western Philosophy. We debated interpretations of
Dostoyevsky on different mountain trails, the Arizona sun
bearing down on us as we lingered in the striking beauty of
our surroundings.

I became close with Frank's wife, too. Betsy heard my
horror stories from the party dorm I was staying in and lob-
bied the ASU administration to have me transferred to a
quieter, academic-themed housing unit. A few days after I
moved into my new room, she showed up at my door, her
arms filled with curtains and a quilt she'd bought especially
for me.

IN KANDAHAR, THE POLITICAL situation remained unchanged. The Taliban continued to attack Afghan soldiers
and government officials. Suicide bombings remained common. Yet even as this violence continued, the city was slowly

modernizing. Influenced by international television programs and the advent of the internet, my generation chafed against the constrictive, traditional culture that had always defined Kandahar. Restrictions gradually loosened. Restaurants in Aino Mena cordoned off a special family dining area where women were allowed to eat. New malls opened that allowed men and women to shop together.

My mother threw away her two burqas. She had always despised the tentlike blue covering, the heavy fabric that obscured everything from the curve of her chin to the shape of her ankle. She especially hated the thin mesh that covered her eyes, allowing her only the tiniest glimpse of what lay outside. It became acceptable for her to wear a black abaya, a long flowing covering that resembles a dress. The abaya is more flattering than a burqa, with sleeves and thinner fabric and a slight cinching at the waist. It comes in different styles and can be hemmed with layers of multicolored embroidery. She concealed her face with a niqab, a type of covering that leaves a few inches of skin uncovered between a woman's eyebrows and the bridge of her nose. For women in the Western world, this attire would have felt unbearably restrictive. But for Moor and other women in Kandahar, even this small change was liberating.

THROUGHOUT 2017, I TRAVELED across my new country. Emily took me on a vacation to the Grand Canyon. In Kandahar, I'd seen picturesque silhouettes of looming mountains, of groves studded with blushing pomegranates. But I had never witnessed this kind of stark beauty. I marveled at the vibrant gradients visible on every rock formation, at the cavernous emptiness that hovered above the canyon floor. Looking out onto the landscape as the sun dropped below the horizon, I felt as though I were floating above a magical world.

We were only a few hours' flight away from California, where the Khan Academy offices are located. A year earlier, when I was still living in Kandahar and trying to obtain a visa, Emily had emailed Sal Khan and set up a video meeting for both of us. I was so excited to see the man who'd taught me addition and trigonometry and calculus that I could barely answer any of his basic questions.

Now Emily emailed him again to see if we could meet in person, and he invited us to visit the Khan Academy offices. We landed in San Francisco and drove south to Mountain View. In person, I expected Sal Khan to be larger than life, an imposing personality aware of his tremendous influence on the world. But instead, I found him to be humble, down to earth. He gave me a tour of the entire building and ended up in front of his office, a small corner room lined with chalkboards, windows, and a charcoal-black door. I stood in the doorway as an employee piped, "This is where Sal records all his videos!" As if in a dream, I was thrust back to my Kandahar bedroom where I'd watched early videos on fractions, in which Sal drew a pizza and divided it into fourths. I remembered the desk where I had sat late into the night in Karachi, watching him analyze SAT reading comprehension passages. I remembered the first Khan Academy physics videos I'd watched, on Newton's laws and friction. It was difficult to comprehend that this was the place where my knowledge had originated. How had I made it here, to the other side?

Enjoying my travels and newfound freedom that year, I was reminded of how lucky I was to have escaped Kandahar's grasp. I traveled to New York to visit Baba's distant cousin. I imagined we'd explore the city together, snack on Afghan desserts, and tell jokes in Pashto. Instead, I found the man to be domineering, steeped in conservative Kandahari culture. He forbade his two high-school-age daughters to go out alone or even to lock their phones with a password. I was repulsed by his attitude, possessed with an urgent desire to leave their home. I told him I was leaving for the day to explore New York City, that I would return to his home for dinner. Baba's cousin turned to me, unrestrained distaste twisting his features, and said, "I don't understand how your father let you come alone to the United States. I would rather die than send my daughter alone to a new country."

A FEW WEEKS LATER I returned to Arizona. There I met another person who would influence the direction of my new life. Cynthia Keeler, a new physics professor at ASU, had initially heard about me from a friend who'd read the *New York Times* article. She offered to meet me, and so a few days later I walked to her office in a nondescript physics department building on campus. Within minutes of our introduction, she jumped up from her chair and approached the small blackboard next to her desk, writing out formulas and theories I'd never heard of. She tried to explain string theory, one of the most difficult concepts in physics. I understood little pieces of what she was saying, and she kept explaining, her enthusiasm unwavering.

Emboldened, I suddenly blurted out, "Can we meet like this every week? Maybe you can help me read scientific papers in quantum physics. I want to learn enough so I can do research with you this summer." Maybe she was thrown by my forwardness, but she agreed.

Professor Keeler assigned me papers on string theory and quantum gravity. The readings were so confusing, I couldn't even understand the one-paragraph introductory abstracts at the top of the first page. As other students dressed up on Friday nights to go out to fraternities, I pored over formulas and methodologies and conclusions. I looked up other papers to try to decipher the ones Professor Keeler had given me. I was spending twenty hours a week studying outside class.

Eventually, I highlighted the paragraphs I still couldn't interpret, and every week she walked me through the papers line by line, explaining vocabulary and concepts so animatedly that I followed her every word.

Months passed, and the papers slowly came into focus. I asked Professor Keeler to assign me more difficult readings. I enrolled in a graduate-level quantum physics course and received an A. I Skyped with Frank Wilczek, discussing my new knowledge of quantum computing and machine learning.

At the same time, I continued to self-study in other subjects outside science. I read books about Afghan history and politics that chronicled the horrific consequences of foreign involvement in Afghanistan. I enrolled in "Justice," an online Harvard course about moral philosophy taught by Michael Sandel. On weekends, I read the professor's book *Justice: What's the Right Thing to Do?*, which chronicled theories of philosophers from Aristotle to Rawls. I learned for the first time about the idea of universal human equality. Throughout my life in Kandahar, I'd assumed Afghans were inherently unlucky, that our lives were ultimately doomed by our own inadequacies and by fate. I believed we were governed by different standards than citizens of other countries, that the bar to our happiness was set higher than we could ever reach. My studies changed my perspective. For the first time, I considered myself as a human first, a being deserving of rights, independent of the place where I was born.

But rather than bringing empowerment, my new outlook brought pain. I found it impossible to square theoretical concepts of equality with the political reality in Afghanistan. Over the phone, Baba told me the Taliban had begun to murder with abandon. They killed government officials haphazardly, without any regard for their rank. Some of our distant relatives were low-level employees of the Afghan government who barely earned enough to feed themselves. Still, the Taliban killed them. "Afghanistan is so fragile," Baba told me. "It can collapse in an instant." Within weeks, I had to revert back to my old ideas about Afghan tragedy as fate. The only way for me to understand the violence was to believe that Afghans were beggars who could not be choosers, a people who should dream only of staying alive.

IN MARCH 2018, Professor Keeler nominated me for a quantum physics program at the California Institute of Technology, or Caltech, in Pasadena. The program was a four-day workshop tailored to undergraduate students interested in pursuing a PhD. I was accepted, and in late November I flew to Southern California. The heat was milder than I'd expected, a breezy contrast to the searing Arizona sun I'd grown used to. On the shuttle ride to Caltech, I stared out the windows, marveling at the soaring, deep green palm trees that curved up toward the cloudless sky. I stayed in a beautiful hotel with a sandy, tiled exterior and little balconies that looked out onto the historic downtown. Every morning my roommate and I woke up and stood next to each other in front of the mirror in the bathroom, applying makeup and adjusting our blouses and straightening our nametags. Then we rode the elevator downstairs and took a shuttle to Caltech's campus, where we attended physics workshops. People around me chatted casually about astronomy and quantum gravity, and soon I surprised myself by turning in my seat to join the conversation. I'd never been somewhere where existing was so easy, where every hour that passed was both invigorating and uncomplicated. I forgot for long stretches of time about my history, the fundamental experiences that set me apart from the young American-born students around me. But sometimes, when I met an impressively young postdoctoral fellow or a student my age who'd already published academic papers, I wondered if I might have been like them if I hadn't been born in Afghanistan.

FRANK HAD SUGGESTED I meet John Preskill at Caltech, one of the foremost pioneers in quantum physics research. Thanks to his introduction, I ducked out of a workshop early on the final day of the program and headed toward Professor Preskill's office. I lingered as I walked across campus, admiring grassy lawns and burbling fountains.

I nearly gasped as I turned the corner and saw the Annenberg Center for Information Science and Technology. I stood paralyzed for a moment by the view. The building was stunning, a modern complex composed of blue-toned rectangular windows that reflected images of nearby palm trees and the surrounding mountains. The redbrick pathways to the ground-floor doors were lined with fragile reeds and newly planted trees.

I rode the elevator up to Professor Preskill's office and knocked lightly on the door. He emerged, a man with slightly graying hair and thin-rimmed glasses, and welcomed me inside, where we fell into an easy conversation about my education journey and his recent research. An hour after I entered his office, Professor Preskill glanced at his watch and told me that he had a meeting with his researchers. I gathered my things and began to leave when he turned to me casually and asked, "Sola, do you want to come and meet the rest of the team?" I tried unsuccessfully to hide my excitement as I followed him into a conference room. He introduced me to his colleagues, and then the meeting began. I listened closely as they went around the table discussing working papers and grant applications and new research proposals.

The Caltech physics program ended at lunchtime on the Sunday after we'd arrived. After exchanging phone numbers with the friends I'd made over impromptu lunches and delayed lectures and late-night chats, I checked out of my hotel room and headed to the nearby botanical gardens I hadn't yet had a chance to see. I walked for hours through the sprawling property, admiring the brilliant roses and delicate lily pads and trees that drooped over a wood-plank bridge. I didn't want to leave.

When I arrived back at ASU the next morning, I sat at my desk and typed out an email to John Preskill asking if I could return to Caltech that summer to conduct research with him. He responded the next day, saying he would love to have me. It was all I could do to keep from jumping across my dorm room. I'd never felt such childlike, unburdened glee.

The months at ASU flew by, and within an instant I was back at Caltech. This time my physics research focused on understanding black holes. I worked every day at the building I'd marveled at on my first visit. I attended casual lunch gatherings with Professor Preskill's group outside in the breezy California summer, talking about topics related to our research but also discussing literature and art. I spoke for hours with postdocs, trying to understand the pioneering research they were conducting. As a culmination of my work, I presented my research in a campus classroom in front of Professor Preskill and several scholars from all over the world. It was my first time speaking in public, one of my first times being judged purely on my academic merits, and I found it exhilarating.

Throughout the summer program I stayed in a suite on campus with seven other young women, all conducting summer research in different departments. For the first time, I understood the pleasure of living in a dorm with like-minded people, and I did my best to embrace it. I befriended almost everyone living on my hall and even adjusted to the ever-present din of neighboring parties. The university planned outings for us. I took pictures with my new friends as the sun sank behind Griffith Observatory, leaving behind hues of pink and purple that disappeared as we ran back to the shuttle, still sweating in the sunless heat. We attended faculty dinners hosted outdoors, under strings of bobbing lights. We planned our own activities, too: midnight hikes, dips into the freezing-cold Pacific Ocean. My suitemates and I all hailed from different countries, and so we tried to introduce one another to our respective cultures, eating out at a Korean shaved-rice shop, an Afghan restaurant, an Indian buffet, an Italian pizzeria. We stayed up late, sitting on the floors of one another's rooms, laughing together. My new friends discussed their college adventures—boyfriends, parties, drunken escapades—as I listened, my eyes wide with shock. Three months passed in an instant.

The day before we were to board flights to various corners of the United States, my suitemates and I ventured out to a local souvenir store and bought seven friendship bracelets, each adorned with a different charm. I spun mine around on my wrist as I waited in the L.A. airport to board my plane, breaking into intermittent smiles.

CHAPTER TWENTY

THE FUNNIEST JOKE IN KANDAHAR WHEN I WAS GROWING up was based on the title of a classic Indian Bollywood film called *Kabhi Khushi Kabhie Gham*, or *Sometimes Happiness, Sometimes Sorrow*:

> An Indian and an Afghan meet at the airport. The Afghan asks, "How's life?" The Indian responds, "Oh, you know. Sometimes Happiness, Sometimes Sorrow. What about you?" The Afghan says, "In Afghanistan, life is Sometimes Suicide Bomb, Sometimes Air Strikes."

We would laugh uproariously as we delivered the punchline. It was funny only because it was so true. As Taliban insurgents launched suicide attacks in Kandahar and the prosperity from the American invasion faded, moments of happiness grew fleeting. We found that the only times of lightness were those we created, and so we developed a dark sense of humor to callous us against reality.

The truth of living sandwiched between bullets and rockets is that you cannot cry for every life lost or fear every imminent attack. You cannot think about a recent uptick in suicide bombs as you travel to the bazaar or listen too closely to the rockets whizzing over the park, or you will never leave your house. The destruction will be crippling if you choose to dwell on it, and the life you saved for yourself won't be worth living.

So when a bomb goes off, you crack a joke about a popular Indian movie. You laugh and try your best to live fully the life you still have, without indulging in fear of violence you deem both indiscriminate and inevitable.

Living in the throes of violence in Afghanistan, I was unaware of how jarring this mindset must have seemed to those living outside. But in the fall of 2019, after I returned from Caltech to Tempe, security deteriorated in Kandahar province. I read in the news about journalist murders and targeted assassinations. Roadside bombings grew more frequent. An airstrike attack killed twelve people. Non-Taliban militias formed on the outskirts of the city and reportedly kidnapped scores of women and young boys for ransom. Conditions in the villages grew so deadly that hundreds of displaced people swarmed into Kandahar city, seeking refuge from the violence. Many Kandaharis believed the province would soon revert back to civil-war-era conditions with brutal fighting between Taliban, militia, and government forces.

A year passed, and the situation worsened. In November 2020, gunmen disguised as police officers stormed Kabul University's campus. They threw grenades, sprayed the campus with gunfire, and captured hostages from the throngs of students, some of whom, spurred by desperation and fear, threw themselves out of classroom windows. It took six hours to end the brutal siege. The attackers left behind the bodies of twenty-two students and a grieving university, its grounds wet with blood and riddled with bullet holes.

Months earlier, in February 2020, President Donald Trump had announced a U.S. peace deal with the Taliban. The United States agreed to withdraw from Afghanistan in exchange for mostly unenforceable concessions from the Taliban. The Americans also promised the release of five thousand Taliban prisoners from Afghan prisons. The deal almost completely sidestepped the legitimate Afghan government. At the time, President Trump was spouting such wild proclamations that we didn't believe he would actually withdraw and make an already dangerous situation much worse by removing the modicum of security that the American forces provided.

I called home every day, willing someone to pick up the phone. As I waited, my imagination teemed with devastating possibilities the way an ugly, putrid stain blooms across fabric.

I worried that Baba's store in the center of Kandahar would be ravaged by a suicide bomber. I wondered if my mother was safe, tucked into the recesses of our compound.

One day my father picked up the call. *The situation is very bad, Baba,* I wanted to tell him. *What are you going to do? You are not safe!* But before I could say anything, he held the phone up to the window so I could hear the sound of bombs exploding across the city. "That one missed us by a few streets!" he said, laughing. Living thousands of miles away from it all, I was jolted by his humorous delivery of such wrenching, terrifying facts. My distance illuminated the danger they were in. I found it impossible to joke about bombs the way I had when I lived at home, subject to the same risks that they were. I hung up a few minutes later and sat on my dorm room bed, plagued by utter helplessness.

It was painful to process the geographical chasm in our family. My siblings and I lived abroad, my nieces and nephews spoke English and Norwegian and attended school. They spent their holidays on class ski trips and on trains headed to other European countries. They returned to Afghanistan only every few years.

It would have been an immense comfort to know that Afghanistan's grasp on us all loosened with every successive generation. But in addition to my parents, not all the members of our family had managed to escape. Nadir and his wife, Shabana, still lived in our family compound with their three children, my little cousins Hamid, Ayan, and Nadia. When I lived in Afghanistan, Hamid was a toddler old enough to listen to my stories and pepper me with unending questions. He had wide eyes and a head of tousled brown hair. His mother dressed him in Western-style long-sleeve shirts with multicolored stripes that made him look as though he'd just stepped out of an American children's picture book. From the moment he could walk, Hamid had followed me around every day. He parked himself on the kitchen floor as I washed dishes, bounced on my bed as I watched videos about Pascal's triangle, and cried when he had to stop playing with me and go to sleep. Between study sessions, I danced with him to the newest Bollywood songs, my feet moving in double time while he bobbed unsteadily, his hands stretched out for balance. We took selfies on my phone making silly faces. I pursed my lips and crossed my eyes until I looked so ridiculous that he collapsed into gig-gles and I snapped the picture.

When I left Afghanistan, Hamid was only eight years old. In America, I marveled at pictures his mother sent me of him laughing with his little siblings or posing solemnly in a new *kameez*, already so much taller than I remembered. I tried to crack a joke or ask him about school through lag-ging video calls, as a dozen other family members crowded around the camera to say hello, but it was impossible to have our own conversation.

But by the age of eleven, Hamid began to call me on his own, when no one else was around. When the phone rang, I closed my dorm room door and leaned back in my desk chair. At first we talked for hours about my work, his friends, and the new Pashto words his baby sister Nadia had learned. But soon I realized there was more to Hamid than the mischievous little boy I had left behind. "I want to leave Afghanistan, Sola, like you did," he confided in me. He was practicing English on his own, using YouTube videos and English movies to perfect his accent. He tried a few sen-tences on me, and I laughed out loud, astonished. His gram-mar was still uneven and his vocabulary limited, but every word he pronounced sounded as if it had come from a suave American actor rather than a young Afghan boy.

Soon Hamid was studying almost as much as I had. He created an account on Khan Academy, where a placement test indicated he was at a third-grade math level. The in-struction in Kandahar was so poor that even though Hamid was one of the most advanced students in his school, he had to start his self-studies practically at the beginning. He worked his way through decimals and geometry and basic algebra, watching videos alone in his room just as I had a few years earlier.

I helped Hamid sign up for online English tutoring with a teacher from South America who helped him conjugate properly and expand his vocabulary. Eventually, he read short stories and articles in English and prepared to take the SAT, which he hoped would allow him to come to America.

On some of our phone calls, I talked to Hamid about why I'd left Afghanistan. His cheery disposition dissipated on the other end as I described days spent at home cooking dinners and washing laundry instead of attending school. "Will these things happen to Nadia, too?" he asked me quietly one afternoon. I wanted so badly to tell him that everything would be fixed by the time his baby sister grew up, that she would go to school and eventually graduate from university. I wanted to joke that she might make more money than him and then to hear his laughter punctuated with relief.

But I remembered how Agha had done the same thing to my mother so many generations ago, how the disappointment had been a crushing blow she could never forgive. I told Hamid the truth, and we both sat quietly, each unsure what to say to the other.

A few months later Hamid got in trouble at school. He stood up in class and challenged the teachers, asking them to explain how they'd derived certain equations or why chemical interactions occurred the way they did. He wanted to get to a deeper understanding, but all his teachers were merely reading aloud from textbooks. They didn't have enough knowledge to answer him, and they resented him for asking. "No one else is asking these things," one teacher told him indignantly. "There must be something wrong with you, you must be crazy."

But still Hamid continued. He wrote compositions on why women should have equal rights and submitted them to be graded in a school that didn't even allow girls. He sent me poems and short stories written entirely in English, critiques of Afghan society that sounded as though they'd come from a burgeoning intellectual. "There are not women rights," he wrote. "The job of women is only to cook dinner and lunch. Women cannot learn because many men say that women must stay at home. They cannot go to any place for seeing beautiful scenery or experiencing something new and wonderful. But a man can do anything, he can learn and have fun, but women can't, according to tradition."

My pride toward him was dampened by fear. I called him urgently, told him to stop speaking up in class, to write what everyone else was writing, to blend into the background. I worried that his teachers or even his classmates would report him to the principal, who might take some kind of drastic action. He promised to listen to me, and I felt relief, instantly replaced by gnawing sadness. I imagined Hamid waking up every morning, humming his favorite Indian pop song, jumping down the stairs, engaging his mother in forceful debate over breakfast. As he walked toward school, I imagined him reining in his personality, remembering my warnings, sacrificing his carefree nature to fear. *Have I created this problem?* I wondered. Perhaps, blinded by my own freedom, I'd cultivated in my nephew the kind of unquenchable curiosity that promised opportunity in America but brought danger at home. I felt for my mother, suddenly understanding what I had put her through. In Afghanistan, you have to fear for the future of an educated child.

THE DICHOTOMY BETWEEN MY LIFE in America and Hamid's in Kandahar was striking.

I was pursuing research in a groundbreaking field with the potential to transform the future of technology and America's role on the global scientific stage. A postdoc from Caltech named Angelo Lucia and I began working together to develop algorithms that could be run on quantum computers. Until this point, most of my quantum research had been extremely theoretical. I was thrilled to now work on something that had real-world applications.

I also accepted a job at Tufts University outside Boston from Peter Love, whom I'd also met during my summer at Caltech. I planned to work with him on a project related to quantum algorithms, the same general subject I was working on with Angelo.

I called Moor over Skype to tell her about my new job. "This is great news, Sola!" she told me, her eyes shining with pride. She laughed. "Everything that got you into trouble in Kandahar has now led to your success in America." She paused, then grew thoughtful. "There is nothing sweeter than your first paycheck," she said, remembering. "There is a different feeling in earning your own money."

I packed up my dorm room the next week—my book collection, the quilt from Betsy Devine, my American clothes—and flew to Boston. As the plane touched down at Logan airport, I reflected on how quickly my time at

ASU had passed. I'd spent most of my years there studying in my dorm room, finding it difficult to make connections with the eighteen- and nineteen-year-old Americans outside my door. I hadn't even officially graduated from the university because Professor Love's job offer, with its promise of impactful, real-world research, was more enticing to me than another year in Tempe. I was looking forward to this next chapter in my life, a chance to experience America in a new light.

In Boston, I'd found a small house to rent through a Facebook search. I knew that I would live with two housemates and have my own bedroom, but in all the chaos of moving, I hadn't taken time to investigate anything more about my new home.

The Uber pulled up to my new address, and I stared out the window. The house had two stories and was adorned with sky-blue paneling and a white roof that had browned with age. Cream-colored rusted pillars held up a sagging second-floor balcony. The entire structure looked unsteady, as if the first floor might collapse at any moment under the weight of the second one.

I slid out of the car and set my bags onto the cracked sidewalk, next to a tiny garden sparsely filled with dried-out bushes. I climbed a few stairs to a scuffed front door and knocked tentatively, suddenly nervous.

The door swung open, and my new housemates appeared dressed in undershirts and crumpled jeans. I fought back a smile for a moment, imagining the scandal that would break out in Kandahar if anyone knew I was sharing a house with two men. "Hey!" They nodded at me. "Come on in!" One of the housemates gave me a quick tour, pointing out the tiled bathroom and the kitchen piled with dirty dishes. I crinkled my nose at a persistent, skunky smell that I'd later discover came from the marijuana they smoked most evenings in front of the TV.

I started work at Professor Love's group the next morning. I had our space in the Tufts physics and astronomy department to myself, since most researchers preferred to work at home during the COVID pandemic. I spent hours alone, researching and writing what would eventually become my first published paper.

At home, I ventured into the kitchen once a week to prepare a massive batch of Afghan-style potatoes or fried eggplant. Every evening, as my new housemates dissolved into peals of laughter and exhaled copious amounts of foul-smelling smoke, I microwaved a bowl of leftovers and ate in front of my laptop while fast-forwarding through Bollywood movies I'd watched a dozen times before.

IN JANUARY 2021, JOE BIDEN was inaugurated as the new president of the United States. I'd been in downtown Boston when the election results were called, suddenly immersed in a frenzy of honking horns and screams of unhampered joy. Though I was ineligible to vote, I was thrilled with the results. I was hopeful for a future in America without Trump's racist innuendo and harsh immigration policies. I believed Biden was an empathetic leader. I thought he would reverse many of the rash, irresponsible decisions made during the Trump administration.

The next months blurred together. I managed to find a better place to live and moved to a new house in Cambridge, this time with two girls from Brazil. I endured my first East Coast winter, a harsh contrast to the temperate months I'd experienced at ASU. I bought my first winter coat, boots, and gloves. The hairs in my nostrils froze when I went outside. Sometimes it grew dark outside before four-thirty in the afternoon.

Eventually, spring drifted across Boston.

In April I woke up to President Biden's announcement that he planned to conform with Trump's U.S.-Taliban agreement and withdraw all American troops from Afghanistan in 2021. He delayed the complete withdrawal until September 2021, exactly twenty years after the 9/11 attacks.

The immediacy of what was happening didn't strike me at first. Since Trump had initiated talks with the Taliban in 2020, the possibility of a withdrawal had lurked within the recesses of my mind, but it had never sounded like a reality. Based on what Baba told me, American forces in Afghanistan were like the foundation of a crumbling building: imperfect and unsteady but still profoundly necessary to the structure's survival. They were not engaged in direct combat but provided essential logistical and air support to the Afghan military. They seemed to flow in and out of the country at regular intervals, never disappearing entirely, still maintaining a tenuous peace.

I called home later that April morning. "How are you?" I asked my father, and he gave his usual response, updating me on the political situation in Afghanistan rather than on his own personal life. We talked about Biden's announcement. Like most Afghans, Baba didn't believe the United States would fully withdraw. He reminded me that President Barack Obama had made similar pronouncements during his administration, yet American troops had remained.

But Biden's announcement didn't fade into the background as the others had. Instead, in May, he began withdrawing troops from the country. Presented with an opening, Taliban forces seized control of several districts in northern Afghanistan, a region that has historically posed the fiercest opposition to their incursions. I clung to the few news reports exiting the country and studied maps that demonstrated how quickly the Taliban forces were progressing. A searing pain clenching between my ribs would unexpectedly contort my body with dread in the early mornings or on the walks I took through my Boston neighborhood.

For almost a decade, I'd thought about Afghanistan in terms of what it had stolen from me and my family. It was because of Afghanistan that my mother had been condemned to a life of regret. It was because of Afghanistan that I'd spent my childhood wrapped too tightly within the walls of our compound. It was because of Afghanistan that I was shredded between two worlds, unable to find peace in the halls of academia because of the worsening violence at home.

But watching the country shatter awoke in me a dormant love for my country. Afghanistan meant war and restriction, but it also meant family. It meant students at Kabul's universities as well as girls like me, still stuck at home in conservative provinces, studying from their bedrooms. It meant vibrant weddings with hours of dancing, traditional music imbued with yearning and sorrow. It meant pomegranate groves and breathtaking mosques and the rivers Baba would take me swimming in as a little girl.

I knew Taliban rule would rob us of our country's essential promises, would sterilize our culture through fear. The threat of this fundamental loss coursed through me, sparking the incomparable pain that comes from watching your country die.

SUMMERTIME CAME TO BOSTON. At Tufts, I worked on several new quantum computing projects and wrote a research paper on quantum algorithms that would eventually be published. For years, I had consumed knowledge developed by other people. It was electrifying to finally become a creator, to release my own ideas into the world.

At the same time, the American withdrawal unfolded rapidly in Afghanistan and the Taliban swept across the country. By early July, they controlled nearly a quarter of Afghanistan's four hundred districts. They planted land mines and rained rocket fire down on Kandahar's airport. The Afghan government attacked entire villages in its fight to maintain control. One of our relatives died at home, caught in crossfire from Afghan and Taliban forces. On the news, I saw pictures of terrified children running through the streets, of a young boy crying over his father's dead body.

On July 2 the United States announced it had left Bagram Air Base, the largest American air base in Afghanistan. American troops abandoned the base in the middle of the night, without updating any members of the Afghan military. The new Afghan commander in charge of Bagram didn't even learn that U.S. troops had left until two hours after they were gone. Looters took advantage of the poor coordination, storming the base and stealing everything from computers to gas canisters.

A week later the Taliban advanced on Kandahar. They imposed a curfew, and anyone who left their house after ten o'clock at night risked getting shot. They managed to cut internet and cellphone access in the city for a time, presumably as a show of strength and to limit communication that could interfere with their operation. I found out about what was unfolding only the next evening, when my mother managed to reach me with an old cellphone operating on a different, spotty network. After the call, I sat in my Boston bedroom, frozen. I scrolled through my recent text messages with Moor. I saw pictures of her smiling beside Javid, who had visited earlier in the summer, and videos of my baby cousin Nadia dancing on the living room floor, her tiny arms spread, her checkered headband falling in front of her face, her eyes beaming. I closed the phone and lay still across my bed, wide awake as darkness fell on my new home.

When asked about the situation in Afghanistan that day, President Biden responded, "I want to talk about happy things, man. . . . It's the holiday weekend. I'm going to celebrate it. There's great things happening."

One week later Taliban forces breached Kandahar. I stayed in irregular contact with my parents through voice messages they sent whenever they could connect to the cellular network.

They told me that Afghan forces had managed to repel

some of the Taliban's advances, but the fighting remained close to the city. The night had echoed with the disorienting sound of machine-gun fire. The noise grew so loud that one of my cousins living in a nearby district fainted from fear. By the morning, the Taliban were just six miles from our compound.

I called home, pleading with my parents to leave Kandahar. But Baba was in denial of what was unfolding around him. "The Taliban will not take over," he told me. "The Americans will never leave. They have spent so much money over twenty years, and they have made such big promises. They will never leave like this." As we spoke, he told me he could hear the sounds of gunshots from the city boundaries.

I managed to connect to a video call with Hamid that evening. "Download some math and English videos," I said to his grainy silhouette, trying to take his mind off of what was unfolding around him, to preserve his enthusiasm for some kind of future. "You'll be able to study then, even if they take away the internet."

"I don't care about these things anymore!" he cried. He was worried that the fighting would escalate, that an airstrike would hit our compound. "I just don't want to die," he said into the phone, as tears streamed down his face.

The next day, when President Biden was asked if he bore any responsibility for lives lost after the U.S. troop withdrawal, he responded emphatically, "No, no, no! It's up to the people of Afghanistan to decide what government they want."

Over the next few days, I called my parents every few

hours. Instead of greeting them with the traditional *salaam*, I began every call by asking, "Is everyone alive?" Moor told me that Hamid was so frightened of the airstrikes that he was unable to eat, that even one spoon of food was enough to make him throw up. Nadia, just five years old, told her mother she wished she had never been born. Moor asked me to talk with them, to reassure them that everything would be okay. But I struggled to find words of comfort when I knew they were empty lies.

Moor and Baba had no way to ascertain exactly what was happening around them since journalists were not allowed to report or publish. Instead, my parents relied on Facebook posts from people across the city to get accurate information. One evening I called them again and begged them to leave. "It is too dangerous for us to go now," Baba told me solemnly, trying to temper my wild fear. "The Taliban have blocked most of the roads out of Kandahar that could take us to Kabul or Pakistan." My stomach twisted with despair, and then I was suddenly filled with anger. For decades, my father had insisted on staying in Kandahar, even as it became too dangerous for his daughters to attend school, even as violence escalated with every passing year. Now he was trapped with my family inside the city as the Taliban closed in. How could he have let it come to this?

Moor, Baba, my aunt and uncle, and my cousins sat at home as the fighting unfolded around them. They tried not to think about what seemed inevitable, fearing the suffocating chokehold of Taliban control, a return to the brutality of the 1990s. They remembered the isolation of two decades earlier, the sense of spinning away, untethered from the rest of the world. They remembered poverty and extreme hunger and dilapidated, uninhabited hospitals. They remembered Talibs stoning adulterers and cutting off the hands of thieves. They remembered how time had stopped in a horrible nightmare, how Afghanistan had been like an animal carcass, ripped apart and left for the vultures.

CHAPTER
TWENTY-ONE

I am thinking of you my beloved Kandahar
I am trying to forget you but can't forget you . . .
Kandahar your blood and my blood is one

—KHALIQ AZIZ,
"SONG TO KANDAHAR"

ON AUGUST 13, 2021, THE TALIBAN CAPTURED KANDAHAR.
I stayed awake the entire night as my city fell, scrolling through social media, trying to find the latest updates. By the morning, it was over. Talibs crowded into the backs of white pickup trucks and rode through the streets, their white flags flowing in the breeze like a provocation. The same day, the Taliban also took Herat and Ghazni, two politically strategic cities.

Moor managed to call me later that day. There was a silence on the phone as we both processed the immensity of what was happening. "I will need to buy new burqas," she finally said, her voice thick with sorrow.

On August 14 I fell asleep in Boston to the sound of

newscasters speaking in assured, tempered tones. They acknowledged that the Taliban were gaining ground, that things were bad. But they insisted Kabul was very secure, protected by international troops and Afghan forces. I accepted their assessment, believing the fight for Afghanistan's capital might drag out for months or even years. I allowed myself a fragment of hope that Afghan forces would eventually secure control over Kabul and move to other provinces, slowly liberating each one from the Taliban.

But when I woke up the next morning, Kabul had fallen. President Ashraf Ghani had fled the country, and the Taliban flooded the capital, facing little resistance. Talibs in long beards and black turbans posed for a photo in the captured presidential palace, their faces unsmiling and their hands wrapped around rifles. Just a few years earlier I had visited Kabul and marveled at the bustling city. Now I imagined Kabul University closing. I imagined medieval violence exacted in the streets. I imagined young women accustomed only to light headscarves rushing out to buy burqas, just as Moor had in Kandahar.

I watched with the rest of the world as Kabul's runways teemed with crowds of people trying to escape. I tried to turn away but couldn't as some Afghans, fueled by sheer desperation, clung to the wheels of a U.S. airplane as it took off. Later I'd see videos of black specks hurtling toward the concrete as the plane tilted upward and faded into the distance. I'd wonder what they'd been thinking as the airplane climbed higher, the moment they realized they faced certain death whether they held on or let go.

———

THE DAY AFTER THE Taliban seized power, Moor went to watch her favorite morning television show, hosted by two female anchors and broadcast every morning from Kabul. But the show was missing. Maybe the anchors had fled to another country, or maybe the Taliban had taken the program off the air. Moor told us later she cried as she realized what was happening, that overnight Afghanistan had begun to descend again into the devastating blackness of twenty years earlier. Her strongest fear was that she would never see any of her children again. "Who will come to visit a country controlled by the Taliban?" she asked me over the phone.

When I talked to Hamid, he told me an eerie silence had swept across the city. The belligerent sounds of fighting that had plagued them for weeks had faded. The only noise they heard was at night when, still high on their victory, Taliban fighters shot triumphant rounds of gunfire. No one knew how long this period of uneasy stillness might last, but the Taliban's reign seemed cemented.

Then one night in late August, news circulated throughout Kandahar that the Taliban were planning to close key land borders with other countries. No flights were operating out of the country. The border closings would effectively eliminate any path from Kandahar out of Afghanistan.

My mother was inconsolable. "In the last regime I lost my career," she told my father. "In this one I will lose my children." She said she couldn't live again under the Taliban's cold brutality.

Baba realized the window to leave home was closing

rapidly. He decided the two of them would try to escape the country. The rest of the family, including Hamid, Ayan, and Nadia, planned to follow soon after. Later Baba would tell me, "I left Kandahar for your mother."

That night they packed lightly, taking only a few bags of clothes and documents. The next day Baba hired a driver to take them to the border of a neighboring country. He rode in the passenger seat while Moor sat in the back. For the first time, he didn't stay behind to protect the compound or save his business. It was his silent admission that they would likely never return home.

They drove past Aino Mena and Kandahar's rivers. They passed Taliban fighters loitering on the streets who let them go, unaware they were trying to leave the country. My parents sat together in the car for hours, consumed with their own thoughts, barely speaking a word aloud.

Eventually, they reached the border.

The crossing was overrun with throngs of Afghans, all trying to cross without the legally required paperwork. Hundreds of people were trying to shove their way through to the neighboring country. Families clung together, and fathers hoisted their little children onto their shoulders so they wouldn't be trampled. A loud din of running motors and urgent, clamoring conversations filled the air.

My parents left their car and driver and walked quickly. Baba pushed a path for them between the crowd, and they forced their way to the other side. Rows of drivers were lined up at the border, waiting for new migrants. Baba helped Moor into a car and urged the driver forward.

The sky brightened into afternoon. They drove along a single-lane highway toward the closest major city. Emptiness stretched around them for miles. Occasionally, a truck or sedan passed them, then faded into the dusty landscape. The sun glared, its shining rays licking the roof of the car like flames.

I knew my parents had decided to leave. Hours passed without any updates, and I waited, unable to turn my attention to work or even cook a meal. I stared for hours at my computer, refreshing news sites and Twitter feeds. The world was horrified by the unfolding humanitarian crisis. I read global criticism of Biden's decision to withdraw. I saw articles about American strangers trying to hire planes to get Afghan children out of the country. I watched interviews with U.S. translators and young Kabuli women, their faces obscured for safety.

THEN IN THE SPACE of only a few seconds, my mother's life changed forever. Without any warning, my parents' driver swerved to avoid an oncoming vehicle. Their car skidded across the highway and careened off the road. It flipped and rolled wildly, landing in a ditch.

Minutes passed. They lay within a pile of hot, mangled metal, covered in broken glass, unable to understand what had just happened. Eventually, the driver carefully disentangled himself and stepped out onto the side of the road, unharmed. My father managed to get out after him. His arm and fingers were slashed, and blood gushed across his white *kameez*. His pain turned to icy numbness as he realized Moor was still trapped inside.

They called to Moor, peering into the wreckage for a

glimpse of her face. Finally, they found her lying still, crushed by the weight of the car. They repeated her name over and over, but she didn't respond.

Baba and the driver reached into the car's interior for her, trying to maneuver her small frame through broken seats, shards of glass, and twisted metal. Eventually, they pulled her out and laid her gently on the side of the road. She was unresponsive. Her eyes fluttered occasionally, but no other part of her body moved. Her *salwaar kameez* was drenched in blood, but she didn't make a sound or cry in pain.

I don't know how Baba managed to get her to the hospital, but hours later he called me. "There was an accident," he told me. "Moor is hurt."

My stomach clenched. "What do you mean?"

He told me about the crash, how the car had flipped down the highway and that now my mother wasn't moving.

My body shook uncontrollably. My empty walls seemed to fall in on me.

Hours later Baba sent me a video of my mother lying immobile on a hospital cot, her neck restrained by a brace, her face expressionless. Her palms lay open, her fingers curled slightly inward. The doctors had wrapped her in a black-and-white blanket, pressing her blood-soaked *salwaar* against her skin.

I sat on the edge of my bed in my Boston house, clutching my phone, waiting for someone to explain what was happening. I stared at the video of Moor on my screen, and then I was consumed by racking sobs, choking on tears, barely able to draw a breath. Morning rose on the horizon outside my window, and I stayed still, dizziness clanging between my temples.

Eventually, Aisha and Roya called, then Yousef and Nadir and Javid. At first we could barely speak to one another, silent in our shared sense of helplessness. Then we broke down, dissolving into panicked tears. In all our other desperate moments, during Taliban fighting and suicide bombings, Moor had been there. As we'd jumped at the sounds of gunfire, she'd sat still beside us, resting her palm atop our heads and pulling us closer. Whenever she sensed we were worried about something, she used to crawl into bed beside us and drape her arms over our shoulders until her steady breathing lulled us to sleep. Now, as the magnitude of our crisis set in, emptiness took hold.

The next day Baba called again. Moor's spine was broken, he told us. She was paralyzed from the neck down. The doctors believed she would die within the next few days.

THE MINUTES PASSED WITH agonizing slowness. I stood in the corner of my bedroom and processed every update numbly. *Her broken spine is pressing against her throat,* a text read. *She's struggling to breathe. She still isn't moving.* The doctors put Moor on a ventilator when she couldn't breathe on her own. Her oxygen levels plummeted, hovering around the minimum saturation required to keep her alive.

Moor made it through a few days but didn't get any better. A week passed, and she showed no signs of improvement. I slept in fifteen-minute increments. I didn't eat. I was tormented by the miles between us, seized with crippling anguish. I wanted to rush to her, but I wasn't allowed to leave the country on my humanitarian parole visa.

Every morning for four months, I woke up unsure if my mother was still alive. I took weeks off from work and stayed huddled in my room. I scrolled through photos taken decades earlier of me swaddled in Moor's lap or grasping for her hand. I searched for my mother in the pictures Baba sent of snaking tubes and hospital gowns and hair matted against a pillow.

At night I dreamed of Moor skipping through Kabul University. I dreamed of her laughing gently as I danced to wild Bollywood music in our kitchen. I dreamed of her reading next to me in the garden, sitting among the coral roses and blooming trees, her fingers lifting every few minutes to turn a page.

I HAVE NOT SEEN my mother in six years, since the day I left Kandahar. Today Moor is a quadriplegic, paralyzed from the neck down. Sometimes in the weeks and months that passed, her oxygen levels dropped so low that my siblings and I were certain she would not survive. We called one another, but sorrow seized our throats and we couldn't talk. We stayed silent on the phone, thousands of miles apart, crying together for a miracle.

Somehow, though, even in the midst of tragedy, our lives moved forward. Aisha got a job as a medical translator in Birmingham, helping pregnant, injured, or sick Afghan immigrants access care. It was her first time pursuing something outside the home since she'd been forced to leave school so many decades earlier. Roya, who still lived in Norway with her husband and two children, enrolled in school to become a daycare worker. Yousef began practicing neurology in a small town in Denmark. Javid pursued an MBA and a master's in artificial intelligence, studying remotely at Moor's bedside and flying into Denmark every few months to take his exams. And after months of applications and interviews and paperwork, Nadir and his family were granted asylum in a Western country.

The blackness that settled over me after Moor's accident never lifted. But still my life in America continued. I returned to work and was accepted to several entrepreneurship programs to explore business ideas around quantum computing and drug discovery. I made friends all over Cambridge. With some, I traded research ideas over lingering meals near the Tufts campus, explaining my ideas about quantum physics applications over bowls of pasta or tall cups of coffee. Frank Wilczek had a house in Concord, Massachusetts, and I met up with him often, usually for meandering walks where we discussed everything from U.S. politics to philosophy. I went to orchestra concerts by a group of musicians from a nearby conservatory, and I celebrated Eid with other Cambridge Muslims at Tufts. Sometimes, in the middle of laughing at someone's joke or listening intently to a story, I'd realize that I was living the life I'd dreamed of so many years earlier. The distant vision that had sustained me as I scrubbed dishes and wrung laundry and studied into the morning hours was finally before me. But these glimmers of happiness were still fleeting.

Moor is now stable enough that we think she will live. In November 2021 she received an emergency visa to leave the border country and move to Greece for better medical care, but her condition remains mostly the same. Her existence is thin, reduced to the most basic elements of survival. I mourn the years I have spent apart from her, building a new life as the one she knew came to a close. I wonder often why she was robbed of what little she had, just as she was on the edge of freedom.

On the weekends, I go on bike rides the way I used to when I first moved to the United States. As I pedal on rocky trails, past glistening lakes and lush trees, I chase the lightness I felt then, the sense of a new beginning. But no matter how far I ride, I cannot escape the interminable pull of home, the images of building skeletons and empty schools and Talibs cruising through Kandahar's streets. I cannot escape the thought of my mother, lying immobile by the side of the road. Afghanistan is a pain I'll never be able to disentangle from. I left, but it claimed the ultimate price.

A NOTE FROM AUTHOR
MALAINA KAPOOR

DEFIANT DREAMS IS A COLLABORATION BETWEEN
Sola Mahfouz and me. Over the course of a year, I
wrote as Sola described her life to me, moving beyond the
simple facts of her story to illustrate the immensity of what
she experienced over the past twenty-six years. I drew from
my own Indian American background to write about everything from the flavors and spices she grew up with, to the
importance of marriage within her culture, to the cavernous sense of loss that often comes with displacement. Late
into the night, we spoke about the intense emotions and
fears that pushed her forward through her teenage years.
And I lived the final chapters of the book alongside her. By
then, we were no longer merely partners in a book project,
but two deeply close friends.

ACKNOWLEDGMENTS

I T'S A HUMBLING EXERCISE TO REFLECT FROM TIME TO time on my life and realize that without the help of some individuals, it wouldn't be the same one that I am living now, the one I am happy to own. I will order the people as they appeared in my life. Of those individuals, my grandfather stands first in line with his inspiring story of self-determination and placing the highest value on education, especially English. He said English is like opening a window to the world that exists beyond the mountains of Afghanistan. Many years later, word by word, I built that window in the walls of my mind and flung it open to a new life. My mother comes after him, sharing his positive outlook toward life no matter how deep the darkness was and is. When I was a girl, I would say to my mother that I am grateful to have Moor, and my mother would always reply, "I am happy to have you."

After my mother, my sweet younger brother is next. In the early days of my education journey, he supplied me with books, pens, a comfortable chair, the internet, and most important, the belief that I was his equal. Then comes my father, who didn't stop me from leaving Afghanistan, allowing me space where I could exercise my freedom, and my older sister, whose credit card I used to buy books online when I was in Kandahar. My cousin Mirvise helped me improve my spoken English. Emily Roberts, my friend, did everything to help me get into college and immigrate to the United States, a path with countless challenges. Her help in the early months of my immigration smoothed my transition to this new country. I also thank my immigration lawyer, Sheryl Winarick, for working on my immigration case before I came to the U.S. and after.

Next to one another stand my advisors: Peter Love, Frank Wilczek, and Elizabeth Langland, dean at ASU. Each one has enhanced and shaped my intellectual life profoundly and respected me for my intellectual curiosity, as I respected them. From Peter Love, I learned how to write clear scientific papers and develop sound judgment on research topics, and he encouraged and supported me in my various academic pursuits.

Through interaction with Frank Wilczek, I realized that thinking originally and beautifully is the highest virtue I should strive for. I also appreciated how fun it is to have an all-encompassing view of the world. With Elizabeth Langland, I began to explore fiction at a much deeper level and shared with her where it reflected my life or the lives I have seen in Kandahar. She didn't give me a puzzling look when I told her that I see in Kafka's *Metamorphosis* aspects of my life as an Afghan woman. Her vast knowledge, as a former English professor, of all types of fiction and reading my stories and then discussing them with me over Zoom calls, allowed me to develop a writing style where I can express myself thoroughly and clearly.

Elizabeth Slavitt is the friend who first believed that my story could be a book. I also want to thank Barb Kunz for help on the journey of this book. Malaina, my great friend, whose deep awareness of the world and empathy pushed me to dig deep into my emotions. My friendship with Malaina has enabled me to bond with her family. This warm human connection reminded me of what it means to have a family after not seeing mine for years. With them, I don't feel alone.

I am immensely grateful to Sal Khan, my first teacher, for creating Khan Academy, which has changed my life in the best possible way. Thank you to him and his wife, Umaima Marvi, for selflessly extending their helping hands to help with my family's immigration when Afghanistan fell to the Taliban.

I thank Duvall Osteen and Susanna Porter, my literary agent and my editor, for believing in the story that I wanted to tell and extending support to me beyond the writing of the book.

The presence of all these people in my life has made me a better human being, and without any of them, my life would be incomplete. I also extend my gratitude to everyone who helped me and whose names I am not able to mention here.

—SOLA MAHFOUZ

WHILE WRITING *DEFIANT DREAMS*, I SPENT COUNTLESS hours reflecting on the ugliest depths of humanity, on the oppression, brutality, and fundamental inequities that set the backdrop for this book. But I was also moved by how many people sacrificed their time and energy to support us in telling such an important story. I'm so grateful to these colleagues, friends, and family members who helped me to still believe in the goodness of people, to remember the power of light.

Thank you to my agent, Duvall Osteen, who took a chance on me just a few weeks before my eighteenth birthday. I've been so lucky to experience your contagious enthusiasm, unwavering commitment, and warmth over the past few years.

Thank you to my editor, Susanna Porter, for your insightful comments and your kindness. Thank you also to Sydney Shiffman, Andra Miller, and everyone else at Ballantine who helped put *Defiant Dreams* into the world.

Thank you to Elizabeth Slavitt for being an incredible mentor and friend, and for your generosity throughout this book process. Thank you to Sal Khan and Umaima Marvi for always believing in me and motivating me to seek new heights. Thank you to Seema and Shantanu Sinha, Prabha Kannan, and Amar Kendale for your constant encouragement. To Preeti and Zafar Iqbal, my dear masi and masa, thank you for your essential life advice, your love, and your support.

Thank you to my co-author and close friend, Sola Mahfouz. Sola, your friendship has been one of the greatest gifts to come from this book, and your incredible story has changed the way I look at the world. Here's to many more years of long phone calls, late-night musings, book clubs, and Bollywood movies.

To Dada and Dadi, who live on in our memories. I know you both are looking down on me always. To Nana and

Nani: you are my greatest inspirations. You have taught me the true meanings of perseverance and strength. I am so grateful for the extraordinary sacrifices you made to give us the freedom of life in America. I miss you every minute we are apart and treasure every moment we spend together.

To my brother, Zidaan. From the moment you were born, you brought us all more lightness and joy than we imagined was possible. You are my partner in crime and my biggest cheerleader—I move through life more easily knowing you are always by my side. Thank you for making me the luckiest sister in the world.

To Daddy. Your fortitude, optimism, and wisdom drive me forward. Each one of your stories and sayings stay with me, and I turn to them in moments of uncertainty. I love you most for the laughter you bring to my life, the spontaneous adventures and jokes that are funny to no one but you and me. And I am grateful every day for the sacrifices you made so we all could have this life together.

Finally, to Mama, who spent countless hours helping me to edit every draft of this book. From the time I was a little girl, you taught me to dream freely, to walk confidently, and to work hard for what I wanted to achieve. You are my anchor, my confidante, and my best friend. I love you more than you know.

—MALAINA KAPOOR

ABOUT THE AUTHORS

SOLA MAHFOUZ was born in Afghanistan and immigrated to the United States in 2016 to attend college. She is currently a quantum computing researcher at Tufts University Quantum Information Group. In her free time, she reads and studies different styles of fiction and writes about the rugged homeland she has left behind. She lives in Boston, Massachusetts.

MALAINA KAPOOR is a writer from Redwood City, California. She previously served as a Fellow at PEN America, where she advocated for international human rights, press freedoms, and election integrity. Malaina served on the management team of a refugee resettlement organization and was the producer of *In Deep*, a nationally syndicated public affairs radio broadcast program. She has received national awards for her poetry, personal essays, and short stories. Malaina will graduate from Stanford University in 2025.

ABOUT THE TYPE

This book was set in Dante, a typeface designed by Giovanni Mardersteig (1892–1977). Conceived as a private type for the Officina Bodoni in Verona, Italy, Dante was originally cut only for hand composition by Charles Malin, the famous Parisian punch cutter, between 1946 and 1952. Its first use was in an edition of Boccaccio's *Trattatello in laude di Dante* that appeared in 1954. The Monotype Corporation's version of Dante followed in 1957. Though modeled on the Aldine type used for Pietro Cardinal Bembo's treatise *De Aetna* in 1495, Dante is a thoroughly modern interpretation of that venerable face.